the Unofficial Guide™ to Hiring Contractors

Duncan C. Stephens

D1234216

Macmillan • USA

Macmillan General Reference
A Simon & Schuster Macmillan Company
1633 Broadway
New York, New York 10019-6785

ISBN: 0-02-862460-2

Manufactured in the United States of America

10 9 8 7 6 5 4 3 2 1

First edition

To my wife, Eileen, an excellent editor who knows when to let things get by.
Betsy Amster, my editor-turned-agent, who remembered the good times.
Ruth Turner, who asked the first question.
Molly Burns, Holly Brown, Laura Poole, and John Jones, the real editors.
—Duncan C. Stephens

Acknowledgments

It is fairly common for an author to say, "This book would have been impossible to write without the help of the following people . . ." He then goes on to acknowledge and thank his wife, children, typist, proofreader, golfing buddies, and pet gerbils.

I too have a long list of people to whom I am indebted, not just for their support and inspiration, but because their help was an essential part of the project. These are the homeowners, contractors, builders, bankers, architects, and subcontractors who shared their experiences and hard-won remodeling knowledge with me in long, often eloquently humorous, entertaining, and informative interviews. Here they are, more or less in the order in which I met them:

Howard Romero, designer/builder, Vermont; Mark Woodward, builder, Vermont; Heather Marks, homeowner, Vermont; John Rahin, architect at Black River Design, Vermont; Mark Alvarez, homeowner, Connecticut; Susan and Gus Southworth, homeowners, Connecticut; Debby Watson, homeowner, Connecticut; Susan Sobilinski, inn owner, Connecticut; David and Katie Heim, homeowners, Pennsylvania and New York City; Michael DeZinno, former contractor, Connecticut; Jarron Basinger, contractor, Connecticut; Frank Husband, remodeler, Connecticut; Theodore Ceraldi, architect, New York; Lore and Ron Basil, homeowners, New Jersey; Mark and Chris Ahasic, brownstone owners, New York City; Stephen J. Sweeney, homeowner, Connecticut; Lydia Straus-Edwards, architect,

Connecticut; Robert Hanbury, designer/remodeler, Connecticut; Liz Strasser, homeowner, New York; Hal Wright, homeowner, Maine; Jim Clark, banker, Connecticut; Carol Bacon, banker/homeowner, Connecticut; Michael Walsh, banker, Connecticut; Bret Zuraitis, designer/remodeler, Connecticut; NAHB Remodelers Council, Washington, D.C.; National Association of the Remodeling Industry (NARI), Arlington, Virginia; American Institute of Architects (AIA), New Haven, Connecticut office; Steve Pryor, electrical contractor; Edmond Santopietro, interior decorator; Ronald Stokes, pool builder; Patrick McLaughlin, duct cleaner; Bill Daly, Alarm Systems; Dana Fox, home inspector; Chris Wolf and Chuck Olmstead, Ken's Hardware; Mr. Mann, pest control; Thom Bardugone, The Paint Brush; Dan Denver, pool owner and nuclear engineer.

And the many friends and strangers who, once the subject of remodeling came up, contributed brief stories and insights on what they had learned during their remodeling process.

I certainly have to include Randy Crump and his crew, the remodelers on our project; my wife Eileen, who suffered through both the remodeling and book writing exerience with me; and Betsy Amster, who edited my work and makes me wonder if maybe she should be listed as coauthor.

Thank you all. I hope the results make you feel your time was well spent and that you get some gratification from knowing others may be able to avoid a few of the mistakes you had to live with.

Contents

The *Unofficial Guide* Reader's Bill of Rights

We Give You More Than the Official Line

Welcome to the *Unofficial Guide* series of Lifestyles titles—books that deliver critical, unbiased information that other books can't or won't reveal—the inside scoop. Our goal is to provide you with the most accessible, useful information and advice possible. The recommendations we offer in these pages are not influenced by the corporate line of any organization or industry; we give you the hard facts, whether those institutions like them or not. If something is ill-advised or will cause a loss of time and/or money, we'll give you ample warning. And if it is a worthwhile option, we'll let you know that, too.

Armed and Ready

Our hand-picked authors confidently and critically report on a wide range of topics that matter to smart readers like you. Our authors are passionate about their subjects, but have distanced themselves enough to help you be armed and protected, and help you make educated decisions as you go through your process. It is our intent that, from having read this book, you will avoid the pitfalls everyone else falls into and get it right the first time.

Don't be fooled by cheap imitations; this is the genuine article *Unofficial Guide* series from Macmillan Publishing. You may be familiar with our proven track record of the travel *Unofficial Guides*, which have more than three million copies in print. Each year thousands of travelers—new and old—are armed with a brand new, fully updated edition of the flagship *Unofficial Guide to Walt Disney World*, by Bob Sehlinger. It is our intention here to provide you with the same level of objective authority that Mr. Sehlinger does in his brainchild.

The Unofficial Panel of Experts

Every work in the Lifestyle *Unofficial Guides* is intensively inspected by a team of top professionals in their fields. These experts review the manuscript for factual accuracy, comprehensiveness, and an insider's determination as to whether the manuscript fulfills the credo in this Reader's Bill of Rights. In other words, our Panel ensures that you are, in fact, getting "the inside scoop."

Our Pledge

The authors, the editorial staff, and the *Unofficial* Panel of Experts assembled for *Unofficial Guides* are determined to lay out the most valuable alternatives available for our readers. This dictum means that our writers must be explicit, prescriptive, and above all, direct. We strive to be thorough and complete, but our goal is not necessarily to have the "most" or "all" of the information on a topic; this is not, after all, an encyclopedia. Our objective is to help you narrow down your options to the best of what is available, unbiased by affiliation with any industry or organization.

In each *Unofficial Guide* we give you:

- Comprehensive coverage of necessary and vital information
- Authoritative, rigidly fact-checked data
- The most up-to-date insights into trends
- Savvy, sophisticated writing that's also readable
- Sensible, applicable facts and secrets that only an insider knows

Special Features

Every book in our series offers the following six special sidebars in the margins that were devised to help you get things done cheaply, efficiently, and smartly.

1. "**Timesaver**"—tips and shortcuts that save you time.

2. "**Moneysaver**"—tips and shortcuts that save you money.

3. "**Watch Out!**"—more serious cautions and warnings.

4. "**Bright Idea**"—general tips and shortcuts to help you find an easier or smarter way to do something.

5. "**Quote**"—statements from real people that are intended to be prescriptive and valuable to you.

6. "**Unofficially**..."—an insider's fact or anecdote.

We also recognize your need to have quick information at your fingertips, and have thus provided the following sections at the back of the book:

1. **Resource Guide:** Lists of relevant agencies, associations, institutions, Web sites, etc.

2. **Important Statistics:** Facts and numbers presented at-a-glance for easy reference.

3. **Glossary:** Definitions of complicated terminology and jargon.
4. **Index.**

Letters, Comments, and Questions from Readers

We strive to continually improve the *Unofficial* series, and input from our readers is a valuable way for us to do that. Many of those who have used the *Unofficial Guide* travel books write to the authors to ask questions, make comments, or share their own discoveries and lessons. For lifestyle *Unofficial Guides,* we would also appreciate all such correspondence, both positive and critical, and we will make best efforts to incorporate appropriate readers' feedback and comments in revised editions of this work.

How to write to us:

Unofficial Guides
Macmillan Lifestyle Guides
Macmillan Publishing
1633 Broadway
New York, NY 10019

Attention: Reader's Comments

The *Unofficial Guide* Panel of Experts

The *Unofficial Guide* editorial team recognizes that you've purchased this book with the expectation of getting the most authoritative, carefully inspected information currently available. Toward that end, on each and every title in this series, we have selected "official" experts comprising the *"Unofficial* Panel" who painstakingly review the manuscripts to ensure: factual accuracy of all data; inclusion of the most up-to-date and relevant information; and that, from an insider's perspective, the authors have armed you with all the necessary facts you need—but the institutions don't want you to know.

For *The Unofficial Guide to Hiring Contractors,* we are proud to introduce the following experts:

Jack Tucker Mr. Tucker is a nationally renowned teacher in home sales training. He designed and runs his own seminar, "Building Wisdom: Construction Training for Sales Reps" (now part of the National Association of Home Builders training). He also oversees a popular website (www.buildingwisdom.com), which includes information about Tucker Resources, Inc., public seminar dates, construction chat rooms, frequently asked questions by homeowners, and free copies of all construction paperwork needed to build a home.

Owen Devine   Mr. Devine, a fraud investigator for a Fortune 500 company, has investigated numerous fraud cases involving offenses perpetrated by contractors and construction companies. He has served as Investigative Analyst in the Manhattan District Attorney's Office, and has received extensive training from the National White Collar Crime Center and the Association of Certified Fraud Examiners.

Introduction

The moment you first moved into your home, you probably felt a tremendous sense of relief. All the visits with the realtor were finally over; all the documents surrounding the financing, inspection, and insurance were finally signed, sealed, and delivered. Barely did you have time to relax in your new living room, however, before you realized that you are now responsible for maintaining a surprisingly complex combination of systems. And there's no way you and your partner can do it all yourself. Keeping everything running requires the skilled knowledge and abilities of a mind-boggling number of trades- and craftspeople, repair workers, and service providers.

Whether you're an expert around the house or a total klutz, this book will keep you from making a few big (and many small) mistakes. We'll help you find and deal with people who can do the work for you and who can give you the confidence and knowledge to deal with costs, personalities, and the dozens of choices you'll have to make as you try to maintain and improve your home.

To tailor the information in this book to meet your specific needs, we have made some educated guesses about you, the reader. We suspect, for example, that you are not the easygoing, everything will-work-out-for-the-best-in-the-end kind of personality. You probably hate to get involved in something you don't understand well. Whether it's your vacation or a session with a furnace repairman, you like to know what's going on, what needs to be done, and how much it will cost. In other words, you want to feel comfortable with the process and secure in the outcome. So take a deep breath and read on. Together, we'll get through whatever repair or home improvement you're contemplating.

Trusting Those You Hire

In addition to worrying about things you don't completely understand, you might have some doubts concerning the motives of the people you ask to help you. Because they know all about it (whatever "it" is) and you know next to nothing, it's hard to ignore the suspicion that they might try to put something over on you, sell you something you don't really need, or overcharge you.

Unfortunately, some of your suspicions are well-founded. Dissatisfaction with home construction, repair, and remodeling are among the largest categories of complaints to local Better Business Bureaus and state Consumer Protection Departments. We have all heard about the aluminum siding, replacement windows, and driveway paving scam artists who prey on the elderly and unwary. Among the things this book will do is help you recognize scams and provide a way to protect yourself from them. If you should fall victim, I offer some avenues for redressing your grievances. Scam artists are out there, but most contractors are honest, hardworking, knowledgeable people. My job is to help you find them.

The first item of advice we give you is going to be the hardest to follow. You may be an assertive, confident, perhaps impatient, take-charge type of person, but when dealing with tradesmen and craftsmen, pretend you're not. Although you are the one paying the bills, if you try to demand, challenge, accuse, or belittle your contractors, you will get only minimum cooperation, no sympathy, and possibly a result different from the one you seek to orchestrate. In this world, you tend be treated the way you expect to be treated. If you expect people to be honest, they will usually treat you honestly. If you expect everyone to try to cheat you, they probably will.

Our first bit of advice is to keep doubts and suspicions to yourself when you meet with prospective contractors. Be friendly and open. If you have questions, by all means ask them, but try to set a tone of mutual respect. You might be a top CPA, lawyer, or Sanskrit scholar, but your contractor can cut a compound miter in crown molding, rewire a home, design an energy-efficient HVAC system, and so on. You can't and probably never will.

It's impossible to know everything about every aspect of your home. Even if your father taught you the basics of home repair and you have some mechanical ability, the equipment, appliances, and materials change every year. Contractors do not expect you to be all-knowing and usually will patiently explain any complications and your options. Even the most sympathetic contractor, however, might be tempted to lead you astray if you exhibit a total lack of understanding. Although you might require the services of a skilled craftsman from time to time, you are the engineer-in-residence at your home. One clue to your status as a knowledgeable consumer is how you handle simple, everyday maintenance and repair problems.

You can change a lightbulb without calling an electrician, and you have learned that your vacuum cleaner works better if you occasionally empty the bag. But do you change the air filters in your furnace once a month during the heating season? Do you defrost your refrigerator when it needs it? Do you unclog your garbage disposal? Do you know where the circuit breakers are located and how to reset them if the lights go out?

Here's a list of fairly easy tasks the average homeowner can handle without summoning help:

- Fixing a leaky faucet
- Draining and shutting off outside faucets before the first freeze
- Unclogging a toilet with a plunger
- Cleaning at least first-story gutters
- Replacing a broken window pane
- Tightening a loose doorknob
- Knowing how to open and close your fireplace flue
- Unclogging sink drains
- Caulking window and door frames
- Getting sliding drawers back on track
- Changing batteries in smoke alarms

These tasks are not gender-specific. Women are just as capable of mastering the skills as men. If you've never had a good instructor, ask a neighbor, a relative, or a friend to teach you. You could also hit a bookstore or a library for any number of household repair and maintenance manuals.

This book isn't written to teach you how to do it yourself. It is for people who are contemplating hiring a repairman, a contractor, or a craftsman to do work. We'll suggest several ways you can work with these people to save some expenses, but our primary objective is to help you avoid problems and misunderstandings—from selecting professional help through the diagnostic, planning, and (for larger jobs) contract negotiation stages to living with a work in progress and, finally, wrapping it up neatly at the end.

First in difficulty is getting a repair worker to actually come to your home; a close second is finding a competent one with whom you're comfortable. In fact, the more skilled a contractor is, the harder it is to break into his busy schedule; just finding one can be a lifelong project. Some people even refuse to give out the name of a favorite auto mechanic or carpenter for fear that he will become too busy for them when they need help.

The first place most people look for contractors is the Yellow Pages. However, many really good carpenters and contractors don't advertise anywhere because they don't have to. Instead of looking under "Contracting," try looking under Contractors—Altering & Remodeling, Contractors—Building, or Plumbing Contractors. These listings usually consist of firms looking for major building or remodeling projects rather than individual craftsmen or repairmen, but they might help lead you to what you're looking for. Your local daily or weekly newspapers probably have a section in which local tradespeople can run small advertisements. You might find a jack-of-all-trades listed that could solve several of your problems. Don't forget to ask around, too. As we will remind you time and again throughout this book, friends, neighbors, church members, hardware or lumberyard clerks, and many others can help you find contractors and tradespeople whose reputations for quality work have spread by word of mouth alone. You also should check bulletin boards. If you do hire someone, get to know him. He can be your best source for other craftsmen in your town and probably won't hesitate to tell you what he thinks of their skills and personalities.

Don't be discouraged by seemingly negative reports from competing contractors or subcontractors. Craftsmen of all trades tend to have a somewhat inflated opinion of their own skills and serious doubts about everyone else's. Chapter 2, "Bids and Contracts," provides a list of questions to ask that can help you get better information and form a more accurate appraisal of prospective contractors.

In addition, don't be put off by the number of complications and problems that construction projects can entail; these problems don't all come up on every project. With the help of this book, you just might be able to have a comparatively stress-free building experience. We've interviewed scores of builders, contractors, and homeowners. Every one of them stressed the importance of preparation. One thing is very clear: more time spent planning directly translates into less money spent building (or tearing out and rebuilding). Don't skip Chapter 1, "Your Planning Process and the People Who Can Help," no matter how impatient you are to look up your specific project and get started.

We've organized the book to first take you through many of the general issues surrounding contracting. We then walk you through several specific projects and the challenges peculiar to them.

Part One of this book discusses creating the plan and completing the contract. We'll tell you where to get ideas and how to evaluate what you want and need. You'll see some detailed questions you must work through if you want your project to be a complete success. We'll also guide you through the first steps of where to look for help, including finding names and checking referrals. We'll then demystify the process of bids and contracts, showing you the pros and cons of various approaches.

In Part Two, we'll show you what you can do ahead of time to make the project as easy as possible. You cannot expect your contractor to do all the work—*you* have to take responsibility to start well and to keep things running smoothly. You must be informed, work out a system with your partner, and always stick to the timetable you have committed to with your contractor. This part also simplifies the decision-making process, helping you make decisions room by room. The process will inevitably test your patience at home. We'll give you strategies for handling the disruptions to your routine, finances, and relationships.

In Part Three, we put you in the position to keep the work under control. You have to prepare yourself for the almost inevitable overruns of cost and time. We'll help you understand why these overruns happen, how to avoid them, and how to deal with them when they do occur. We'll even walk you through mistakes and disputes of various kinds to help you prepare for dealing with them effectively, particularly as the job nears completion. Finally, we'll teach you what the punch list is (and just as importantly, what it *isn't*) and how to use it and callbacks effectively.

In Part Four, we begin to discuss specific remodeling projects, starting with redecoration and remodeling. Do you need to remodel or can redecoration meet your needs? When is an interior decorator right for you? Do you already have spaces in your home that you can reorganize to create new rooms without major construction? We'll help you answer these questions.

You might decide to remodel when you learn how much of that cost can be recouped when you resell your house. If you decide to remodel the kitchen or a bathroom—the two most popular remodeling projects for a home—we'll take you through the process of lining up possible contractors, choosing the right one, and learning the basics so you'll be informed throughout the process.

In Part Five, we examine system repair and replacement. You, like many people, probably take your water heating, air heating, ventilation, and air-conditioning systems for granted. When they need repair, however, you need to be ready with information about the kind of repairs you need, the varieties of systems available, and how to get the most out of your systems. We'll then discuss hiring an electrician. Do you need one? How can you find a reputable one? How can you avoid scam artists? We'll give you similar information about insulation installers, discussing the kinds of insulation available and how you know whether you need to add more. We'll also provide details about how to improve your home's energy efficiency.

Part Six looks at refurbishing the inside of your home—appliances, painting, wallpaper, and flooring. We'll tell you how you can save money by replacing your appliances instead of fixing them. We'll also give you choices of how and when to hire professionals, such as combining a professional contractor and do-it-yourself work when painting. You'll also be prepared for the wide variety of flooring options you'll face.

In Part Seven, we discuss how to protect yourself and your home from various pests—chemical, fire, and living (insects and humans). We start by looking at the unseen problems of carbon monoxide and radon. How can you detect them and get rid of them? We'll then alert you to a problem you probably didn't even know about—the many allergens that can accumulate in heating ducts. After reviewing the choices you have in smoke detectors and fire alarm services, we look at living pests—burglars and insects. We'll help you avoid confusing yet seductive claims about "free" security systems, and we'll clarify how long extermination jobs should take and how much they should cost. We'll also look at home inspection and the code of ethics you *must* expect from your inspector.

In Part Eight, we'll look at major contracting you might need for the outside of your home. We start with roofing and reveal what the process involves, the materials available to you, and how to protect yourself from rip-offs. We then cover siding (no, not *all* siding firms are fly-by-night cons), painting, and windows. We let you know how to find a good contractor and what activities to expect from one. Finally, we look at pool maintenance and protection.

You are about to embark on an experience you will remember every time you look around your home. My goal is to have those memories be as pleasant as possible for you.

Create the Plan and Complete the Contract

PART I

GET THE SCOOP ON...
Why planning is so important ▪ Where to find
ideas and inspiration ▪ Questions about your
lifestyle and home ▪ Putting ideas and plans
on paper ▪ Asking for help

Your Planning Process and the People Who Can Help

Chapter 1

Planning well is essential to any home project; every subsequent step depends on it. Planning is also the least expensive part of a project. If you wait until the walls are up to decide the space is too small or too big, it can cost lots of money to change. In the planning stage, however, you can make changes with an eraser. During the planning stage, you and your partner can discover whether your tastes are compatible and can begin to work out some compromises.

Your planning process has probably been going on for months or even years. Small hints may have been dropped along the way. "We really should have a second bathroom." "Wouldn't it be nice to have more room for entertaining?" "If we had a larger window here, we could look out over the garden." If you bought this book, you're probably starting to get serious about acting on these plans.

In this chapter I'll tell you where to get ideas and how to decide what you want this project to accomplish. I'll also help you get your ideas down on paper so others can work with them. Because you're probably new at this, you may run into some questions you can't answer yourself. I'll tell you where and when to ask for help.

Planning is essential

Any remodeling project will be easier, less stressful, and less expensive if you have a clear understanding of what you want to do and if your ideas are in a form you can communicate to your builder or contractor. Obviously, some jobs—such as replacing a hot water heater or repairing your furnace—require little or no planning. But if you're going to move or remove walls, put an addition on your house, or even remodel a single room (particularly a bathroom or kitchen), creating a plan makes you face your alternatives and work out any personal differences before anyone is sitting around on a time clock.

A good architect or contractor undoubtedly will sit down and make you think your project through before he starts working or even submits a bid. Taking a few evenings of quiet contemplation to get your ideas and goals down on paper will greatly improve your chances of having a successful project. You will look like an informed consumer by being able to show what you want.

Researching: where to get ideas

Planning occurs in two phases. The first is the dream phase, which may have been going on for years as you visited your friends' newly remodeled or newly purchased homes or as you subscribed to magazines

Unofficially . . .
Don't limit your imagination by thinking about money during the planning stage. This is when you should put your dreams on paper. By thinking big, you might find a way to make this a multistage project, or your bank might like what you want to do so much that it'll offer you a bigger mortgage.

such as *House Beautiful, House and Garden, Home,* or *Colonial Homes.* You'll know you're moving toward phase two, reality, when you start marking the pages containing layouts or decorations you like or even tearing out pictures and filing them in folders.

Start going over the magazines and the pictures with your partner. You might assume that you have similar tastes because you both have accepted the space where you currently live. That space came with the house, however, and now you are going to change it. One of you might be thinking stark modern; the other might be dreaming of an English cottage. Keep looking and you'll probably find a common middle ground.

My wife, an architecture buff, has been clipping pictures for years and has files divided into kitchens, bathrooms, living rooms, windows, cupboards, bookcases, and so forth. She was planning remodeling projects long before she even had a house. Unless you are trying to take an old house back to its original decor, however, you don't need such a historic series of magazine clippings. Interior decorating and construction move through fads; a collection of a few recent magazines should bring you up-to-date with a wide range of ideas from which to choose.

Look at window styles, types of doors, furniture arrangements, and wall colors as well as room shapes and sizes. Remember, it's your house and you can do pretty much what you want.

Also remember that, although the structural changes will be relatively permanent, wall colors can be changed (unless you are trying to paint over shades of black). Painting is a fairly easy renovation that can transform the mood of a room quickly.

Bright Idea
When looking through magazines for pictures of various room styles, clip not only pictures of what you like but also what you don't like. Showing these clips to your contractor or architect can help communicate your tastes.

Many new wall-painting techniques—such as using a rag or a sponge and transparent layering—offer creative alternatives. First, however, you need to decide which areas or aspects of your home you want to improve.

Evaluating: identify what you want and need

It's a good idea to start your formal planning process by writing down how you currently live and by listing the activities you engage in and where you do so. I've provided a series of questions (see "A planning questionnaire," below) to lead you through what architects call "creating the client's program." It starts by making you really evaluate the way you use your house.

After you have finished the questionnaire, have identified the aspects of your current house that you don't like and want to change (for instance, a tiny entrance that results in a clutter of wet, muddy clothes and boots at the kitchen door), and have discovered anything you want to add (a bigger kitchen), it's time to do some serious measuring to see whether it all can fit and where it could go.

Good planning often depends on asking the right questions. The following questionnaire is designed to make you think about your house as it is now, how you live in it, and what you want to change or improve.

If you hire an architect, he will probably take you through a similar process. A good general contractor (GC) also will accomplish the same thing—although in a different way—because he has to know what you want before planning can begin.

A planning questionnaire

This list of questions was drawn from a questionnaire created by architects at Black River Design in

Vermont. They assign it to their clients as homework for both new houses and remodeling projects.

General questions

1. What are the major shortcomings of your house as it is? Functional shortcomings? Aesthetic shortcomings?

2. Do you use your house differently in winter than in summer?

3. What special interests or activities require special spaces?

4. What eventual size or square-foot number do you have in mind?

5. What is your approximate budget for this project?

6. Do you have target start and finish construction dates in mind?

    Start date   _____

    Finish date   _____

7. Do you plan to make future changes beyond this project?

Questions concerning your lot and house site

8. Can you locate a copy of your site plan? (Check with your town clerk.)

9. What do you like about your house site?

10. What are the drawbacks (noisy road, future building site next door)?

11. What direction does the prevailing wind come from?

12. Where are north, south, east, and west in relation to your house?

Timesaver
If more than one person is involved in the project, each should work on the questionnaire separately, numbering comments on separate sheets of paper. This accelerates the process and elicits unpressured opinions from each person. Differences can be worked out later, as you compare your comments.

13. What outdoor activities are important to you (gardening, entertaining, barbecuing, kids' play area, and so on)?

14. Do you enjoy, tolerate, or despise mowing the lawn and trimming bushes?

Car questions

15. How many vehicles do you have? Any boats? Campers?

16. Where will they be stored or parked? In the garage? In the driveway or on the street? Under a covered carport?

17. Is the garage part of your remodeling plans? Do you plan to add to it? Are you planning to use the garage space for something else?

Storage questions

18. What equipment do you own (tractor lawn-mower, power lawnmower, wheelbarrow, snow blower, bicycles, canoe, boat)?

19. What else do you own that requires storage (garden tools, hoses, garbage cans, outdoor furniture, grill, toys, sports equipment)?

20. Would you consider a freestanding shed? Is there room for one?

21. Do you have space for a workshop? What would you do in it?

Deck, terrace, and porch questions

Depending on what part of the country you live in, covering a deck or terrace or screening in a porch can extend your outdoor season.

22. Covering a deck with an awning or a roof and enclosing it with screen or glass can create a

greenhouse, almost another room. It can be used year-round. Would this solve your space problems?

23. For what activities would you use outdoor space? Eating, playing, entertaining, year-round gardening?

Stage of life questions

24. Are you and your partner young, married, expecting a child or more children? Do you need an adult privacy room? A kids' playroom? A separate TV area?

25. Do you have older children needing separate bedrooms? Is adult privacy a necessity? Do you need an office area for both adults and children to do homework? Do you need an area for a computer?

26. Do you have adult children that no longer live at home, creating extra rooms? Do you need a guest bedroom for visiting children and other guests? Do you need entertaining-area improvements? A hobby area?

27. Could rooms be utilized for dual purposes (such as putting a hide-a-bed in an office, den, or TV room to make a guest bedroom)?

28. How do you want to use the space? For relaxation, entertainment, watching TV, working?

29. The traditional living room often is the least-used room in today's homes. How do you utilize this room now? How could it be modified?

30. Do you need a large room for entertaining?

31. For what functions do you want to create separate areas?

32. What functions could you combine (entertaining, kids' play area, adult TV watching, reading, listening to music, playing music, exercising)?

33. What kind of work do you do or will you be doing at home (paying bills, keeping records, doing office work, earning a living)?

34. How will you accommodate these functions? Options include creating and using a great room or a study, a den, a TV room, a family room, or an enclosed porch.

Eating questions

35. Where do you like to eat? In a formal dining room (another underutilized space in today's homes), at a dining table off the kitchen area, in the kitchen, in a breakfast nook, or at an island or eating counter?

36. How separate or connected do you want the cooking and eating spaces to be?

37. How often do you entertain?

38. How often does the whole family eat together?

Kitchen questions

39. Who does the food preparation? One or more people? How many at a time?

40. How often do you shop for food? (If you shop every day, you need less storage space; if you shop once a month, you need a lot of storage space.)

41. How much food storage do you have now? How much would you like to have?

42. When guests come over, do they always end up in the kitchen?

43. Do you have any special preparation or cooking requirements for your kitchen?

44. Is the design of your kitchen in the proven sink, stove, refrigerator work triangle?

45. Have you selected and priced the appliances you want to replace?

46. Do you need more cupboard space? If at least one person in the household is tall, have you considered having cabinets that go all the way to the ceiling?

Sleeping questions

It usually is dark outside when you're in your bedroom, but morning sun and views can be important considerations.

47. Have you considered using your bedroom as a sitting or TV area (away from children and their after-school guests), a work area, an exercise area, a dressing area, or a vanity area?

48. How big do you want your bedroom to be? Big (over 12 feet square), average, or small?

49. What are your clothes-storage needs? Do you need a walk-in closet(s), a regular closet, or no closet but more space for wardrobes and dressers?

50. Do you need seasonal storage for clothing? If so, where should it be?

51. Do you want a master bathroom off your bedroom?

52. Will your kids have separate bedrooms or will they share?

53. Do you want their rooms close to yours or farther away?

Moneysaver
When you invite kitchen or bathroom design firms to bid on your project, make sure to tell them there are two or three other companies bidding on the same job. This tends to keep their pricing pencils sharp and their numbers a bit lower.

54. Do you expect your kids to spend time in their rooms playing, studying, and so on? Or will they use another location? Remember to plan ahead; they won't be this age for long.

55. Do you want or need a guest bedroom?

56. Should it have a separate bath or will guests share a bath with the family?

57. Can the guest room double as something else (a den, a TV room, or a playroom)?

Bathroom questions

Unofficially . . .
The bathroom and the kitchen are the two most frequently selected remodeling projects. Take time to evaluate both your needs and the many new products and innovations available.

58. Would you like double vanities and sinks (ideal for a family with conflicting morning schedules)?

59. Is there a scenic view possibility for placement of the toilet or tub?

60. Is there room downstairs for a vanity or a half-bath?

61. Is bath time an important part of your day or is it strictly functional?

62. Are you tempted to go all-out and soak, shower, steam, and whirl?

63. Will your dream bathroom fit in your existing space?

Laundry questions

64. Who does the laundry? Mom? Dad? Kids? Have you given all participants a voice in the design?

65. Do you need more room for or a better-organized sorting system?

66. Have you considered different appliance arrangements such as stacking, side-by-side, or opposite?

67. Would you like a permanent set-up for ironing or a convenient fold-down ironing board?

68. Are there other tasks you want to do at the same time that you do laundry?

69. Where would the laundry be most convenient? In the basement with a chute? On the first floor? On the second floor near the bedrooms? Consider the noise issue, and remember to anticipate the inevitable flooding of the washer with tile and a drain.

Fireplace questions

Fireplaces are a traditional focal point of the home, although they're inefficient compared to a wood stove for heating.

70. Do you want a fireplace in your home? If so, in association with what activities?

71. Have you considered a wood stove? If so, in association with what activities?

72. Have you considered the resupply and storage of firewood?

73. Have you considered where the smoke stack for a new fireplace will go?

Solar questions

Particularly in the northern U.S., it makes sense to consider orienting some of your rooms and windows toward the sun (south) to gain active or passive solar heat as well as to brighten the interior.

74. Which of the following rooms would you like sunlit and when: kitchen, dining area, formal eating area, living and relaxing area, bedrooms, work area, study, library, greenhouse, deck, kids' play area? In the morning, all day, or in the afternoon?

75. Have you considered adding passive solar energy space to your house, such as (in the North) larger windows facing south and west? Collectors such as sun rooms or hallways?

76. Is there room for laying out piping to heat water for your home? Can you heat your swimming pool with the sun?

Now you should know more about your home, its strengths, and its weaknesses. You have been forced to think about what you really want, and you're ready to start playing with designs.

Watch Out!
Don't use your own plans. No matter how wonderful your drawings are, have your contractor create his own set of plans for your project. That way, if there are any mistakes or miscalculations, they will not be your responsibility.

Putting those dreams on paper

If you are lucky enough to have an architect's or contractor's drawing of your home, great. Get some tracing paper and start rearranging your rooms. Drawing floor plans of your house and playing with various room, appliance, and furniture arrangements is fun. It's a good way to ease from the dream phase into reality. It is also the best way to provide guidance to your architect or contractor.

Here is a list of the items you will need to get started with drawing plans. Most of these items are available at a local art supply store.

- A pad of quarter-inch graph paper. (Use the scale $1/4$ inch = 1 foot.)

- A drafting triangle.

- A T-square.

- An architect's scale ruler so you can translate feet to quarter-inch increments without having to count squares.

- A quarter-inch-scale furniture indicator and house plan and plumbing inking templates.

- A pad of tissue paper for tracings.

■ A couple of hard-lead (2-H) pencils (for detail work) and several soft-lead pencils (for creative sketching).

With these tools, you can outline the proposed dimensions of the rooms in your home or of an addition, and you can trace in the actual furniture and appliances you plan to put into the space. These templates also allow you to draw conventional doors and various bi-fold doors and to figure out the required room and swing direction for each.

The next step is to measure the inside dimensions of your house or at least the rooms to be remodeled. (You don't have to measure the outside.) For this, you'll need a 25-foot retractable tape measure (preferably with the lever lock feature). Get one that's at least three-quarters of an inch wide so you can push it without buckling. Don't try using the cloth tape from your sewing basket—you won't be happy.

Now draw a basic plan of the space you're looking at. First, simply sketch out the dimensions. Second, translate your rough dimensions into scale (one-quarter inch = 1 foot). Rather than redrawing this basic plan over and over as you try different ideas, you might run off about 20 copies of the original. Or you can do what architects do: Lay sheets of tracing paper over your original drawing and, using soft-lead pencils, try successive quick variations. One advantage of this method is that you can make changes to the original window, wall, and door sizes and locations.

Take the versions you think come closest to what you want your space to look like and put them on the graph paper. When we were exploring ideas for expanding our small ranch house, we came up with

Timesaver
Keep track of your variations by numbering them and give a brief description of the idea you're expressing. If you don't, you'll wind up with a pile of papers and confusion. Here's a good example: "Drawing #4. Making two small rooms into one bigger one."

four completely different variations. Two involved adding a new section to the back of the house, one called for a room over the existing garage, and the fourth suggested adding a second floor. We drew separate plans for each of these ideas. Our two-story approach also involved extending the back of the house about 4 feet.

When and where to look for help

Unlike a college exam, there are no rules that say you must work alone on this plan. You can definitely invite people to advise you. When my wife and I came up with our four options, we had no idea what they might cost or whether they were even possible according to the natural laws of construction and gravity. It was obviously time to ask for help. We called in four general contractors, went over our ideas with each of them, listened to their suggestions, and got rough estimates of the cost of each alternative. Of course, there are also other places you can go for help.

You must plan ahead if you want your remodeling or repair projects to go smoothly—or at least, as smoothly as construction work can go. Everything you do from this point on depends on your plan. If you are vague and indecisive about your wants and needs, you are asking architects, designers, and contractors to read your mind.

Unless you plan to do all the construction work yourself (usually not a great idea), the time will come to bring in expert help. That time may come during the planning stage if you run into some problems. You might want expert help, for example, if you are contemplating removing an interior wall and are concerned about the roof falling in or if you and your planning partner simply can't agree on the direction you should go. It helps to have a third-party individual who understands design and construction principles, if nothing else, to act as a referee.

The more information you can gather in the beginning stages, the better the chances your project will come out the way you want it to, the fewer surprises there will be as the job progresses, and the closer it will come to costing what you expect.

Help is available from a variety of sources. An architect or contractor could take over the entire project, or a local carpenter could look at your plans, possibly make some practical suggestions, or simply get to work. The following sections tell you what kind of help is available, where to find it, and what you can expect each person or service to provide.

Hire an architect to design your project

You can, of course, retain an architect to design your entire project. During the preplanning stage, you will describe your ideas to him or her. An architect brings a great deal of experience to your project as well as originality and creativity. The fee for such services is usually a percentage of the overall cost, for which you'll get a full set of construction plans and a schedule or list of the materials and supplies needed. He or she might also help you review the bids.

Hire an architect to manage your building project

Architects can also represent you during construction with regular inspections and meetings with the contractor and subcontractors. The architect can serve as your "clerk of the works" (an old term that means "watchdog"). This might seem to duplicate what the contractor should be doing, but

Bright Idea
Even if you decide to do all the work yourself in your spare time, you still might need someone to come in and fix any errors you make on the job or, more likely, to finish it when you and your partner run out of patience with living in a half-built kitchen.

contractors often tell me they appreciate having another professional available to work out solutions to problems as they arise. This also tends to keep the homeowner (you) off the contractor's back. This approach represents an additional cost to you, but architects often claim they save a customer more than they cost.

The size of your project might determine whether or not you need an architect, but don't feel you are insulting a professional with a small job. I once checked with a local architect and found that his current jobs ranged from a two-car garage plan for a difficult site that would cost about $22,000 to build, a small kitchen renovation budgeted at $3,000, and a new million-dollar house.

Architects are comparatively easy to find because they are usually listed in the Yellow Pages of your phone book. For recommendations, check with friends or neighbors who may have retained an architect in the past. Call two or three architects, describe what you are looking for, and make an appointment to meet with them if they are interested. I suggest that the first meeting be in their offices where you can look over some of their recent projects, judge whether their design philosophies agree with yours, and make sure they have a license from the state. Any second meetings should be in your space.

Rent an architect

If you know you need some expert advice, but you don't want to take on the additional cost of an architect, it's possible to retain an architect on an hourly basis to go over your plans and make suggestions or to solve any puzzles you've created. It might be a good idea to avail yourself of this service at the

Watch Out!
Some architects take every project and bend it to fit their own personal design philosophy. If you hit on one who just won't listen to you and ignores all your suggestions, thank him for his time and move on to the next one. Find someone you can work with comfortably.

beginning of your planning process. An architect can walk through your space, listen to your ideas, and sketch out various approaches you might not have considered. I wish we had been aware of this possibility when we were working on our project. An architect might have checked the attic and noticed that our chimney slanted 2 feet toward the front of the house. Call a few local architects, describe what you want, and ask what hourly rate they charge for consultation work.

Retail experts: your local lumberyard or building supply store

Many lumberyards and building supply stores have an estimator on the premises who can estimate what your materials will cost based on your plans. He can prepare a list of the materials you need plus the numbers, styles, and sizes of windows and doors. A lumberyard probably won't be able to compile similar schedules for your plumbing and electrical supplies. For these estimates, you should go to a plumbing supply store and an electrical supply store.

These estimates do not include the cost of a contractor and the labor costs of any necessary subcontractors. The estimators, however, might be able to furnish a ballpark figure and possibly give you the names of some good contractors in the area. In return, they appreciate the opportunity to bid on your project's building materials.

Kitchen and bath specialists

Kitchen and bath remodeling specialists are listed in your phone book and regularly advertise in local papers. They specialize in designing and building kitchens and bathrooms. One advantage of using these companies is that they have a lot of

Unofficially . . .
No project is too big or too small for a small- or medium-sized architectural firm. They won't be insulted if you invite them to help. Many architects consider hourly consulting on smaller house projects to be the most creative and fun part of their profession.

experience with these projects. Another advantage is that they might have skilled tradespeople on their payroll or regularly use certain reputable subcontractors; therefore, they will have better control over scheduling. (See Chapters 8 and 9 for more details about designing your kitchen and bath.)

Remember, these companies make their money selling their services and products; they may push you to the higher end of your budget limits. You can protect yourself by asking two or three such companies to come in, design, and offer bids. There is usually no charge for designs and preliminary consulting.

Make sure to get a list of previous clients who hired the company for jobs similar to yours. At the very least, call these previous clients on the phone; if possible, visit them to see the results. Most homeowners welcome the chance to show off their new kitchens or bathrooms, and you can gain better insight into the quality of the work. Use this same approach with all the firms or individuals you invite to provide proposals and bids. (For more details, see the section "Doing your homework: how to really check a contractor's referrals" later in this chapter.)

Design/remodeling firms

The design/remodeling combination concept is comparatively new in construction. As you read the descriptions of what architects and contractors do, you might decide you want to employ both professionals—many people do. Some contractors have recognized the benefits of providing both services under one roof and have hired a designer to provide the planning service.

At one time, locating such a firm in your area would have been a problem, but these days it's

getting easier. According to the National Association of Home Builders (NAHB), there were only
278 certified graduate design/remodeling firms in
the United States in 1993. In 1997, there were over
500 registered firms. To be recognized as a certified
graduate remodeler (CGR), a contractor must complete a series of business management courses with
the NAHB.

Another national organization is the National
Association of the Remodeling Industry (NARI).
NARI has more than 6,000 members nationwide,
about one-third of which have completed the
certified remodelers (CR) course. NARI members
can apply for one of three certified courses—
remodelers, lead carpenters, or specialists (such as
electrical or mechanical).

The following are some advantages to using a
design/remodeling firm with a designer skilled in
interviewing clients and translating your wishes into
working drawings:

- **Better designer-contractor communications.**
  Having the designer of your project stay with it
  all the way to completion creates a cooperative
  effort that's hard to achieve with several independent professionals.

- **State-of-the-art management systems and
  computer-aided design (CAD) capabilities.**
  These give many design/remodeling firms an
  efficient means of creating your plans and
  preparing bids as well as the skill to organize
  and schedule the work.

- **One-stop shopping.** If you use a design/remod-
  eling firm, you might have to make only one
  phone call to get the whole job done or to
  correct mistakes. Some firms employ skilled

Bright Idea
Your state or
local Home
Builders
Associations are
among the best
sources for names
of reputable
design/
remodelers in
your area. To get
a list of certified
remodelers from
NARI, call
800-440-6274
or access its
Web site
(www.nari.org).

tradespeople, giving them more control over scheduling; others sub the work out to craftsmen they know and have worked well with in the past.

- **A fixed price.** The design/remodeling companies were among the few builders I interviewed who were willing to offer a fixed-price bid on the entire project.

- **On-time completion.** The combination of in-house professional tradespeople, prebidding interviews, and a complete understanding of the design gives the design/remodeling companies what they feel is the best chance to finish your project on schedule.

Your local carpenter

Your remodeling project might only require a simple job. Perhaps adding a bow window in your kitchen, putting in a new floor and vanity in the bath, or removing a wall will give you the space or modernization you want. If this is the case, you could call in a local carpenter to talk about the project. He has probably handled dozens of jobs similar to yours.

A good portion of remodeling and repair work is done by local carpenters who handle most of the diverse tasks required on a job themselves or with a couple of helpers. They call in plumbers or electricians only if they run into special problems. The whole project can probably be done quickly, on a fairly informal basis, and with a cost range rather than a firm bid or on a time-and-material basis.

You shouldn't be surprised if a carpenter can handle your entire project. After all, most general contractors start off as carpenters and only get into general contracting when they start having multiple

Moneysaver
You can send the plans created by one design department out to other builders for competitive bids. As one design/remodeling firm employee put it, "We treat each portion of our business separately and don't mind the competition. We do have an advantage in the bidding, however, because we know the job so well."

jobs at the same time. Arrangements with a local carpenter tend to be less formal—be sure he gets the necessary local permits and is properly licensed.

A local carpenter will take measurements, possibly offer some alternatives, call the local lumberyard for prices of materials, and give you a quote. The next time you hear anything might be when he reports that your materials are in and that the project will begin the next morning.

How do you find this gem? The good ones have jobs lined up a few weeks in advance and don't feel they have to advertise. (One reason they can offer lower prices is that they often have a lower overhead from not advertising or marketing.) Your neighbors might even be a little reluctant to give up their carpenter's name. They may need help again! Persist in your search. A good carpenter is worth finding and, if your project is within his scope, should be strongly considered.

General contractors

The general contractor (GC) is the person who takes the remodeling project from your final dream on paper to the new space you have envisioned. Your first contact with a GC will probably be when you invite him to your home to meet you and to see the space you have in mind. Don't be surprised if the GC shows up in business attire carrying a briefcase. Contractors are business people and often are college graduates. On the other hand, he may show up in bib overalls with a ponytail. Don't prejudge.

The general contractor may or may not do any actual physical labor on your project. Ours pounded nails during the framing phase to work off frustration and to get some exercise. He also laid all the tile in both bathrooms because he loves doing it.

> 66
> A replacement-window firm charged our neighbor $10,000 to change all her windows to double panes. We had a local carpenter bid on the same job for our similar-sized house. It was in the hundreds, so we hired him. Two days later all the new windows were in with matched trim painted inside and out. Our neighbor still has to paint her outside shingles.
> —Liz Strasser, Armonk, NY
> 99

All the GCs you invite to look at your project prior to submitting bids (including all the other building types previously mentioned) will go over your plans and ideas with you, will make recommendations, and will tell you how they would handle the job. They should tell you about similar jobs they have done and should give you a list of references. If they don't volunteer this information, ask for it. References should include work they just finished as well as work they completed three to four years ago.

At this stage, you are dealing with all the contractors you have located. If you have the names of 12 contractors, you should do a quick screening job to narrow the list down to the 6 you will actually invite to see the job. You should then do a complete job of checking out these six contractors.

Here is a list of the basic criteria you should consider when deciding which contractors will make your prospective bidders list:

- Look for someone who has been in business at least five years.

- Check for membership in professional organizations such as the National Association of Home Builders (NAHB), your state's Home Builders Association, and the National Association of the Remodeling Industry (NARI) and its state associations. In addition, many building trades have associations of their own such as plumbers, HVAC, architects, and so on.

- Check with your local Better Business Bureau to see whether any complaints have been filed against your prospective contractors.

- Always make sure that the contractor is licensed and insured. The best way is simply to ask to see a license and proof of insurance. Unscrupulous contractors have been known to carry outdated insurance proof or to practice immediate cancellation (carrying current-looking proof on a canceled policy). To cover yourself, verify that these are up-to-date (see the next item).

■ Ask to see insurance certificates for both worker's compensation and general liability insurance. Take down the telephone number of the contractor's insurance agent or company and call to make sure he is currently insured. Asking to see proof of insurance and a state license number is not an insult. The cost of these permits adds considerably to a contractor's overhead and has to be reflected in the bid. By checking, you are indicating you will not try to underbid him with some fly-by-night outfit. A reputable contractor will be glad you asked.

■ Get an up-to-date reference list of previous customers. Call them and ask to inspect both recent and older jobs in person.

Doing your homework: how to really check a contractor's referrals

One homeowner (who set a record for cost overruns at 600 percent) told me that many people came to admire his remodeled home and asked who his contractor was. His home is an old Cape Cod cottage overlooking a beautiful little Maine harbor with a lighthouse in the distance. His visitors got so carried away with the view from his new picture windows that they neglected to get any real information. "Very few ever asked me what I thought of the quality of his work or if I would ever hire him again. My answer, if they had asked, would have been, 'It was terrible and I would never hire him again.'"

Watch Out!
As the homeowner and job-site owner, you are the deep pocket of last resort for injury claims by any uninsured subcontractors you or even your contractor may hire (if it turns out both are uninsured). Your homeowner's insurance should protect you. Make sure it's in effect and that it covers such claims.

He could have pointed out the 3-inch difference in the floor level of the new addition, a stairway you cannot descend without bumping your head, a bathroom door that never closes properly, and a sliding window that can't be opened, not to mention the extra $90,000 spent and the building materials stolen out of the yard.

The following are good questions to ask when checking a contractor's referrals:

- Did you enjoy working with your builder?
- Was the final cost at or near the bid? If it cost more, why?
- Did the work start and end on schedule? If not, why not?
- Did the workers clean up at the end of each day?
- Did you have any disagreements with your builder? If so, how did he handle them?
- Were you satisfied with the subcontractors?
- Would you hire your general contractor for another project?
- Do you recommend that I hire him?

While checking referrals at the homes of a contractor's previous customers, you can also learn a lot about a builder's capabilities and attention to detail by using your eyes. The following are some things to look for as the proud homeowners take you through their new space:

- Check corners and joints where window and door frames and baseboards come together. Are they tight?
- In the kitchen, open the oven, dishwasher, and refrigerator doors. Do they interfere with each other?

Moneysaver
If you ask vague questions, you'll get vague answers. Take a page from a good reporter's notebook. Ask open-ended questions using the famous who, what, why, when, and (for construction) how much?

- Open and close inside doors, cabinets, and drawers. Do they work smoothly without binding?

- Check for paint runs on the walls and woodwork.

- Remember any good ideas you see to use at your place.

- Does the addition or new work blend with the previously-existing home?

How to choose your contractors

Many homeowners and virtually all towns and government agencies choose their contractors based on the lowest bid. I don't go along with this philosophy, as you will see in the next chapter and thereafter.

One contractor friend once suggested to me that you shouldn't hire any contractor you wouldn't invite home for dinner with your family. What he means, of course, is that you will be living with this person for the life of your project. It should be someone you respect, are comfortable with, and like.

A contractor can be a big help in your initial planning with both his basic knowledge of the mechanics of construction and his experience with similar projects. You should make it clear from the start, however, that you are still going to solicit other bids.

When you have narrowed your list down to two or three contractors using the many objective measurements available to you, trust your gut for that final selection. Go for the one that just feels right.

Watch Out!
All contractors have a short memory for disasters and tend to be optimists. The time estimate for the job is based on the assumption that, for the first time in the history of home building, everything will work smoothly. You should mentally add half again or even double the time given.

After you select the person or firm to head up your project from the bids you receive (see Chapter 2), you can expect the following:

- A detailed list, a written description, and a plan of the work to be performed
- A list of the materials needed by quantity and/or brand name
- A list of jobs expected to be subcontracted
- An estimate of the time the job will take
- A starting date

When selecting any of the services people described in this chapter, you should follow some basic guidelines:

- Get at least four written estimates based on the same plans and specifications.
- Never pay more than 10 percent or $1,000 in advance, whichever is lower (see Chapter 2, "Bids and Contracts").
- Progressive payments should not exceed the cost of time and materials for work already completed.
- Make sure your contractor gets all the necessary building permits (see Chapter 2, "Bids and Contracts").

Just the facts

- Go through the questionnaire and identify the issues on which you and your spouse agree and disagree.
- Ask for help from architects, lumberyard draftsmen, and other specialists.
- Work on your own plans; it will give you a knowledge of your home and an appreciation of the complexity of remodeling.

Moneysaver
It's more satisfying to start tearing out walls than to fool around asking questions and making endless drawings. Planning, however, is the only part of remodeling that's completely free. The more time and thought you spend planning, the less time and money you'll spend later.

Chapter 2

Bids and Contracts

In this chapter I will introduce you to how contractors prepare bids and estimates and explain why good contractors frequently lose out to shoddy builders. You will learn about the three main types of bids and the advantages and disadvantages of each from both your viewpoint and your builder's. I will also provide some criteria you can use when evaluating bids and some tips on how to do a little post-bid negotiating. Finally, I'll review how you can select the winner.

You've decided what you want done and have narrowed your ideas to a specific plan and written a description of the new appliances and fixtures and any physical changes. Now you're ready to send your project out for bids.

Bidding 101

As a homeowner with a project ready for bid, you will receive dollar amounts in three progressive forms, as follows:

- **Estimate.** A ballpark figure of the cost of a project. Because many homeowners use this figure

Bright Idea
If you want accurate bids, you must supply each of your bidding contractors the same set of plans and criteria with as few unknowns and surprises as possible. I encourage you to enlist the aid of an architect to draw up your project or to select one of the plans submitted by potential contractors.

to select a contractor, estimates tend to be on the low side. In the hands of an experienced builder it can be quite accurate, but it is still basically a guess and is subject to change.

- **Bid.** A cost figure usually based on a *take-off* from the plans with actual dimensions, the number of electrical outlets, the cost and amount of materials, appliances, and calculated labor time. This is a more accurate figure and is the one your builder is more apt to live with, but it is not legally binding.

- **Contracted price.** The cost for which your contractor will actually do the job, as described in the contract. It is a legal document.

There are three basic forms of bids you might receive:

- Time and materials
- Cost per square foot
- Firm price

Each bid method or form has its advantages and disadvantages. A lot depends on the size and scope of your project and your confidence in the contractors.

Time and materials (or cost-plus)

For this type of bid, the contractor estimates the amount of materials and time the job will take, adds 10 to 15 percent for his profit, and comes up with a rough estimate of the cost. You then can take this estimate to a bank for your loan.

Advantages: The final cost is based on the actual time spent and materials used. If surprises or problems crop up, they will be added to the cost. If all goes according to plan, however, you will not owe any extra.

Disadvantages: A high level of trust is required for this approach. You or your architect should do some informed monitoring to let your contractor know someone is paying attention. In the hands of an inexperienced builder, this method can run up some serious costs as he tears out mistakes and spends time figuring out how to do the job.

Cost per square foot

This method works best with new construction such as a whole house or a new addition or wing.

Advantages: You can get a bid quickly, but it depends on the availability of up-to-date cost data for your area.

Disadvantages: Cost per square foot is almost useless as a basis for a contract—it is just too vague. For remodeling existing space, it is totally useless. Cost per square foot can give a ballpark figure for new construction because there are fewer unknowns or surprises. It does not, however, allow for such upgrades as specialized wall treatments or paneling, terrazzo floors, or high-end lighting and bathroom fixtures. When remodeling, you have these same variables plus the initial destruction process. You won't know ahead of time whether the old bathroom floor can hold up the new hot tub or if the whole plumbing and electrical systems will have to be reworked.

Firm price

The contractor, working from your architect's plans or his own, does a complete take-off for materials and supplies, calculates his and all the planned subcontractors' time and profit, and offers you a firm price. He also calculates cost allowances for any appliances, plumbing fixtures, lighting fixtures, and cabinets.

Moneysaver
You will pay a bad carpenter as much per hour for slow, sloppy work as you do a good carpenter for fast, accurate work. In the end, however, you'll pay even more for sloppy work because it takes longer to correct mistakes.

Advantages: If your contractor runs into surprises—delays due to weather or scheduling complications for items described in the contract—they are his responsibility. The price remains the same to you. Sounds like the best deal, right? Not necessarily.

Disadvantages: If your contractor has to come up with a firm price he can live with for your remodeling project, he'll have to include a large "fudge factor" to cover the unknown and unexpected surprises that invariably come up as the walls come down. Also, if you change your mind after the job is bid on, changes become extras that get billed out as time and materials. That so-called firm price can go up considerably.

Which bid type to use

If forced, I could come up with some situations in which I thought a firm bid would be the best way for a homeowner to go, but with limitations. There should be no more than one, maybe two, trades involved (carpenters, plumbers, and so on), and most of the surprises would have to be eliminated. A roofing contractor might be a good person to ask for a firm bid. Painting, inside or out, is another area in which most of the variables (other than weather) are known in advance.

Using my guideline of single-trade applications, possible situations can also include carpeting, floor sanding and finishing, and bookcase building. I also just had a firm bid on a new furnace including installation. When it comes to bathroom and kitchen remodeling, however, when the contractor can't see through the walls and under the floor, a firm bid just won't hold.

Timesaver
You can take some time off the bidding process by requesting firm bids on single-contractor projects such as installing a new roof, sanding and refinishing your floor, or painting the inside or outside of your house.

For each form of bid, the information provided with the bid request must be the same for all bidders. Bidding on construction projects might well be where the term "comparing apples to oranges" originated. If each contractor has a different set of plans and if each plan calls for different materials and specifications, the bids are useless.

Your job as the homeowner is to settle on the floor plan you want, reproduce it, and get it out to all the prospective bidders. Even better, you could do some leg work and come up with a list of everything you want installed in the remodeled rooms such as appliances, tubs, toilets, light fixtures, water fixtures, replacement windows, floor coverings, and so on.

It is even more useful to both you and your bidders if you include model numbers and brands. (Note the retail prices on your copy of the bid request.) With the information distributed, you can now peruse the bids you receive and be able to compare them appropriately—no matter which form of bid your contractors use.

Bright Idea
Instruct each bidder to prepare a bid based on the plan, descriptions, and materials as handed out. Then ask each bidder to note any areas where problems might arise—such as rotten floor boards, old piping, outmoded wiring, and so on—and calculate these costs. Now you can compare apples to apples and oranges to oranges.

Why do bids range so widely?

Let's say you decide to remodel the upstairs bathroom in your 1952 raised-ranch home. You want a new, built-in tub, a new toilet, a modern sink and vanity, and a new linoleum floor. You invite two contractors to bid on the job.

Contractor #1 submits a bid covering 40 hours of labor to remove the old tub, toilet, and sink and to install the new items. At $40 per hour, that's $1,600. He then makes a $1,000 allowance for the new items; new fixtures and materials will be selected by the owner (you) at a later date. Any additional labor or materials necessary but not listed in the bid or contract will be charged extra on a time-and-materials basis. Total bid: $2,600.

Contractor #2 is an experienced builder who knows that homes more than 40 years old are probably ripe for plumbing problems. His bid includes removal of the old tub, sink, toilet, and fixtures plus replacing the old galvanized pipes from the basement to the bathroom with copper. He noticed some water damage around the tub, so his bid includes replacing the underlayment as well as laying the new linoleum floor. When he asks about the tile around the tub, you tell him you assumed new tile would be part of a new tub installation (not the case). His bid includes replacing the Sheetrock backing as well as new tile. Any additional labor and materials necessary but not listed in the bid will be billed extra on a time-and-materials basis. Total bid: $7,300.

Which bid should you take? After you see the reasons for the differences, it will be obvious that the higher bid is the more accurate one. In the actual bidding process, the differences are not usually so well-defined. In the hands of a less-than-straightforward contractor, that low bid could balloon to $10,000.

In the experience of my wife and me, when it came time to pick the piping for our new second-floor bath, the contractor offered me the option of half-inch or three-quarter-inch copper tubing. "The half-inch tubing is less expensive," he said, "but you could get the thrill of scalding hot water in your shower if someone flushes the downstairs toilet." I opted for the three-quarter-inch pipe.

Magazine and newspaper articles often promote firm or fixed bids as a means to protect yourself from add-on costs. One builder I talked to observed, "A firm bid from a contractor costs a lot because he has to protect himself from all the surprises that could be encountered in a remodel as the walls are opened up." In the event that there are no surprises, you are still stuck with the original, significantly padded bid.

The challenge in bidding is to come up with a means of arriving at a price that is fair to both the contractor and the homeowner. I recommend taking the following steps to accomplish this goal:

1. Keep the bidding on the basic proposal separate from any contingencies or surprise factors. Have the contractors list areas where they think problems might be encountered and then have them estimate these costs separately. Make your plans as complete as possible with a detailed list of the quality of the materials and fixtures you expect.

2. Do some prebid pricing of your own. Go to appliance stores, plumbing and lighting fixture showrooms, and the kitchen cabinet and window-display sections of lumberyards. Price the items or the level of quality you want. This lets you know how realistic those allowances for selected items are.

3. Do some extra work prequalifying your contractors. First, only consider companies that have been in business for at least five years. Next, really check their references. Visit some of their former jobs and talk to their clients. Finally, select a contractor you trust and feel comfortable with to work on your project on a cost-plus or labor-and-materials basis.

Timesaver
Uncover surprises before asking for bids. If you want an accurate bid, open up the walls you intend to remove or alter and let the contractors see what they will be working with. A couple of hours of wallboard removal work by you or a contractor takes the surprises out of the project and removes the need for the insurance factor.

Negotiating after a bid

There are no rules forbidding you to talk to your bidders after you receive their offers. You can ask them to explain why their number is higher or lower than other bidders, and you can possibly clear up any misunderstandings about the project.

In any project involving different subcontractors (electrical, plumbing, carpentry, painting, and so on), your bidding contractors have probably solicited bids from other firms or individuals. Each of these subcontractors might have added some "insurance" factors to protect themselves against surprises. Your contractor might be able to ease their doubts and get them to lower their bids, particularly if you have shown in your meetings with the contractor that you are open-minded and willing to adjust to unanticipated costs if they are justified.

Consider the following progression of steps for narrowing down your choice of contractors when soliciting bids:

1. Collect the names and qualifications of as many contractors as possible to provide a representative pool from which to select.

2. Narrow this list down to the best six and invite each one to meet with you to talk about the project. Listen to their ideas, get to know them a little, and really check up on their qualifications, history, and referrals.

3. From these six, invite four to actually submit bids.

4. From the four bids, throw out the highest and lowest if there is a wide discrepancy between the two.

"
One owner wanted to hire me but had lower bids. I explained that my bid included the possibility of problems with the foundation. When he agreed to pay half the cost of fixing such problems, I was able to drop my bid by $3,200. I got the job at a price that was right for both of us.

—Jarron Basinger, contractor
"

5. Invite the two in the middle range (or if all are comparatively close, all four) to explain their numbers and possibly to negotiate further.

6. Use the final figures plus your gut intuition to select your contractor.

If you are confused by the bidding process, think of the plight of the poor contractors. They have to try to balance their bid between trying to be the low bidder and still covering the costs of yet-to-be-discovered problems. Their competition might be neophytes who don't know what they're doing or a desperate firm willing to bid low just to meet its payroll for another month. There's a saying in construction that, in the competition to be the low bidder, the guy who gets the job is usually the one who offers the least accurate bid.

You might think that, after you have checked out your contractors, reviewed all the bids, and chosen one, you are done with the paperwork part of the selection process. This is not the case. You still need to read and sign the contract your contractor prepares for you.

If you've ever bought a used car at a high-pressure lot, you have encountered a typical fine-print warning about the contract being the entire agreement—anything the salesman might have told you counts for nothing. Don't assume anything that isn't in the contract.

You might be having some trouble keeping track of the terms *bid, proposal, agreement,* and *contract.* They respectively relate to different phases of the same process. In fact, they might even be the same document. It is simply a proposal or bid until you sign it and then it becomes the agreement or contract.

Watch Out!
The contract is not just a routine formality. It forms the basis for the work to be done, the price, and how you and your contractor will interact. Read it and understand it before signing.

What is a contract?

In simple terms, a contract is an agreement between you and your contractor (or plumber or architect) in which you describe what you want done and your contractor describes what he will do in the bid spec, who and what he will use to do it, how much it will cost, and the terms of payment. What could be simpler? As one builder observed, however, "It starts out as an agreement until something goes wrong and the lawyers get into the act . . . then it becomes a contract."

Who should write the contract?

The contractor should write the contract, but it doesn't necessarily have to be on the contractor's form. Whoever writes the contract gets to put in and leave out what he wants. There is an advantage to this. Some states mandate that a contract must contain certain things, but usually they are so basic that they offer little or no protection. Connecticut law, for example, only mandates that the company or contractor's name and address, the state contractor license number, and both signatures appear.

There are two distinct parts of a contract. In the first part, your job and the work to be performed are described and the price and payment agreement are stipulated. The second part, often referred to as the *boiler plate*, states the standards to which the contractor will adhere, the responsibilities of both you and your contractor (the bid spec), and how differences will be resolved. This part can be lengthy because it covers a wide range of contingencies that could (but probably won't) come up.

AIA forms

Instead of blindly accepting your contractor's contract form, you might look into the standard contracts available through your local or state AIA chapter. These standard forms have been developed over 80 years of trial and error. If you employ an architect, he will undoubtedly use an AIA form for his contract with you. The architect will then prepare another contract for you and your contractor using another AIA form.

One reason to use an AIA contract form is that it saves someone a lot of typing. More stipulations and contingencies are covered than you could ever think of yourself—certainly more than you'll ever actually use. Almost every situation you and your contractor could get into is covered in these forms by a definition, a way to determine responsibility, or an explanation of who has to do what. If you and your contractor can't come to an agreement at some point in the future, the forms invariably include a section in which the parties agree to go to arbitration rather than to court.

How to order AIA contract forms

AIA contract forms can be ordered over the phone through your state AIA. You can find your state's number from virtually any architect, from the phone book, or by calling the national headquarters at 202-626-7300. You can also order directly from the AIA book store at 202-626-7541. The store accepts credit card payment, can ship anywhere, and does not require a minimum purchase.

The forms are updated continually. Order numbers might change, but the store will know what you are talking about based on the numbers listed here. Costs range from $1 to $10. The following is a partial list of contract forms you might order and read (order numbers are in parentheses):

Bright Idea
The finely printed stipulations, contingencies, and calls for arbitration (which should appear in any contract) read much like a prenuptial agreement and could cast the same shadow of doubt over the proposed union. In the AIA preprinted form, however, they are less likely to be taken personally.

Unofficially...
The contract does not necessarily have to be on the contractor's form with only the addendums he chooses. Use the forms provided by the AIA for an unbiased and legally defensible description of the duties and obligations of all parties in a construction project.

- (A101) Owner-Contractor Agreement Form—Stipulated Sum

- (A107) Abbreviated Owner-Contractor Agreement Form for Small Construction Contracts—Stipulated Sum

- (A111) Owner-Contractor Agreement Form—Cost Plus Fee

- (A191) Standard Form of Agreement Between Owner and Design/Builder

- (B141) Standard Form of Agreement Between Owner and Architect

- (B141) CM Standard Form of Agreement Between Owner and Architect—Construction Management Edition

- (A201) General Conditions of the Contract for Construction

AIA also offers a number of pamphlets with advice and counsel about many aspects of construction. You should order enough different forms to educate yourself about the various options open to you. Some forms are designed to be used in conjunction with other forms (such as General Conditions of the Contract for Construction). Upon request, the AIA will send you a list of all their forms. AIA representatives can explain these forms when you call. I think you'll be impressed with their service and helpful attitude.

How to use the forms
The forms are designed for one-time use. You and your contractor fill in the blanks as you go. You are then permitted to make up to 10 copies for distribution to the parties involved. Each form comes with detailed and understandable directions for its use

and with clear warnings about unauthorized reproduction.

What a contract should contain

The following are the basic elements that make up a contract:

1. Name of the firm offering the service
2. Company's address and telephone number
3. Name of the president of the contracting firm
4. Firm's state license number
5. Name(s) of the homeowner(s)
6. Address of the homeowner(s)
7. What the contractor agrees to do
8. What it will cost
9. Payment schedule
10. When the work will start
11. When the project will be done
12. The current date
13. Statement of the right of rescission regulations
14. Signature of the homeowner(s)
15. Signature of the contractor

The preceding items make up a bare-bones contract. In the next section, we'll cover an example of an actual contract.

What a construction agreement looks like

You could try a quick study of agreements when you are handed one by your contractor, but you should probably make a trial run first. Here I have reproduced an actual contract created by a reputable design/remodeling firm for a kitchen project. It is a good example of the style and wording you can

Watch Out!
Every construction trade has a language of its own that contains terms, shorthand descriptions, and code words. Don't pretend you understand; you could get in trouble. Ask your contractor for a translation. He will not be annoyed. In fact, he will respect you for taking the initiative to educate yourself.

Remodeling pro-
posal. (page 1)

Page 1 of 2 pages

SAMPLE KITCHEN REMODELING PROPOSAL
Building Company Name
Address/Telephone Number

A

PROPOSAL SUBMITTED TO:_____ PHONE:_____ DATE:_____

STREET:_____ JOB NAME:_____

CITY, STATE, ZIP:_____ JOB LOCATION:_____

ARCHITECT: _Builder's design_ DATE OF PLANS:_____ JOB PHONE:_____

B

We Propose hereby to furnish material and labor—complete in accordance with specifications below, for the sum:
(Written Total) Sixteen thousand nine hundred and five   Dollars ($16,905).

C

Payment to be made as follows:
15% down payment, 25% when work commences, 25% when roughs are completed,
25% when fixtures are set, balance upon substantial completion.

D

*All material is guaranteed to be as specified. All work to be completed in a workmanlike manner ac-
cording to standard practices. Any alteration or deviation from specifications below involving extra costs
will be executed only upon written orders and will become an extra charge over and above the estimate. All
agreements contingent upon strikes, accidents, or delays beyond our control. Owner to carry fire, tornado,
and other necessary insurance. Our workers are fully covered by workmen's compensation Insurance.*

Signature of builder.

_____

E

Note: This proposal may be withdrawn by us if not accepted within _____ 5 ____ days.

We hereby submit specifications and estimates for:

"Kitchen Remodeling"

TO INCLUDE:

Plans/Permit—Permit not included. Simple kitchen layout plans included.

Demolition/Cleanups—provide plastic at door openings and drop-cloth runners on finish floors.
Cleanups as work progresses. Remove existing underlayment and finish floor.

Cabinets/Counters/Removals—remove and discard existing cabinets, counters as directed by
owner. Existing refrigerator moved to another adjacent room for temporary use during project.
Old appliances discarded by homeowner unless specified otherwise.

F

Structural—relocate walls at pantry for new layout. Create new stub wall with Sheetrock corner-
bead edges. Walls and floor patched and repaired.

Underlayment—builder to install APA plywood underlayment per manufacturer's specs with
screws and ring nails.

Walls/Ceiling—½" Sheetrock applied to new walls and repaired ceiling area. Taped/spackled
three coats and sanded smooth. Ceiling to be sprayed with medium-density spray after scraping
and using stain-kill paint sealer. Wallpaper removal, if required, is not included.

Remodeling proposal. (page 2)

F

Plumbing—disconnect existing equipment (assumes all valves are operational and supply lines are adequate). Connect new fixtures and appliances (appliances by owner). Sink and faucet allowance to be $200.00. ISE garbage disposer included. Ice maker hookup included.

Electrical—disconnect existing appliances and fixtures. Relocate table hanging light. Add new recess light (supplied by builder) in sink soffit. Existing plugs updated with GFI plugs as per code. Add four recess lights (Brand and model numbers) off existing switch (change to dimmer) in kitchen.

Heating—none included.

Cooking Ventilation—no duct work included. Recirculating hood fan planned.

Flooring—new sheet goods vinyl flooring (to be selected—TBS) installed after installation of new underlayment. Figure $18/s.y. retail cost plus tax for flooring allowance. Provide and install vinyl cove base under cabinet toe spaces and behind the refrigerator. Metal edges may be necessary at junction of other floor materials.

Cabinets—Cabinets to be chosen. Kraftmaid pickled maple cabinets budgeted. ($4,000 allowed). Installation cost included.

Counters—built up edge plastic laminate counters with 4" splash included. Owner to wallpaper above the splash.

General Carpentry—baseboard replaced and install new materials similar to existing. Other trim to remain unless specified otherwise. Assumes that window and door trims are not cut or notched from previous kitchen layout and thus can be reused as is.

G

NOT INCLUDED:

Appliances—supplied/delivered by others/owner. Set by builder.

Paint/decorate—by owner.

Electrical Fixtures—by owner unless specified otherwise.

H

TOTAL BUDGET = $16,905.00

I

Approx start date = xx/xx/xx

Approx completing date = xx/xx/xx

J

Connecticut Home Improvement Registration # 000000

K

Contract Addendum has been read by customer and is part of this agreement.

L

TERMS: All unpaid balances after 30 days will run at 1½% per month on the unpaid balance, 18% per annum. All costs of collection including a reasonable attorney's fee will be charged to customer in the event this matter is placed for collection. You have three days to cancel this contract.

M

Acceptance of Proposal - The above prices, specifications, and conditions are satisfactory and are hereby accepted. You are authorized to do the work as specified. Payment will be made as outlined above.

N

Date of Acceptance:_____

Signature _____

Signature _____

expect in a fixed-price, firm bid or (as the AIA calls it) a stipulated-sum project.

The letters from A to N in the left-hand margin indicate some translations and interpretations of the sections provided on the following pages. I'll take you through this sample proposal line by line, and you'll see what each item could mean to you in terms of extra money and services.

A. Name, address, etc.

This section is mostly self-explanatory. It contains some of the essentials such as your contractor's name, address, and telephone number. If you don't see the contractor's license number here, make sure it appears elsewhere. Some contractors put their number under the start date on page 2.

B. We propose . . .

This is a very brief description of what the remodeler agrees to provide—materials and labor. Also listed here is the quoted price, which, as you'll soon learn, is not what the job will cost you in the end.

C. Payment schedule

Watch Out!
One of the first clues that you're being hustled is a demand that you make a decision today. Another clue is a demand for a large up-front payment. If these warning signs appear, keep looking for another contractor.

This contract calls for 15 percent of the total price at the time of signing and an additional 25 percent when work commences. This means you would pay 40 percent of the total price as a down payment—an amount higher than I generally recommended.

This particular amount of up-front money is not unusual when remodeling a kitchen or bath because so much of the job involves purchasing expensive cabinets and fixtures. You might make the first check a joint check with your contractor for the supplier. Other payments are due when "rough carpentry" is complete (25 percent) and when the fixtures are set (25 percent). That leaves 10 percent for the final payment, which is made after the punch list items are taken care of and the homeowner is satisfied with the job.

D. Standard fine-print paragraph

This statement offers the homeowner some standard guarantees for the quality of the work done and the materials used. Ideally, terms like "workmanlike manner" and "standard practices" ought to be defined in the attached addendum. Even if they're not, you can be sure they mean something to an arbitrator or judge.

Notice the statement, "Any alteration or deviation from the specifications below involving extra cost . . . will become extra costs over and above the estimate." With this statement, the contractor is protecting himself from surprises and requested changes by the owner. He is also taking the businesslike approach of stating that all such changes must be in writing. He further protects himself by stating he is not responsible for on-time completion or additional costs due to circumstances beyond his control.

The insurance issue is handled by having the homeowner(s) insure the home and by having the contractor cover his own workers.

E. Time limit on bid

The remodeler has set a five-day time limit for the homeowners to accept the bid. It is not uncommon for clients to sit on proposals for weeks, months, or even years and then expect the amount quoted to remain the same.

F. To include . . .

This is a good argument-saving section. The contractor lists everything he is going to do on the job

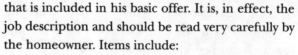

that is included in his basic offer. It is, in effect, the job description and should be read very carefully by the homeowner. Items include:

Watch Out!
Do not apply for local construction or building permits yourself. Make your contractor apply because the person who applies is held responsible for compliance.

- **Plans/permits.** The fact that the permit is not included means the homeowners must apply for their own permit. In this case, the issuing agency holds the person requesting the permit responsible for conforming to local regulations. The builder should be the one who applies for the permit, and the clause should be revised to read "Builder will apply for all permits. Owner will be billed for any fees involved."

- **Demolition/cleanups.** Many contracts don't cover this subject. I would like to see the phrase "Broom clean at end of each day." It should also specify who is responsible for getting rid of the trash. The disposal of building refuse is becoming an expensive and time-consuming part of construction, often requiring special dumping permits and fees. Find out how your local community handles the problem.

- **Cabinet/counters/removals.** Notice that this clause makes provisions for the homeowners to have the use of the refrigerator (in the living room) for the duration of the project. It also requires the owners to dispose of the old appliances, a point you might want to negotiate.

- **Walls/ceiling.** The remodeler offers a clear picture of what will be done to the walls and the ceiling, but he is also protecting himself against the unknown. If the owners decide the wallpaper must be removed, an extra cost will be incurred. This could mean one of two things: either the removal of the wallpaper is only a remote possibility, or the contractor has left out the cost in order to offer a lower bid.

- **Plumbing.** The contractor further protects himself by clearly stating his assumption that "all valves are operational and waste and supply lines are adequate." If they are not, replacing them means considerable additional cost to the homeowner. Like with the wallpaper, the need might be remote or it could be a hidden cost. A $200 allowance for the sink and faucet might not be enough. To avoid unpleasant surprises, homeowners should select and price their fixtures ahead of time so they'll know the actual costs.

- **Electrical.** Increased lighting and more outlets are major considerations for a new kitchen. The contractor seems to have addressed these considerations.

- **Heating.** Because the space is staying the same, the existing heating arrangement should be sufficient. If a new wing or a second story is added, an HVAC engineer should calculate whether your existing heating system can handle the additional load. My wife and I added an entire second floor, doubling the size of the house, and our 1945 furnace didn't have to be replaced.

- **Cooking ventilation.** New ductwork is not needed with the type of hood fan called for in this project.

- **Flooring.** Homeowners would be wise to price the flooring they want in order to know whether the allowance is sufficient. Metal edges might be necessary, and it's unclear whether they are covered by this agreement (probably not).

Moneysaver
Most building codes do not require an elaborate hood over an island stove-top counter. A simple bathroom-type ceiling exhaust fan vented outside is sufficient, considerably less expensive, and more sightly. (Also, many new cook-tops come with built-in down-draft vents.)

- **Cabinets.** The cabinets have yet to be selected by the owners, but the builder has based his allowance of $4,000 on a particular brand and model of cabinets. If the owners select a more upscale brand or style, the cost could easily double or triple. It is best to price the exact cabinets you want in advance, including cabinet and drawer pulls, a specific hinge type, and any other accessories or variations. Notice that installation is included, as it should be.

- **Counters.** The owners have agreed to purchase and put up the wallpaper, probably to save some money. We did this in our kitchen, and it was a simple one-evening job . . . that we did three years later.

- **General carpentry.** Notice the contractor's assumption that the window and door trim is usable. If trim has been notched or cut, the homeowner's cost will rise.

G. Not included . . .

This is an excellent heading to include in a contract. It helps avoid misunderstandings and incorrect assumptions. Some of the items that might be listed under this heading include:

- **Appliances.** The proposal doesn't include the cost of appliances. If a stove, refrigerator, microwave oven, or dishwasher is called for, the owners can expect to spend considerably more money than the total quoted in the proposal.

- **Painting or decorating.** The purchase of paint or wallpaper is the responsibility of the owners, who will presumably do their own work to save some money. If you're working on a tight budget, doing your own work is one way to save money, but the cost of the materials is often overlooked. Be sure to calculate them in your overall cost estimates.

- **Electrical fixtures.** It seems that most of the electrical fixtures are covered in this proposal, but any additional fixtures or upgrades are not. The homeowners should make a list of all the electrical fixtures they want and should compare that to the list supplied with the contract.

H. Total budget

This section shows the cost of what the builder has agreed to perform and provide. You can be sure this is not what the project will cost in the end. We know the owners have to buy all the appliances, some light fixtures, and any wallpaper or paint. They also possibly pay permit fees and trash-hauling fees for their debris and old appliances and hope that the existing plumbing and trim are usable and that they can live within the allowances for cabinets and new flooring. After the owners add in all these eventualities, they will know the total cost.

I. Approximate starting and completion dates

Because this project is being done by a designer/builder who has standard subcontractors, these dates might be accurate if there are no surprises. Because these dates are preceded by the term "Approx.," they fall into the category of things determined by law. You probably won't know what the legal limits on start and finish dates are until you wind up in arbitration.

J. State home improvement registration number

This number is necessary on any proposal or contract. In Connecticut, for example, if the contractor's license number is not on the contract (as well

Bright Idea
One way or another, you end up paying for all the elements required in your remodeling, such as appliances or fixtures. Be sure to keep an accurate budget of all the items you choose to purchase on your own; the prices of these items will not be reflected in the bid. Otherwise, you'll have an unrealistic sense of how inexpensive your project is.

as his name, address, and firm name), the homeowner is not legally obligated to pay him for his
work.

K. Contract addendum

The addendum states that the homeowner has read
the attached pages (not reproduced in this book),
which contain definitions of terminology used in
the proposal and the general conditions of the contract (consult AIA forms). The material contained
in the addendum is probably useful only if there's a
serious disagreement between the owner and the
builder. It is written in legal but understandable
English and should be read before signing the
proposal.

L. Terms

The terms describe what will happen if the homeowners don't pay on time. It also alerts the owners
that they have three days to change their minds after
they sign the proposal (right of rescission).

M. Acceptance of proposal

With their signatures, the homeowners accept the
offer. This changes the proposal into a contract and
authorizes the builder to start work (after the three
days have passed).

N. Date and signatures

This section requires the signatures of everyone listed on the mortgage or deed as owners of the house.
The date of acceptance starts the clock running on
the homeowner's right to cancel.

I have reproduced this contract and the "translation" to familiarize you with the language and techniques used to describe the work to be done and its
cost. If your contract has phrases such as "assuming
present fixture to be workable" or other references

calling for a perfect world, ask for an explanation of what could happen and even what it could cost.

Just because a contract is neatly typed does not mean you can't add items or write in items. Make sure you and your contractor both agree and both initial the additions.

Just the facts

- Make sure your bid request includes a list of everything to be purchased and installed and a complete, detailed remodeling floor plan.

- Study the bids to determine why the low bids are low and why the high bids are high.

- Suggest that each bidder bid on the job as described and then prepare a list of possible surprises, additional tasks, and additional costs.

- Calculate the real cost of your project by reviewing the kitchen-remodeling contract to learn what each section means and why the final cost of even a "simple" remodeling plan might bear little resemblance to its projected cost.

Coping with the Project

PART II

GET THE SCOOP ON...
Meeting your work crew's basic needs ▪ Dealing
effectively with the chaos ▪ Staying on
schedule and within budget ▪ The art of
compromise ▪ Room-by-room checklists

Surviving the Remodeling Ordeal

Chapter 3

You might not have the Occupational Safety and Health Agency (OSHA) looking over your shoulder, but your house will become a workplace for your contractor, his crew, and the subcontractors for the duration of your project. Just like the local factory, pleasant and organized working conditions make for happier and more productive workers. In this chapter I'll show you several things you can do to gain your crew's appreciation and loyalty and speed the work.

Even if you hire a contractor to handle your remodeling job, many things still require your attention and a good deal of your time and effort. Remember all those items marked "TBS" in the contract? If you haven't already done it, now you have to go out and make those selections.

If you and your partner are the only ones making selections, it can be hard to get a majority vote on any items you can't agree on. I'll suggest some ways to make decisions together and discuss the various items needed when remodeling any specific room. You really should make all these changes prior to signing the contract. You have to do it sometime, so do it now. If the bid is to mean anything, these items need to be in the bid if the contractor is supplying them.

As stressful as your visits to plumbing-supply and lighting-fixture display rooms might be, they'll begin to seem like a peaceful oasis compared to the noise, dust, confusion, and disruptions going on in your once-peaceful home. It's not easy living with a remodeling job, but I'll offer some suggestions of how to take some of the hassle out it. Through it all, try your best to maintain an attitude of respect. And by all means, keep your sense of humor.

What you can do to create a better workplace

For a while, your home will be your contractor's workplace. The more efficiently the space is organized and the more comfortable he and his subordinates feel there (within reason), the more productive they will be. The following suggestions can help you set up a workspace that will facilitate and expedite your project:

- **Create a convenient work and storage space for your contractors.** This saves them time every morning and saves you money. If you're smart, you'll clear out your garage or basement and give it to the contractor. (The car, antique convertible or not, can stay outside in the rain.) This gives him a secure place to store his tools and building materials.

  You'll save yourself a lot of grief if you accept the idea that the space where the contractor is working and the place he's storing his tools and

Unofficially ...
There's a sneaky reason for devoting space to your contractor. If all his tools are at your place, he'll keep coming back. You'll also get a few more minutes of productive work time each day. The contractor won't have to pack up all his tools and cart them off to his truck at the end of the day and then unpack them again the next morning.

equipment is not yours anymore. It belongs to him for the duration of the project—if he tells you to get out, get out.

- **Conduct a tour of your facilities.** The first morning on the job, show the workers which bathroom they can use and provide some towels, paper or otherwise. Also provide them with some glasses and permission to drink the water.

- **Be a gracious host.** Provide for your contractor's needs. Turn over the use of some of your amenities. Your crew also has to eat. Clear off a shelf and let them put their lunches and soft drinks in your refrigerator. You might even show them how your microwave works and let them heat up their lunches.

It's both wise and hospitable to have a pot of coffee and some doughnuts waiting for them when they come in. This might also cut out the necessity of their 8 a.m. trip to the local quickie mart and might give you some more productive time. No crew on a contracting job does anything in the morning until they get their coffee and sugar fix.

- **Free up your phone.** Another necessity for a contractor is access to a telephone. (In this age of cellular phones, however, he's likely to be more self-reliant.) He needs to check on dozens of details each day, from delivery of the next round of materials to the availability of subcontractors. If you or your partner are around the house during the day, you might consider filling in as your contractor's answering service. It saves him from coming down a ladder every time the phone rings, and it makes you feel like part of the operation.

> **❝**
> Some homeowners give you a hose to drink out of, but most of the time you have to ask. It would be nice if the homeowner said, 'Here is the bathroom, I've put a pot of coffee on for you, and there is soda in the refrigerator.'
>
> —A contractor
> **❞**

▪ **Give your contractor permission to answer your phone.** This can be helpful if both of you will be out for the day. Our crew got pretty good at taking messages. (Make sure a pad and pencil are handy by the phone.) It can be a little startling to have the plumbing subcontractor inform you as you come in that your Rotary Club dance has been moved to the Elk's Club, but it makes their job easier.

▪ **Adjust your schedule if necessary.** Let the workers get to work on time and on their schedule. Many construction crews start as early as 7 a.m. Find out what time your GC intends to start his day, and get yourself and your family up and out before that. Contractors have told me about families that keep them waiting at the front door while they finish their morning showers and breakfast. This is a dumb way to spend a contractor's time and your money. Eventually, he will punch his time clock from the time he rings your bell, not from the time he starts work.

▪ **Get out of the way.** You can also clear out the room or rooms to be remodeled. If it's your bedroom, move completely out and take all your clothes with you. Set up cots and clothes racks in another part of house. Do not try to move into a space at night and move out again the next morning. It doesn't work.

If the project is a new kitchen, empty all the shelves and cupboards into boxes and set up dining facilities somewhere else. Work out with your contractor exactly how long you'll have use of your stove, sink, and refrigerator and when they will be unhooked. Be prepared to wash dishes in the bathroom sink for a few days. (You may have to wash them twice—after you eat, and before you eat, to rinse off the plaster dust.)

Your contractor will try to hold down the amount of plaster dust and dirt as much as possible by putting up plastic curtain walls. But those are about as effective as that strip of tissue the barber puts around your neck to keep the hair off your collar. One step that does work pretty well is to curtain off any bookshelves that are not part of the project using plastic sealed completely with masking tape around the edges. Books are difficult to clean, so this can save you time later. Move any delicate machinery such as computers and stereo equipment out of the house if at all possible. If you can't store it somewhere else, put it in plastic garbage bags and seal them well with twist ties.

Your responsibilities during a construction project

Even after you've moved your stuff out of the rooms to be worked on, sealed off the bookshelves, and cleaned out your garage and basement, you aren't done yet. You still have a lot you're responsible for during the project. Your ongoing duties fall into the following categories:

- Regular consultations with your GC
- Emergency meetings to handle surprises encountered on the job
- Making the hundreds of decisions and choices about the fixtures, materials, and colors that will go into your new space
- Enduring the hours of paperwork needed to approve and sign change orders, check the work as it progresses, and write checks

> **66**
> Our crew would rehook up the water and electricity before they left each day, so we always had the basic stuff in the evenings and mornings. But the refrigerator was in the living room for the duration of the project and the stove, too, for part of the time. We ate out a lot.
>
> —Mark Alverez, homeowner
> **99**

Consulting with your general contractor

Meet with your GC on the site at least once a week (preferably Monday mornings). At these meetings, he can outline goals for the week, indicating how these tasks will affect your family and giving you a list of the items you have to select or buy and bring home. In fact, it's really best if you hold a meeting every morning; that way, you can take in the information and get your assignments in smaller, more digestible (and more accurate) chunks.

The types of information your builder might tell you include:

- "Today we'll be tearing out the wall between the kitchen and the dining room."

- "I'll call you at work on Wednesday so you can come over and see how the new space looks."

- "You should select the kitchen sink and the plumbing fixtures you want this week so they can be here in two weeks when we'll need them."

- "I'll need a check from you for the wrecking crew's work on Wednesday."

- "By the way, we won't be coming in Thursday or Friday."

If you're living in the house, you'll get to inspect it every night. You might leave each morning before the workers arrive, however, and get home well after they leave for the day. It's possible to go a long time without running into your GC if you don't make the effort. Arrange your schedule accordingly. Drop by to join the crew for lunch. (You might even treat them to a pizza now and then.) Whatever you do, keep the lines of communication open. If you're not talking regularly, you'll be in trouble. If face-to-face meetings are difficult to arrange, you might keep the lines of communication open by leaving each other notes.

Handling emergency meetings

There will be times when you're at work and something will come up on the remodeling job that requires an immediate decision. Forewarn your employer. If he has ever had any construction done, he will understand. A good contractor will have other tasks to put the crew to work on while they wait for you or your partner to show up. If it's a crucial detail, however, work might have to stop entirely until you get there. On your way home, prepare yourself mentally for spending more money to fix the problem.

The following are some possible job-stopping emergencies:

- They found an old brick chimney behind the wall between your dining room and kitchen. This can be good news or bad news; either way, it changes things.

- When they ripped up the linoleum in the kitchen, they found old, random-width oak flooring. This is usually good news.

- When they opened up the wall behind your bathtub, they found water damage and rotten wood. Bad news. (You must have gone with the low bidder, or this would not have been a surprise.)

- They found dry rot in the sills. (Sills hold up your house.) Very bad news.

- The French doors you ordered three months ago have come in, and they're not what you ordered. Do you want to send them back and wait another three months, or will they do?

Bright Idea
Remember your human relations skills when you leave notes for your GC. You might think you're leaving a gentle reminder; he might think you're screaming at him. Try starting with a compliment on the work been done and then make your suggestions or ask your questions.

Surprises and emergencies are seldom good news. Your builder would rather not have you around while he's working, so a call usually means he has found something that involves increased costs or a change in plans you must approve.

Don't become part of the problem

There are plenty of bad builders in the world. There are also difficult and unreasonable clients. It would be poetic justice if they always got together on the same projects, but it doesn't happen that way.

Keep the lines of communication and cooperation open between you and your builder. Don't stop talking. If it starts to go bad, small problems will start growing into big hassles. Later in this section, I'll give you a list of do's and don'ts that can help smooth your relationship with your builder, his crew, and the subcontractors as they work on your project.

I tried to behave myself during our remodeling project. I made the selections I had to make on time, I ignored the hundreds of white plastic coffee cups, and I didn't demand that the crew turn down their portable boom box. The hardest time I gave my builder and his lead carpenter (yes, I dealt directly with them) was showing up with a revised set of plans every week or so. In my own defense, I was not asking for drastic changes. One set of plans called for a few changes in door-swing directions, another moved some wall plugs and switches around, and one plan even tripled the number of telephone outlets. Thankfully, the builder respected these changes.

The builder and his crew referred to these revisions as Duncan's Plan of the Week, and I inevitably found them a couple days later under a pile of sawdust with footprints all over them. Our builder

Unofficially...
You probably don't see yourself as a potentially difficult personality, but every contractor I've interviewed has a story about a client from hell. You'll get more cooperation from your contractor if you work as a team rather than as adversaries.

didn't actually throw them away—he just didn't pay much attention to them. When it was time to hang the doors and mark the locations for plugs and switches, however, he did ask me where I wanted them. Because I had gone through the exercise of drawing new plans, I knew.

Here's a list of do's and don'ts for homeowners:

- **Don't put your personal priorities ahead of your builder's.** Time is of the essence unless the builder's requirements conflict with your bridge game, a lunch date, or the need to make a living. Here is how one builder described a job he was on: "Time meant everything to the client," he said, "So we rented pneumatic nailers to speed things up. We would be working away nicely and all of a sudden the nails wouldn't go all the way in. We had lost compression. It seemed the wife had washing she felt had to be dried that day so she kept unplugging our compressor and plugging in her drier. I would go downstairs and unplug the drier and plug in our compressor. After four trips to the basement, we went back to swinging hammers. She couldn't grasp the concept that a compressor doesn't have to be 'running' all the time to be useful."

- **Don't squander your financial resources.** The bank's approval of financing for a major remodeling project puts more cash in your bank account than you might ever have seen there at one time. This is a heady experience, and not everyone handles it well. Some homeowners have purchased a new car using remodeling funds while building an addition. They later claimed they couldn't afford several of the remodeling features they originally wanted.

Moneysaver
Avoid the temptation to misspend money borrowed for major remodeling by putting the money in a joint escrow account. This requires the signature of both the homeowner and the contractor to withdraw funds.

■ **Don't expect to use your contractor's discounts.** Homeowners are often intrigued by the contractor's discount at the building-supply store and begin to think they have some right to it. A businesslike contractor does not allow charging privileges, except perhaps for specific items such as light fixtures. Most are reluctant to offer this favor because they have had undesirable experiences with it.

■ **Don't expect your contractor to be neat.** If you are a neat freak by nature, try to suspend these urges during a remodeling project. If you don't you are going to be very unhappy. Let the crew make as much mess during working hours as they need. Many contracts call for the job site to be "broom clean" at the end of each day. This gets the major problems out of your way, but it also raises a cloud of dust to mark their departure.

The remodeling period is a good time to take advantage of all the lunch and dinner invitations you've been saving up for the past year. Invite your neighbors, friends, and family to tour the project after working hours occasionally. This gets them involved, alerts them to your plight, and might result in more invitations to visit, eat out, and let your kids sleep over.

■ **Don't pull the "Oh, while you're here" ploy.** Just because there is finally someone in your house who can actually fix a leaky faucet, patch a hole in the plaster, or build a set of bookshelves, you cannot automatically appropriate these skills for your own pet projects. These little jobs represent additional time not included in the price of your project. You can and should pay for them in one way or another so the contractor is not cheated.

- **Don't use your professional credentials to intimidate your builder.** I asked some contractors if there are any types of homeowners or particular professions they especially avoid. One said, "Engineers are difficult because they are looking for quality and tolerances that simply do not exist in home construction with its use of wood." The legal profession also seems to hold a special place in the hearts of the building trades. Lawyers sometimes have been known to refuse to pay their bills and to dare the builder to take them to court, even while admitting that the work was done perfectly.

  Some contractors feel that accountants or anyone who works with numbers can be difficult, but one design/builder likes the idea and tries to put the professional skills of his clients to good use. The designer told me, "If you can use the skills of your clients to help save them money, all the better. You are going to be up to your hips in contracts; if the guy's a lawyer, let him take care of that problem. Give him the sample contract out of the AIA book. Let the CPA help you keep track of the invoices and billing."

- **Don't try to supply materials for the job.** I was guilty of this one. I now suggest that you let the builder have the 10 percent commission on the materials he buys for your job because that at least covers overhead. Renovations and remodeling jobs are not usually heavy material users, but you can put your GC's schedule out of whack by not getting the basic supplies on time

Bright Idea
If you have some tasks you would like the crew to work on, ask for an estimate and treat each one as a separate project. Let them decide if they have time to spare or want to do the jobs.

or by ordering the wrong items. Let the pro take care of it.

- **Don't change your mind from day to day.** Indecision is the biggest complaint builders have about homeowners. When you can't come to a decision about the location of the door into your bedroom or the fixtures for the bathroom, it causes delays. When you change your mind after the door has gone in, forcing your builder to tear it out and do it over again, you create chaos on the job site. In both cases, the cost and time of the project increases.

- **Don't withhold the final 10 or 15 percent payment when it's due.** As I'll discuss in Chapter 6, the final payment on a construction or remodeling contract usually contains most of the profit your builder makes on your job. Don't wait to pay until every single detail meets with your approval. You wouldn't hold back 10 percent of the cost of your steak from the butcher until after the barbecue is over. Why make it so tough for your GC?

- **Do keep accurate records of the changes you order.** For your sanity and your builder's, insist that clear, detailed records of changes be kept. They are the best defense against last-minute billing arguments that destroy what might have been a pleasant business relationship. A change order should be written up and signed by both parties. It is, in effect, a new contract. It would also be wise to include the contractor's cost estimate for the change in question.

- **Do treat your contractor the way you would like to be treated.** Work under the assumption that

Unofficially...
You most likely went to your GC's previous customers to check his reputation. In turn, his future potential customers will ask your opinion of his work. Use this, not the last 10 percent, as your leverage.

people are honest and will try to help; I find they usually are and do.

- **Do be willing to compromise.** If you follow the suggestions throughout this book for how to select a contractor, you should be dealing with an honest, capable building professional. There might still be mistakes and misunderstandings, but you should deal with each other with mutual respect rather than as adversaries. Be open to discussion, be reasonable, and listen. Try to find out what went wrong and why. Then work out a compromise that hurts each of you a little (a sign of a good settlement). Most of what you think is wrong isn't necessarily wrong, it just isn't the way you thought it would be.

- **Do keep the kids out of the way.** No matter how many kids the carpenter might have at home or how wonderfully the crew gets along with your toddlers, children should not be allowed in the work area during working hours. There are simply too many things that can happen—all of them bad. Power saws, noise, dirt, guys swearing . . . they are all magnets to small children. To keep the kids out of the house, sign your future life away in baby-sitting trades with the neighbors. If you can, schedule your project for when school is in session. If it must be in the summer, send the kids off to camp or for a vacation with your extended family.

- **Do pay your bills on time.** Pay your bills when they are presented in accordance with the bill-paying procedure outlined in your contract. Don't make your builder hound you or beg to get paid.

Moneysaver
Try to talk out any differences you have with your contractor. If you have hired an honest builder, he has a right to expect to deal with an honest client. Besides, unless you are a lawyer, going to court is an unsatisfactory, expensive way to settle problems. Both parties usually wind up losing.

Watch Out!
You and your spouse might have completely different ideas about how to shop and make selections. This can cause a lot of stress. Work out selection techniques you can both live with over coffee between show-room visits.

Decisions, choices, and options

During the course of your project, you will have hundreds of decisions to make and choices to nego-tiate. Your job is to have the fixtures, appliances, door styles, tiles, flooring, and so on not only select-ed but delivered and ready for your contractor to install as they are needed. If he has to wait, it will cost you money and time.

You are an integral part of the supply chain for your building project. Hopefully, you've already selected and ordered the major items that have to fit in a certain space or that have a lead time of several weeks to deliver. Kitchen appliances, for example, need to be selected long before new cabinets or countertops are installed so that accurately sized spaces or holes can be made for them.

During the remodeling process, the most taxing, time-consuming, and frustrating activity you'll engage in is making decisions . . . hundreds of deci-sions. You probably expect to choose the kitchen cabinets, the windows, the bathroom vanities, the paint color for the walls, and the new appliances for your kitchen. You'll also be called on to decide between wood, vinyl, ceramic tile, or linoleum floors. But I doubt that you're prepared for the lit-erally thousands of options available and the range of prices.

At first, all stoves, faucets, and floor coverings look good. You then learn about the advantages and disadvantages of each. After a few hours in a show-room, none of them look good anymore because you have no idea how to select just one.

My wife and I only went to one floor-covering showroom. It was late in our remodeling project, and we had already spent many days in showrooms devoted to light fixtures, kitchen cabinets, plumbing fixtures, furniture, Oriental rugs, fabrics, paint, windows, doors, and hardware. We were growing tired of the whole process. We also realized we had not arrived at decisions on some of the previous tours and had to go back.

At some point during the earlier visits, I learned that we had a different outlook on the procurement process. To me, shopping is done with a specific buying goal in mind. To her, buying was a separate process entirely, to be exercised only after a lot of shopping—not necessarily on the same day or even in the same week.

Recommended strategies for decision-making

The following strategies can help you make order out of the chaos and can help protect your sanity.

Do your research

Broaden your reading of housing magazines to include the advertisements and articles about lighting, bathroom fixtures, siding, roofing materials, and appliances. As you are planning, collect pictures of rooms that capture the style or feel you are trying to achieve. Try to have a meeting of the minds about window styles, types of flooring or floor coverings, kitchen and bathroom looks, and of course, budget philosophies.

If you priced some of the larger items during your planning phase, you can give a list of those items along with style and model numbers to your contractor. It's a good idea to collect the technical data sheets supplied by the manufacturers in case your builder needs exact dimensions or installation information.

Your GC should supply you with a list of most of the items you have to select yourself and should give you a series of deadlines for your decisions. You might have to make some decisions before construction actually starts because some of the items you'll need—windows, doors, kitchen cabinets—are part of the basic structure and have to be ordered several weeks ahead so they'll arrive on time.

Keep ahead of the builder

You are part of the supply chain. If the builder starts to construct the counters in your kitchen and you haven't picked out the stove or refrigerator yet, he has to stop work until you do. The electrical fixtures have to be on hand when the electrician is ready to install them, or he has to come back again. You can put off selecting the paint and carpets for a while, but the windows and doors have to be on-site early in the process.

Know the lead times for delivery

Be aware of how far in advance you have to make your selections and place your orders. Good intentions and bad performances just add to frustration on the job. Remember to check delivery times while you're at the showrooms. You might see the item you want on display, but it might have to be ordered from a central warehouse or the manufacturer. Find out these details while you are there. Don't assume anything.

Know your budget numbers and allowances

Virtually every showroom you walk into will have beautiful items that would be perfect for your home but cost 10 times your allowance. As I discuss in Chapter 5, this is where you get the chance to blow your budget right out of the water. Know how much

Moneysaver
Make a copy of the list of materials and fixtures you need and the amount you've budgeted for each item. Carry it with you when you go to the showrooms.

you can spend. Have it written down and stick to it, or at least stay within the total for that particular group of items. If you feel you really must spend an extra $200 for the light over the kitchen table, spend $200 less on the recessed fixtures.

We used this approach with faucets. My wife made a special trip to a specialty plumbing-display room 50 miles away and came home with a $400 faucet set for the downstairs bathroom sink. It was the kind your parents probably took to the dump when they remodeled in the 1950s—four spokes with HOT and COLD written on the white porcelain centers. Even my wife was shocked by the price, but we made up for it with $60 fake-brass faucet sets in the upstairs bath and the kitchen. They all turn the water on and off properly, and guests compliment us far more often on the $60 sets than on the $400 one.

The question of cost and our budget came into the decision-making process a lot, even in the building materials we selected for the basic structure. When we shopped for fabrics, for example, we tried to select designs that were remnants or on their way out.

Create and keep a schedule

Choosing fixtures and other items is a time-consuming process. You simply can't get it done in your spare time or when the mood strikes. Set time aside when you're both available and just do it. Set up a schedule and keep it. Take a few days off work if necessary.

Do some comparison shopping

Comparison shopping takes time and patience, which you have more of at the beginning of your

Bright Idea
Some emergencies and basic home-building duties will inevitably call you away from your job. Rather than surprise your boss at the last minute, explain in advance what will be going on and get approval or at least understanding in advance. Paying off your home-improvement loan is no fun if you've just lost your job.

project than toward the end. Ask your contractor to recommend showrooms you should visit. You can add to his list by searching the Yellow Pages.

Showrooms tend to specialize in particular lines; going to several places enables you to see the full range of what is available. Give yourself the chance to compare not only quality and selection but prices. Get prices wherever you go. Let the salesperson know what your project is and make it clear that you're comparison shopping.

Negotiate and bargain

To get a better price, you don't necessarily have to move down in quality. Most of the products you'll buy enjoy a comfortable mark-up, and you owe it to yourself to at least ask for a discount. You certainly won't get if you don't ask for it. Call it a contractor's discount, a quantity discount, or if you've been to other shops, call it an opportunity to meet the competition's offer. At the very least, you might get some additional benefit such as an upgrade on padding for your carpet for an average pad's price.

Be willing to travel

You might know the way to all the malls within a 30-mile radius of your house, but chances are you have never been to most of the places you will have to visit to select necessities for your project. They might not be in the best part of town or even in your town at all. Expect to put a lot of mileage on your car during this effort.

In addition to visiting showrooms and display houses, you also might want to go through catalogs. We selected our toilets from a much-thumbed catalog the plumbing subcontractor had in the back of his truck. The sinks came from a little plumbing-supply house a friend of a friend knew about. Many

Timesaver
Check your local papers for home and garden shows, particularly in the spring and the fall. These shows offer an opportunity to check out many suppliers and products and talk to salespeople and manufacturers all under one roof.

lumberyards display kitchens and baths not to mention windows, trim, and moldings. Be sure to check them out as well.

Work out a system with your partner

You and your partner might start out by doing everything together—looking at all the selections, discussing the relative merits of each, and comparing prices. Sooner or later, however, you might find you have differing levels of patience. Sometimes it becomes necessary to postpone a decision to prevent a confrontation. Go home or move on to another type of showroom and let the process percolate for a while. A fresh approach on another day can work wonders.

Some couples divide the shopping duties because either they lack time or their interests differ. It's also perfectly appropriate to leave some things to your contractor's discretion. I chose one of our two toilet bowls (a taller handicap model is great for me, a surprise for our shorter guests) and the plumber chose the second one. The shower heads were of particular interest to me, but the bath and shower faucets were chosen by the contractor by default, because we missed the deadline for deciding, and something had to go in without delay!

Whatever method you use to make decisions, agree on the approach you plan to take. Some husbands completely leave the selection process to their wives. That's not necessarily a good idea. First, remodeling should be a joint venture; both parties should choose what goes into the home. Second, most husbands find they have more opinions than they thought they had—even if they are only financial opinions. So they tend to second-guess decisions already made—a formula for trouble. See

> 66
> I don't know whether it's simply out of exhaustion or something else, but finally something clicks. A little light bulb goes off and you know you've made your decision.
>
> —Katie Heim, homeowner
> 99

Unofficially...
Some husbands
don't like to
make decisions,
but they do like
to second-guess
other people's
decisions. One
way to deal with
this is for the
wife to narrow
down the choices
to two or three
items she likes
and then present
them to her hus-
band. This way,
she gets what
she wants and he
gets to overrule.

Chapter 4 for more information about compromising and decision-making techniques.

Keeping the preceding strategies in mind, the
following section lists some of the decisions you
might have to make and factors to take into consideration when making your choices.

A guide for decision-making room by room

Now that you've worked out a method for making
decisions, it's time to start preparing to actually
make them. For people who like to see things more
neatly arranged, the following checklist covers many
of these items. Use this list as a guide and use the
descriptions to get you thinking.

Special-use rooms, such as the kitchen and the
bathroom, involve additional decisions depending
on how you intend to use them. A media center in a
family room or home office requires a separate list
of decisions.

Build or buy? One fundamental decision is
whether you want your contractor to construct built-
in cabinets, bookshelves, work stations, and filing
cabinets or whether you intend to go the stand-
alone route. My wife and I decided on a combination of both. We had the carpenter build a set of
bookshelves into our master bedroom wall. I built a
tall, country-style pine cabinet to house our old
stereo equipment and the TV, and I set it up in the
family room. I have an office in my home, but the
only special request I made to the contractor was for
a dedicated electrical outlet for my computer.

Make enough copies of the following checklist
that you'll have one for each room you plan to
remodel. The following checklist covers most of
the decisions we had to make for all our rooms,

including the family room and office. If you feel you
need more details, attach a blank piece of paper to
each copy of your checklist and add items as you
think of them. You might also begin to prepare
yourself mentally for going over-budget. The checklist is designed to help you be thorough in your
selection process. Be sure to share the results with
your contractor.

A ROOM-BY-ROOM DECISION CHECKLIST

Room: _____ **Date:** _____

Flooring Material

❑ Wall-to-wall carpeting

❑ Pine planking

❑ Hardwood (strips, parquet)

❑ Ceramic tile

❑ Vinyl (sheet or tiles)

❑ Area rugs

Wall Finish and Material

❑ Plaster, smooth or textured

❑ Wood paneling

❑ Wallboard and wallpaper

❑ Wallboard and paint

❑ Brick or masonry

❑ Ceramic tile

Wood Trim

❑ Baseboards (grade of wood: _____)

❑ Finish (paint or stain)

❑ Door and window trim

❑ Molding (crown, etc.)

Ceiling Material and Finish

❑ Plaster, smooth or textured

❑ Wood paneling, paint or stain

❑ Wallboard with paint

❑ Wallboard with wallpaper

❑ Exposed beams, real or fake

❑ Acoustic tile

❑ Drop ceiling

❑ Other

Hardware

❑ Window locks

❑ Doorknobs and lock sets

❑ Hinges

❑ Coat hooks

❑ Cabinet and drawer pulls

Electrical

❑ Location of switches (will any control outlets?): _____.

❑ Location of outlets: _____.

❑ Which are controlled by a switch? _____.

❑ Location of rewired television cable outlets:
   _____.

❑ Location of rewired telephone outlets: _____.

❑ Location of light fixtures (recessed, mounted, suspended,
   spotlights, floodlights, and table, desk, and floor lamps):
   _____.

❑ Location of rewired electronic equipment (VCR, stereo, speakers, computers, security system): _____.

❑ Location of dedicated electrical lines (outlets on a single circuit breaker): _____.

❑ Prewired security system

Mechanical

❑ Heating method (hookup to central system, auxiliary electric,
   baseboard electric, space heater, radiant in floor or ceiling,
   active or passive solar fireplace)

❑ Air-conditioning (built-in units, window units, central
   system)

❑ Ventilation (exhaust fan, window fan, location of windows)

❑ Method of cooking (gas, electric, microwave oven)

❑ Appliances (color? new? size? location?):

_____

_____.

Windows

❑ Match existing

❑ Insulated glass

❑ Replace or repair

❑ Wood, steel, aluminum

❑ Number of panes (vinyl or metal clad): _____.

❑ Separate storms, type of installation: _____.

Decorating

❑ Paint color (walls, woodwork, windows, trim, doors):

_____

_____.

❑ Paint type (oil- or water-based, high gloss, gloss, semi-gloss, flat)

❑ Tile pattern: _____.

❑ Rug or carpet (pattern, weight, and color)

❑ Fabric type and pattern for drapery, furniture, and curtains:

_____

_____.

Keeping track

One of the immutable laws of remodeling is that every decision you make leads to three more. If you decide to install tile instead of linoleum on the bathroom floor, for example, you need to decide between plastic and ceramic tile, pick a pattern, and finally make sure your GC lays it out the way it's designed to go. My wife and I dropped the ball on that last step. The pattern of black diamonds on white squares we selected became black squares on white diamonds when the contractor laid it out sideways. If you want tile placed a certain way, be there when it's installed.

Getting organized

When you add up all the decisions you have to make, multiply by the two or three showrooms you must visit to make each selection, add in the catalogs and advertisements you need to peruse, and multiply again by the number of people involved in making each decision, you can see that you have to devise a system of keeping track of where you've been and what you've seen—or you'll lose your mind! I suggest you purchase a full-size, spiral-bound notebook with three or four dividers and a heavy cardboard back. Use the first section to keep chronological notes on the job. Take notes at every meeting with your GC; record every telephone call (incoming and outgoing); note important names, addresses, and telephone numbers; date each page; and keep everything up-to-date.

Bright Idea
Use two note-books to record all relevant information regarding your remodeling plans. It is unlikely you will always be with your partner when planning, and each of you should have key information available at all times.

Take the notebook with you when you hit the showrooms. Use the second section to draw sketches and to collect pictures of different fixtures and appliances. Note the model numbers, styles, colors, and prices of the items you are considering. You can also attach business cards from any salespeople you meet.

In the back of the notebook, list everything you decide to buy in a three-column format. In the first column, write down the item. In the second column, write down the estimated cost or the allowance your GC has given you for that item. In the third column, note the amount you actually end up paying. Keep a running tally so you know how much you've spent. You might still go over your limit, but at least with this method it won't come as a surprise.

When great minds don't meet

In the midst of all the decisions you have to make, there are bound to be a few you and your spouse simply can't agree on. The next chapter tells you how other couples have avoided this impasse; it also deals with other emotional costs of a building or remodeling project.

In this chapter, I have begun to give you some idea of what your responsibilities are. Some are things you should do, some are things you have to do, some involve altering the way you deal with people, and some involve getting organized.

Just the facts

- Create a pleasant place for your contractor and his crew to work with access to a bathroom, a phone, water, a refrigerator, and a secure place to keep their tools.

- Keep the lines of communication with your GC open. Schedule meetings on a regular basis and with a positive tone.

- Hold up your end of the job. If you don't perform on time, the work will probably stop.

- Work out a process with your partner for making decisions.

- Decisions have to be made for every room.

GET THE SCOOP ON...
Easing the strain of remodeling ▪ Developing a
shopping process ▪ Compromise ▪ What to do
when you reach an impasse

Chapter 4

Handling the Emotional Toll

Her favorite color is blue; his is brown. He likes country; she prefers modern. She is concerned about costs; he wants only the best. She wants hardwood floors; he wants wall-to-wall carpeting. She wants large expanses of windows; he wants to conserve energy.

When two people come to a remodeling project, they frequently arrive with completely different ideas of what looks good—and yet, decisions have to be made. Compromises are frequently called for. If you and your partner haven't worked out a method for dealing with differences in your relationship, you might as well use your remodeling project as a starting point.

People who have been together for years, who are used to speaking their minds and giving honest (but not always favorable) opinions of their partner's ideas, sometimes find restraint difficult to achieve. Over the years, most couples develop short-hand communication techniques; they can almost

Watch Out!
There should be
a label attached
to remodeling
plans: "Warning!
This project may
be hazardous
to your
relationship."

read each other's minds. Unfortunately, they have also learned each other's hot buttons and how to push them. The decisions necessary for a remodeling project can put significant stress on a relationship.

The best advice I can give you if you are undertaking a remodeling project with your partner is to resurrect and maintain the good behavior and sensitivity that served you so well during your courtship.

Why is remodeling so hard on a relationship?

As you read this chapter, you might be tempted to say, "No way! I have better things to do than fight nonstop with my spouse." But take it from people who have been through it—remodeling is hard on a relationship. This is true for many reasons.

It totally disrupts your daily routine

Think about how grateful you are to see weekend houseguests leave, even though they are wonderful friends? Your remodeling crew "guests" are going to be with you five days a week for weeks or even months, and they start by tearing your house apart.

Remodeling involves family finances

According to marriage counselors, disagreements involving money outweigh every other issue (including sex) as the major cause of stress in a relationship. During a large remodeling project, you're going to make hundreds of decisions that involve spending money—more money than you've spent since buying your house. And, unless you plan extremely well, more money than you've budgeted.

Remodeling involves personal tastes and styles

What looks good and what doesn't is a highly subjective judgment based on a lifetime of experiences.

Each of us has an innate sense of what we like when it comes to decorations and designs. In some people, however, this sense is more highly developed. If you and your partner have strong opinions that are at opposite ends of the taste spectrum, you're in for a rough time as you try to make remodeling decisions together. Unlike deciding what to have for dinner tonight, you're going to have to live with these decisions for years to come. People tend to get uptight.

How to anticipate the trouble spots

This quote may seem discouraging, but that particular builder was in Vermont where, it seems, metropolitan couples with troubled marriages go to spend more time together and heal their relationship. Of course, the old houses they buy need to be fixed up and the togetherness philosophy doesn't work well when people are covered with plaster dust.

If you are single or you don't have to consult with anyone regarding your home repair or remodeling decisions, feel free to skip ahead. On the other hand, if you are working with your spouse, partner, friend, parent, or anyone else whose needs and opinions must be considered, you must develop some guidelines for working together.

Equality

Start by determining whether you both will be equal in the decision-making process. Be aware that being married doesn't necessarily mean equality is required. Some individuals abdicate responsibility and authority to their spouse in the interest of saving time, accommodating impossible schedules, or even due to lack of interest. It's okay for one person to take all (or most) of the responsibility, as long as

Timesaver
A remodeling project will exacerbate any existing differences in a relationship. If a couple is not able to reach compromises both sides can live with, considerable time will be added to the project and its completion will be further delayed.

both parties agree to that arrangement. It's not okay to load all the responsibility onto one person, allow him or her to do all the work, and then second-guess that person's decisions.

The situation that causes the most trouble occurs when one person, usually the husband, says, "I don't care. You choose what you want." What he's really saying is, "I don't care until I have to write the check." This type of person takes no part in the decision-making process until the paint is selected and on the wall. Then he says, "Why'd you pick green? You know I can't stand green."

If you're sharing the load equally, spell out what that means. Does it mean that you will undertake the entire process together or that you will divide up the work? Or does equality simply mean that both of you can exercise veto power? Planning a project and seeing it through is a labor-intensive process. As a result, there is plenty of room for ruffled feathers and resentment if one person feels used or overworked.

The gender thing

Couples working together can cross their wires very easily if they are not careful. Sometimes the problem is gender related. Women characteristically are more opinionated than men when it comes to the home. They come armed with a more specifically defined set of requirements. Men tend to respond more generally and are frequently open to a more diverse range of outcomes.

For some men, however, this openness stems simply from not having given the subject much thought, as opposed to an absence of taste, interest, or opinion. Men I interviewed became quite animated once they warmed to discussions of house design, size,

> 66
>
> Over 50 percent of the clients we have worked for have ended up divorced. It's a sad statistic, and it's one of the big reasons I'm not in the construction business anymore.
>
> —Howard Romero, former designer/builder
>
> 99

and function. Many remarked, after the fact, that they were surprised by their level of interest and enthusiasm. Concerning their previous apathy, many initially believed they didn't have anything of value to offer or contribute.

Decisions about the home have a long tradition of being squarely planted in the feminine domain. In the end, however, both of you will live in the house. It's probably a good idea to prod a bit to get everybody's opinions on the table.

My recommendation for female readers is to set aside some time to involve your male partner in a structured discussion of what you need and want. Familiarize him with some of the design concepts and considerations integral to your project. More often than not, he will evolve from an apathetic bystander into a fully involved participant. Incidentally, the downside of not tackling this problem up front is that your partner might get his education on the job (by initiating changes mid-process). This might be better than no education at all, but it's time-consuming and expensive, and he won't be prepared to join the process until you are fairly far along. When it comes to major repairs or remodeling, it's best to come to the party early and to stay until the end.

Check on your communication skills

Do you let each other know how and what you feel or do you bottle up feelings and opinions? Your chances of weathering the stresses of remodeling are much higher if you recognize that stress can cause serious repercussions, talk about it before you start, and work out a system for compromising.

Good communication transcends the eloquent articulation of your own ideas and opinions. It also

Unofficially...
Although it might seem natural for the woman to take the lead in planning a project and for the man to handle the financing, this division reinforces gender stereotypes and limits the learning experience for both parties.

Bright Idea
Discuss problems openly and in front of the GC if you like the idea of an impartial referee. You'll find the job goes more smoothly when you keep the lines of communication open and filled with feelings, ideas, and suggestions.

involves being able to listen to your partner. Active listening takes listening to an interpretive level, allowing you to derive meaning beyond the spoken word. For example, your wife might ramble on about adding a studio to your house where she can paint or quilt. On the surface, this might sound like a waste of space. After all, why can't she paint or quilt in the family room or den? With active listening, you may recognize that she is not really talking about painting or quilting at all. She's talking about a personal need for privacy, tranquillity, and having a refuge to escape the frenetic activity of the household. Practice listening carefully to your partner. Then probe beneath the surface with well-considered questions, demonstrating not only that you have been paying attention but also that you care.

Evaluate your marriage

Take a good look at your relationship. If it's on shaky ground, the trials of a remodeling project could push you over the edge. Ask yourselves whether this is something you both want or if one of you is going along simply to keep the peace.

Set up and agree to some guidelines

Both of you have to be clear about the rules. One contractor described to me a situation he has encountered more than once. He called it the "Hidden Agenda Syndrome," in which a remodeling project is undertaken to save or delay the end of a marriage. The wife is delighted at first because she is finally getting her dream home. The husband's attitude seems to be, "Give her anything she wants." That can be the sign of either a very generous husband or a man with a guilty conscience. Halfway through the job, the wife often figures out what's going on and sparks begin to fly.

Most couples have not experienced the level of relationship stress that even a comparatively easy remodeling project can cause. It can cause quiet wives to become dominant commanders of work crews and can cause strong, silent men to voice their preference for a paisley print over contrasting stripes.

Meeting halfway: methods of compromise

There are probably as many methods of compromise as there are people who get into situations in which compromise is necessary. It might help you to know what outside influences might affect your negotiations and how other couples, faced with the same situation, have handled the problem.

Certain outside factors can force your hand into making some compromises. The following are some examples:

- You probably only have a certain amount of money to spend. If you agree ahead of time to stay within a budget that is broken down into specific areas such as electrical fixtures, bathroom fixtures, kitchen appliances, and so on, the budget itself can serve as a governor for your decision-making process. You want to have beautiful things, but they must be within your money limitations.

- Space is another compromise-forcing issue. One of you might really want an 8-foot circular bathtub and Jacuzzi combination. If the whole bathroom is only 5 feet by 7 feet, however, it tends to keep the project within the realm of the possible.

- You might not believe it now, but there is a time limit to your project. You'll have to make some

Moneysaver
Although you might have the urge to keep increasing your budget to make room for more expensive items, remember that your enjoyment of the remodeling project will depend not only on the beauty of the work but also on whether you feel you did not spend more than the project was worth to you. Stick to your budget!

decisions today because something has to go in tomorrow. If you're in a deadlock in the showroom, you will have to learn how to compromise by closing time.

Bright Idea
Take stock of your individual interests and skills. If you and your spouse got together under the natural rule that says opposites attract, your chances of reaching a compromise might be better than for two people who are both interested in designing.

A contractor once told me, "There are some cases in which both people are planners or both are detail people and you have a disaster. The client mix I love the best is when one of them is a planner and likes the feel of the organization of rooms and doesn't care what's on the walls or the floors, and the other is interested in interior decoration. They each get to work on the things that interest them, and they let the other one handle the other stuff."

From his experience, decisions—particularly in the planning stage—can go a couple different ways:

■ First, one member of the couple wants something too ambitious, and the other doesn't want to spend the money. The contractor usually suggests a middle ground; for example, the husband doesn't have to spend as much as he thinks and the wife doesn't need quite as big a project as she expects. They've probably been fighting about this for years before the contractor arrived. This contractor quips, "The only reason I'm sitting here is because she's tired of looking at it and he's tired of hearing about it." They usually laugh and that breaks the tension.

■ In the other scenario, one member of the couple is a nitpicker, and the other is a fairly reasonable person. Very seldom do you have a problem with both halves of the couple. The basic rule of survival for a GC is to divide and conquer. One person sits on the money; the other is in charge of the wishes and dreams. The GC becomes a marriage counselor, a minister, a financial counselor . . . at times, even a GC. He has to walk the thin line between alienating the person who will pay him and alienating the person who will be happy enough with the job to say, "Pay him."

Compromise techniques of other homeowners

Many couples devise successful ways to make decisions and to compromise when remodeling. I asked several couples how they handled differences of taste and opinion and money issues. One wife said, "Real differences usually came when money was involved. I don't worry about money. I think it will be there if we really need it or if we want something badly enough. He is very concerned with money. I found it was best to determine how much he had in mind to spend on something before I went out shopping rather than selecting something and then finding out what he had expected to pay. He and I think differently. He tends to be practical, and I'm into practical and pretty."

The homeowner husband said, "Yes, we had arguments and differences and I lost most of them. We have larger windows than I thought we needed, and we have a skylight in the bedroom.

But I must confess I didn't feel strongly about those things. I don't remember losing anything I really insisted on. I was able to convince her to go with the natural wood on the interior woodwork in the addition, and we both like it now. I guess my only pet peeve is the skylight in the bedroom because it wakes me up at 5 a.m. on summer mornings. She still likes it, however."

Another homeowner told me, "My wife and I have very similar tastes. I tend to be a little bit

Unofficially ... As odd as it may sound, I advise any couple contemplating a major remodeling project to get therapy. The stress on relationships created by remodeling projects should not be underestimated.

(actually a lot) more down-and-dirty, and she likes things more buttoned up. But our basic tastes are alike. One place we couldn't agree was on the style of a doorknob for the closet just off the kitchen. It still doesn't have a knob, and you need a Boy Scout knife to get into it."

One couple I questioned had several tactics. They rummaged through magazines and adapted what they saw to their particular situation and tastes. They had what they called the "battle of the pads"— the wife would toss out an idea, he would draw it up, and she would say, "No, no, no. That's not what I meant." Then she would draw something and he would say, "That looks ridiculous." They would go back and forth until they agreed it looked right.

They didn't arrive at all their decisions in one night, however. Several evenings were spent with the wife selling her husband on an idea, which he admitted was not easy to do. "She is a very good seller and does not get discouraged or give up easily," he admitted. "But as it turned out, the ideas she sold the hardest were the best ones."

These are two strong-minded people, but neither ran roughshod over the other. Because the husband did much of the work himself, he couldn't very well be expected to work on something unless he agreed it was a good idea. "I never had to build, move, or take out something under protest," he said. They both had to agree on something before they started on it.

Breaking an impasse

Many projects begin with a feeling-out process because the partners don't know what they want. Gradually, the project begins to sort itself out, and the couple begins to lock onto what they want. What

Bright Idea
Don't feel you have to arrive at a decision or a compromise immediately. When you realize one of you has doubts or serious reservations about a design approach, a fixture, a color, or a pattern, take a break—better yet, sleep on it. You'll be amazed how the battle lines fade and attitudes mellow given a little time.

happens, however, when the partners lock onto two different things?

One homeowner wife said, "We hit impasse situations. I just waited for good opportunities to take up my cause. The power of a drop of water on a stone."

Her husband noted, "She is patient. Very, very patient. That's the solution, really. You just go away from the problem for a while."

His wife agreed, "That's how we solved a problem. We both just stood away from it and let our minds work subconsciously on it. Before long, you start incorporating the other person's idea, no matter how resistant you thought you were in the beginning."

This couple has a large, bold, colorful, floral-pattern fabric on the living room walls of their small New York apartment. The selection of the fabric went considerably beyond which shade of beige would look best, so I asked how they arrived at their selection. The wife told me, "This was something I had to convince him of. He thought a big, busy pattern would make the room look smaller. I showed him dozens of pictures of teeny English cottages and proved that patterned wallpaper actually makes the rooms look bigger. In fact, the more that is in a room and the busier it is, the better off you are. We had some criteria. It had to have a couple of colors in it, and it had to have some coordinated trim designs that went with it."

Her husband says, "She showed me enough pictures of English cottages that I bought the idea, but it took a lot of weekends of going blind looking at fabric samples."

That couple had different views, but they communicated. What happens in the more likely event

Unofficially...
If you find yourselves in a constant state of impasse, you might take a leaf from the basketball rule book. Instead of stopping play for jump-balls when two players have possession of the ball at the same time, use the possession arrow at the scorer's table. The teams take turns getting the ball. You and your partner can take turns winning impasses.

that one member of the couple is not a great communicator? One homeowner told me, "We made a lot of mistakes. There is a lot of stress involved. I'm married to a guy who doesn't communicate. I remember sitting here one evening speculating about how a set of bookshelves might look on the living room wall. I think I might even have gone on and on about it. His comment to me was, 'We can't afford to do that right now.'

One morning, I woke up to the sound of the power saw. I came downstairs and the wall was gone. He was proceeding with the project and asked me if I had any drawings of what I wanted. The last I knew it was a dead issue. Where we got into trouble is that I would openly fantasize about how I wanted to do a room, but what I didn't realize was he was mentally preparing to do it . . . and we never linked up. He was reacting to what he thought I wanted when, in reality, I hadn't had time to think it through properly."

The fascinating thing about these particular homeowners is that they worked on the complete renovation of their home for 10 years and never quite mastered the art of communicating. They were talking, but they were making assumptions rather than making sure they understood each other.

How to handle differences in taste

If you wait until you're in the showroom to discover that you and your partner have completely different ideas of what your house should look like and how it should be decorated, you're in real trouble. It would be easier to arrive at decisions and compromises if there were a right and a wrong. In decorating and outfitting a home, however, many choices will work just as well as others. It comes down to personal taste. Still, there are some things you can do to keep your options within manageable limits.

- First, go back to your file of magazine pictures. Go through them together and point out room arrangements and decorating touches you like. The first time you looked at them, back in the planning phase, you might have been concentrating on floor plans. This time, concentrate on an overall look or atmosphere you can both appreciate.

- Second, try to settle on an identifiable style for your home: country, shaker, Southwest, modern, English cottage, arts and crafts, Victorian, and so on. This helps limit your selections to a manageable number of items that are in that style or at least are compatible with it.

- Third, divide and concur. If you can't agree on an overall style, mix two or three styles. It might be best not to do this in any single room, but if one of you has your heart set on a Victorian look, designate one of the guest rooms for this treatment.

I happen to like dark, forest-green walls; my wife likes bone white. Any compromise of those two colors in the same room would look awful. So I have dark green walls in my office, and the rest of the house is white. We also had a difficult time picking the tiles for the floors and showers in the two bathrooms. It was obvious that we were operating with two different decorative themes, so we split the task. I got to do the upstairs bathroom, and she got to do the downstairs bathroom. I suspect she was looking over my shoulder as I made my selections, but I still got to select my tan tile and desert sage linoleum.

One wife confided to me, "My husband doesn't have any taste. I don't mean he has bad taste. I mean he doesn't have a preference in taste. I think most men relinquish claim to any decisions in the home very early in a relationship. Very few get into fabric swatches and wallpaper sample books."

This is similar to the child who never spoke until one day at the age of eight when he said, "This soup needs more salt." When his delighted parents asked why he had never spoken earlier he replied, "Everything's been fine up to now." The woman's husband, like many of us, probably learned that he could rely on her taste and just went along with it.

Treat compromise like a business decision

Think about how you arrive at decisions and compromises at work, and use the same techniques with your spouse. Don't whine and sulk or rant and rave; instead, treat each other as equal business partners in this venture. Ask and question; don't demand and bully. Suggest alternatives and ask for time to think about your partner's suggestions. If you reach an impasse (and you will), you might take turns getting to make the final choice.

In this chapter, I have tried to prepare you for the work, the decisions, and the possible battles ahead. New construction wears down homeowners because of all the basic decisions to be made almost every day. Remodeling is even more stressful because you're probably living in the mess the work crews have created, and you still have to make all the same decisions.

Bright Idea
If you both are management types, you might try to handle your discussions using professional office etiquette. Use more impersonal and polite phrases such as "What do you think?" or "Well, how about this approach?"
It can help remove much of the heat from your discussions and has the potential to add more light.

Just the facts

- Remember that you and your partner are on the same side in this project and that it will all end eventually.

- Recognize that you're going to feel uptight as you start the selection-and-decision part of your project.

- Don't feel bad when encountering conflicts. Everyone goes through these feelings.

- Draw up some house rules covering finances, division of labor, and methods or tricks for making joint decisions or compromising—and obey them.

- Avoid reaching an impasse with your partner by genuinely listening and by giving it some "time out." If an impasse does occur, try to be diplomatic.

Controlling the Work

PART III

GET THE SCOOP ON...
Where all the money goes ▪ Cost overruns ▪
Where all the time goes ▪ Types of mistakes ▪
Dealing effectively with problems

Chapter 5

Dealing with Problems

One of the most mystifying aspects of remodeling and construction is the amount of unexpected money that inevitably has to be spent. In this chapter, I'll go over some of the areas where this money goes and help you avoid exceeding your budget. And if you do go over budget, you'll at least understand how it happened.

The other mystery is where all the time goes. Everyone said the job would be completed in six weeks, and here you are in the twelfth week. How does this happen? This problem is harder to avoid, but being forewarned might help ease your mind.

No matter how thoroughly you plan and no matter how often you meet with your contractor, there still will be mistakes, misunderstandings, and changes of mind. In this chapter I'll forewarn you about the types of mistakes you might encounter and offer effective ways to deal with them so that skirmishes don't escalate into wars.

Where does all the money go?

If you follow the suggestions in the first four chapters of this book, you improve the chances that your contract will be accurate and complete, that your contractor will be experienced, capable, and honest, and that your project will come in closer to budget. But you still need to prepare for problems.

In this section, we'll explore why things go wrong, where overruns are most likely to occur, and how you can avoid them (or at least keep them to a minimum).

The major culprits: where cost overruns commonly occur

There are generally six areas where your budget goes out of control and your checkbook takes a beating:

- **Behind the walls and under the house.** Surprises can lurk behind your walls. One builder found that all the wiring in a house ran down through a wall he thought would only cost a few hundred dollars to remove. All that wiring not only had to be rerouted, it had to be replaced with wiring that meets today's codes.

- **Weight-bearing walls.** Most builders, and certainly the one you hired, will know where the weight-bearing walls are. If your plans call for a large opening in or the removal of a weight-bearing wall, heavier vertical structural members will be needed, and additional wood or even a steel I-beam are necessary to carry the weight across the span. If this comes as a surprise and increases the cost of the job, you are in the wrong hands.

- **Subtler surprises.** Subtler surprises are common as well, such as plumbing lines that show up in the space where you wanted a window or abandoned chimneys and brick walls that have been covered over and need to be removed at extra cost. The main culprit, however, and the hardest to predict, is dry-rotted or water-damaged wood. If you find this where you expected to find sound material, you suddenly have a project that requires rebuilding, not just redecorating.

■ **Under the ground.** The majority of cost overruns that come to light after the shovels hit the back yard fall into two categories: ledge problems and septic systems. Ledge problems (a nicer way to say rock or granite) change a digging project into a blasting or drilling job, and the costs go up accordingly. Costs for installing or moving a septic system can easily rise if you get bad results from your percolation test. This test, often required by your local health department, measures the time it takes water to seep out of a hole. If the test reveals clay instead of friendly gravel (clay is not a good filtering soil), your septic system can become a major expense.

People who move to a house in the suburbs from a city apartment where toilet flushes just go away often are surprised to discover that, when you have a septic system, your own back yard is the sewage-treatment plant. If this is the first you have heard about septic systems, a word of explanation is in order. The sewage and most of the water from your house runs out through a pipe to a cement septic tank buried in your yard. The septic tank has two or more settling chambers where nature's microbes go to work cleaning up. Comparatively clean water then flows out of the septic tank through pipes with holes drilled in them. These pipes fan out from the septic tank and are your leach field. The water leaches through the holes into the surrounding soil to further the cleansing process. If the soil has gravel or sand in it, that's good. If it's all clay, the problem can be corrected by carting in better soil or by mounding.

Unofficially...
A firm bid doesn't mean you get to stick it to your general contractor every time an unanticipated problem causes a cost overrun. If that were the case, there wouldn't be anyone left in the building business.

■ **In the contract.** If you've read other books and articles about remodeling, you've no doubt encountered authors who advocate the fixed-bid or firm-price contract (or the *stipulated sum,* as the AIA calls it) over the cost-plus contract. I agree with these authors about the disadvantages and dangers of a cost-plus contract, but I disagree with their assessment that fixed-price contracts are low-risk for homeowners. The way they see it, a fixed-price contract forces your contractor to eat any cost increases that result from unexpected problems or delays.

Interviews with contractors, however, indicate that they have recognized the risk of unknown problems for some time and have worked out ways to lessen this risk by writing them directly into firm-bid contracts. The sample kitchen-remodeling proposal from Chapter 2 illustrates this point. Notice the fine print that states, "Any alteration or deviation from the specifications below involving extra cost . . . will become extra costs over and above the estimate."

The contractor further protects himself by specifying that wallpaper removal, if required, is not included. He also clearly states his assumption that all valves are operational and that waste and supply lines are adequate. The sample estimate from Chapter 2 doesn't include the cost of appliances, painting, or electrical fixtures. The allowances it does include ($4,000 for the cabinets and $200 for the sink and faucet) are small.

The design/remodeling firm that supplied this example is highly reputable. As you can see, however, their "firm bid" could easily go up another $10,000 when all the appliances, decorating, electrical fixtures, and assumption corrections are added in. Three possible surprises could be the homeowners selecting a $1,000 sink, a $400 faucet set, and an $8,000 set of kitchen cabinets they "can't live without." This would result in another $10,000 right there. It happens—frequently.

- **At City Hall.** Another person hiding in the wings with potentially costly surprises is your local building inspector. You might be happy with the old electrical panel in the basement, and you may even convince your contractor that a few more circuits will work fine. The inspector, however, is looking for building-code violations. He might require you to buy a new, larger, electrical circuit-breaker panel and to replace all the old knob and tube wiring in your house before he'll give you a certificate of occupancy. Needless to say, this type of surprise can easily short-circuit your budget. You must correct any problems the building inspector finds, or you don't get to move in or even back in.

When selecting everything that will go into the rooms you are remodeling, you will face an array of beautiful products you didn't even know existed. The temptation will be great to indulge yourselves and to justify the extra cost with the idea that "we

Moneysaver
Control your impulses in the showrooms. You yourself might be the reason costs go up. If you or your partner have adopted the philosophy that "we only get to do this once in our lives and we deserve the best," you'd better go back to your bank for a refill.

can spread the payments for this over the 30 years of the mortgage and won't even feel it." You are in for a serious shock. If you decide to go for the $1,200 gold-plated bathtub fixtures, over the 30 years of your mortgage they will cost you about $3,600. Unless, of course, they break—then they'll cost more.

You don't have to buy fancy fixtures to have your bathroom costs go through the roof. If your plumber finds galvanized pipes behind the walls, he will probably talk to you about their remaining life expectancy. He will strongly recommend that they be replaced with copper pipes and that you replace all the old valves and connections. Ask to see all these problems yourself and make your own evaluations.

Keeping cost overruns to a minimum

One sure way to avoid cost overruns is to double the estimate; most jobs would then come in slightly under the bid price.

I also have to emphasize what every building book and contractor says: Keep planning until you know exactly what you want. You might not think I'm saving you any money with this second suggestion—if you find problems before you start, you're still going to have to spend more money— but at least you'll know about them before you go in for your bank loan.

Develop a careful plan and stick to it. The best way to avoid cost overruns is to plan thoroughly in advance and then back up the plans with detailed working drawings (prepared by your contractor or architect). Stick to your plan and keep changes to a minimum. If changes are called for, try to anticipate them.

The main reason I began this book with a chapter about planning is because lack of thorough planning—and the resulting changes and mistakes—are the major contributors to cost overruns. Don't hesitate to change something if you think it will make your house better. Occasionally remind yourself, however, that doing a job over two or three times costs more and demoralizes your crew.

Investigate during the planning stage. The more you and your contractors know about the problems hidden in your house, the more accurate their bids will be. You might let one contractor open up the walls in question to see what lies in wait for him before he actually submits his bid. Sometimes just the age of your house alerts an experienced remodeler to likely problems. Copper piping became the standard after World War II. Before that time, piping could have been brass, galvanized steel, or even lead.

Bright Idea
Visit the work site every day. If you see something that looks wrong or gives you some doubts, talk to your contractor. Get it taken care of before it's built and has to be ripped out to make the change.

Why costs go up quickly and come down slowly

Several homeowners I spoke with noted one of the construction industry's great mysteries: Costs can escalate in the blink of an eye, but they never drop as quickly when projects are scaled back. "Why doesn't an 8 × 10–foot deck cost half as much as a 16 × 10–foot deck?" they ask. "Why does leaving an attic space or bathroom 'unfinished' seem to save so little over the 'finished' cost?"

The reason is that it takes just as many tools to do the smaller job. It takes just as long to set up and break down each day. Every board, no matter how long or how short, has to be cut once and nailed at each end. Whether you paint all day or only touch up one window, an open can of paint has to be stirred. It takes just as long to clean a brush after 10 minutes of use as it does at the end of a full day.

Unofficially...
The more produc-
tive time you can
allow between
the set-up and
the pack-up, the
more efficient
the job will be.

Does keeping track of costs help? Not much. Many businesses start with a plan or business proposal, followed by a budget that lists estimated costs for raw materials, labor, operating expenses, and overhead expenses. As the business goes forward, reports are usually generated in which the actual cost for each item is listed opposite the estimated cost, making comparison simple. Managers know when they are running over budget, and they can usually either make adjustments or negotiate a loan for additional funds.

This is not the case with even moderately complex remodeling. A majority of the materials and supplies are ordered and paid for within a few days of the start of a project. The first load from the lumberyard contains everything from the dimensional lumber, the nails, the Sheetrock, and the underlayment to the flooring for the whole job. It also contains many items for individual parts of the project such as tiles, grout, roofing shingles, and doors. The contractor will have added up the materials needed for all the rooms, and it's almost impossible to attribute each part of the load to a specific room.

How does a homeowner keep track of the costs on a remodeling project? There isn't any way to do it. When it came time for me to write the first of many checks to my builder, he turned over all his receipts for materials and supplies, time cards, bills for the subcontractors, and a total. I'm sure it was all correct, but without reconstructing his entire business, there was no way I could know for sure whether the estimated times and costs itemized in the contract bore any resemblance to this wrinkled pile of receipts. Fortunately, I came to this conclusion very early in the project and didn't spend hours trying to double-check.

When I asked builders and contractors how homeowners should keep track of costs as the job progresses, I began to think that my approach—simply writing the check with few or no questions asked—was the right one. One contractor agreed, "There is no way you can compare the estimate with the actual job. The fact of the matter is the job should feel right to you in your gut."

The clock is ticking: where the time goes

When I asked contractors to explain where all the time goes on a building project, I got dozens of answers, citing everything from natural phenomena and acts of God to human error and miscommunication. Their explanations should give you some appreciation of the problems they regularly encounter in the course of a remodel.

Inn owner Susan Sobilinski, who served as her own GC during remodeling, gave me a great example of the time variable in remodeling. After not having use of a downstairs bathroom for a month, she gave her carpenter a stern talking-to on one of the few days he showed up. "I thought you told me when you bid this job it would only take you seven days," she said. "That's right, I did," he replied, "but I didn't mean in a row."

Weather delays

If you are planning a remodeling project that involves tearing off a roof or adding a foundation and structure to the side, back, or front of your house, it's not hard to imagine the effect a prolonged rainy spell could have on your schedule. If you're working under the happy assumption that you won't be affected by the weather because the remodeling you're doing is all inside, think again.

> **❝**
> I don't want to work for someone who doesn't trust me. At the end of the week, my subs and carpenters tell me how much they have worked. I keep track of my hours, and I turn them in to the client. I trust my subs and my crew. If I didn't, I would have gotten rid of them a long time ago.
> —Frank Husband, remodeling contractor
> **❞**

What do you suppose happens when your contractor, who said he would start your job on August 1, gets delayed three weeks by rain on the job he's doing before yours? Yes, it could delay your start by three weeks. He might also come to you and ask to start your project two weeks before you expect him.

New England, for example, gets 72 days of rain a year. That's one out of every five days. If a contractor or a subcontractor gets three or four days of rain in a row, he will look for a small inside job such as remodeling your bathroom. When the sun comes out, however, he has a problem. Does he leave you without a toilet until it rains again? Or does he delay going back to the original job until the bathroom is done? Whatever he decides can cause problems that ripple through the entire system.

Unofficially . . .
Weather can affect your project in unexpected ways. One contractor told me he loses three days for each day it rains because all the subcontractors have to be rescheduled.

Delivery delays

As you stroll through a lumberyard, your first impression might be that everything you could possibly need is ready and waiting for your GC's order so it can be sent to your site. There is plenty of dimensional lumber, plywood, drywall, siding, roofing, cement blocks, and all the basic stuff. You might notice, however, that all the windows, kitchen cabinets, and bathroom vanities are in little display areas. They're there for you to browse through, select from, and order. The actual delivery time of the items you want can be anywhere from a few weeks to a couple months. That's why you need to decide what you want as early as possible. Otherwise, all work could be halted as your GC and subcontractors wait for the windows or cabinets to arrive.

Your GC can't control the lead time necessary for special orders. Therefore, homeowners must make up their minds as early as possible in the remodeling process. Items such as windows, cupboards, doors, and even some fixtures must be ordered early so they'll arrive on the job site when needed. Windows, for example, can take six to eight weeks for delivery—twice that if it's the busy season.

Scheduling delays

A general contractor has to allow for a frightening number of variables, many of which he can't control. To build even a simple addition to a house can involve up to 18 subcontractors, from the excavator to the landscaper and painter. Many if not all of these subcontractors cannot do their work until the person ahead of them finishes. The framers can't frame until the foundation is in, plumbing and heating people have to wait for the framers, insulation goes in before the Sheetrock goes up, and the electrician must come both before and after the Sheetrock installers.

A contractor I interviewed described being a GC as trying to fight a war with a rented army. No matter how precise his schedule, a GC can't order a subcontractor to be there. If a crew is short-handed or a subcontractor misses his arrival date, the job goes slower and tasks have to be assigned to fill the gap. Part of a GC's job is to keep a list of things that can be done to fill in those blanks in the schedule and keep his crew busy.

Finish work delays

One fall Sunday afternoon, my wife and I were walking the dog past a neighbor's side lot and noticed a foundation for a new house. When we came by the next afternoon, we were impressed to find that the first floor was completely framed. Unfortunately, the speed at which the first few steps in new construction and remodeling are completed is

Watch Out!
If the job calls for 18 subcontractors, and if they all come within two days of their scheduled time (which would be very good service), they will have added 36 days to the projected time. And this is not taking weather into account.

misleading. Homeowners tend to think every phase will go as rapidly, but it doesn't happen that way.

It doesn't take long to tear things apart. Even after the Sheetrock is up, however, the job isn't even halfway finished. In fact, the closer you get to being done in terms of the number of stages, the more detailed the work is and the longer each stage takes. When you get to the part where the work seems to slow to a crawl, you're at the finish carpentry stage.

Finish carpenters are at the high end of the woodworking trades, just a little short of cabinet-makers. They come in after all the rough carpentry is done, the windows have been installed, the kitchen and bathroom cabinets are sitting in their shipping crates, and all the doors and frames are leaning against rough openings. A finish carpenter is the one who puts in the baseboards, frames the windows, puts up the molding you finally decided on, installs the medicine cabinets, builds the shelving in all the closets, and hangs all the doors.

Every board he installs has to be measured twice (if he follows the old adage "measure twice and cut once"), cut (often at an angle that has to be calculated), and nailed. Then the nail has to be set in a little deeper so it can be puttied by the painter. The pounding is slower, with long pauses between nails (unless a pneumatic finish nail gun is used). Speaking of costs, if you're sent out to pick up $1,000 worth of finish-grade lumber, moldings, baseboards, and so on, you won't need any help carrying it to your car. The money doesn't go as far at this stage.

Delays caused by changes you make

No matter how thoroughly you plan, lay things out on the floor, measure, and visualize the proposed space, it always looks different when the walls are up and you actually can walk into it. Sometimes it looks better than you hoped, but frequently you'll realize you've made a mistake. The window should be bigger so you can look out at the view while standing up or sitting down, the kitchen would be more efficient if the sink were on the other wall, a door swings the wrong way, your bedroom closet is too small, or the guest room is too big. Don't feel discouraged. This happens more than you'd think.

Changing your mind after something is already up means the original work has to be torn out, new material must be ordered and delivered, and the job has to be done over again. This takes time. If the Sheetrockers were scheduled to start their work the next day, your contractor might be able to have them start in another room. Hopefully, he will be done with the alteration before they get to the room in question. If not, he will have to cancel and try to get them again later. They might not be available for another two weeks, however; if that is the case, your project will have to wait.

The effect of a change or a mistake on the length of time added to a project is directly proportional to how early you catch it. We walked into our house one evening after the crew had left for the day and noticed that there was an extra window in the kitchen. We were still in the framing stage, so all we saw were 2 × 6's with an extra 2 × 4 open box in them. I met with the contractor the next morning. We went over the drawings to see how it happened. (As it turned out, the framing carpenters had used some old drawings.) Correcting the problem was simple: The framing carpenters simply put a vertical 2 × 6 in the box to fill in the stud pattern. The additional time: about 30 minutes. The subcontractors

Moneysaver
If you feel that a change is necessary, talk it over with your contractor first. He might have some suggestions that can correct the problem without making drastic changes.

Bright Idea
Don't leave old floor plans lying around. Get rid of them before someone accidentally picks them and up and uses them.

who later installed the insulation might have wondered what we were doing, but by catching the problem early, we saved a lot of time and effort. Of course, if we hadn't caught the extra window, the cabinet installer certainly would have—the space it occupied was where his cabinets were supposed to go.

Your-contractor's-got-to-make-a-living delays

As much as you might like to think your project is the most important one in the world (and as much as your contractor leads you to believe this), the fact is that your GC has to line up his next job while work continues on yours. After all, he needs to maintain a steady income. To do this, the contractor has to visit other homes, meet with other owners, and put together bids and proposals. Most of this is done during weekends and evenings, but some day visits might be necessary. He might also have to bid several jobs to get one.

The only time you really have to worry is if the contractor launches the next job well before yours is finished. Just when your job is getting to the time-consuming, detail-work phase, he might have his head in the first phases of the new project. It is a normal construction practice to leave one or two skilled finish carpenters on a site to finish up the first job while taking the rest of the crew to the new one. From your perspective, however, this creates a situation in which not only is the work more time-consuming, but there are fewer people doing it. By this point, you will have become much less sympathetic to your builder's problems, but it might help to know that this is the nature of the construction business.

Your contractor disappears

It seems in every remodeling job a day comes when no one shows up at your house. One day is not too alarming, but if it goes on for several days or a couple of weeks, you might begin to panic. It is safe to bet that you will also not be able to reach anything but an answering machine at your builder's office or home. You start reading the obituary columns in the local paper. Then one morning, out of the blue, you wake up to the sound of a power saw and hammers. They're back.

- **Vacations.** Contractors and subcontractors take vacations, too. Six months ago, when his wife bought the tickets for a trip to Bermuda, he had no idea he would be in the middle of your job when the time came. Builders like to take their vacations in the summer months just like the rest of us. They might have some time in the winter months, but that's because they're unemployed.

- **'Tis the season.** As you schedule your projects, check to see when hunting and fishing season opens in your area. Contractors and subcontractors often can't resist the call of the wild. In Vermont, the opening day of deer season is practically a national holiday. You can only hope your crew is made up of skilled hunters that can get their buck within a day or two. The same phenomenon takes place in other parts of the country on the opening day of trout fishing and so forth.

- **They're only human.** Your builders also might disappear for other reasons. Everything that causes a normal person to take days off from work can also affect builders. They get sick, they

Unofficially...
Clients often complain when a contractor tells them he has vacation plans in the middle of their project. As a result, some contractors prefer not to mention their vacation plans until they've already taken the vacation. If you want to know, you'll have to ask your contractor directly.

have to cope with family emergencies, and they get burned out and need to get away for a few days.

Is there a solution to the disappearing builder syndrome? Not really, but if you're aware that it can and does happen, you won't be shocked, and maybe your builder will level with you so you can calculate the time more accurately.

Look at the bright side. You'll have some additional time to pick out all the things you have to choose. And unless they were so unkind as to leave with the water or electricity turned off, you also get a little peace and quiet for a while.

What to do when things go wrong (and they will)

The purpose of this book is to help your remodeling project be well thought out, well planned, and well organized. But you can't anticipate every contingency or avoid every mistake. So how do you prepare for the inevitable?

One of the architects I talked to presented an interesting approach that eliminated a lot of mistakes—he called them something else. "I'm not sure what a 'mistake' is in construction. There is the problem of homeowners who approve ideas, sketches, and plans all along and never admit that they can't read drawings. The first time they see their house in three dimensions is during the framing stage. When they say, 'That's not what we thought it would look like; can we change it?' That's not a mistake. That's a matter of perception. We have found that most cost overruns occur because the owners make changes as they see their dream coming true. They say, 'You know, I wouldn't mind spending a little more if we could make that window larger.'"

Unofficially...
Face it, there will be mistakes on your job. It's not so much what goes wrong but how you and your contractor react to it that determines how destructive and disruptive the mistakes become.

Mistakes, like sins, come in many forms. There are mistakes of omission, when something that should have been done wasn't done, and mistakes of commission, when something that should not have be done was done or done incorrectly. Then there are mistakes when something is done correctly according to the plans, but it just doesn't look right.

Lack of planning

If a remodeling project is progressing without drawings to go by, mistakes can be made because problems can't be foreseen. Mistakes come from not looking three steps ahead and anticipating problems. Lack of planning can result in finding out the Jacuzzi won't fit through the new bathroom door, tearing out the wall, and then discovering the Jacuzzi could have been taken apart. That's a mistake . . . or two.

Different points of view

Sometimes a mistake, like beauty, is in the eye of the beholder. Our last-minute, "divided-pane" picture window project comes to mind. The contractor and I thought the wooden snap-in grid looked just fine. To my wife, the fake grid was a mistake. Fortunately, it was a mistake that only cost $25. If we had kept the snap-ins, we would have saved about $1,200 (the cost of a true divided lights window), but it would have bothered my wife forever.

Well-intentioned mistakes

For every action, there is an equal and opposite reaction. That law of physics seems to hold true as well for good intentions in construction. The lead carpenter on our project wanted to make sure I had enough head room in the upstairs shower, which is built under the eaves. So when laying out the roof rafters, he raised the peak some 4 extra feet. My wife thought this made the house look like a teepee. She said the roof was completely out of scale. This change was done one morning when the roof rafters went up. We didn't get a vote. We could have insisted on a fix, but it would have cost a lot of extra money, and we weren't even sure the roof would really look out of proportion when it was finished. Unfortunately, my wife still thinks the roof looks completely out of scale, even after years of my pointing out steep-roofed houses.

Another change in that bathroom, discovered later, might have prevented the roof from being raised at all. The original chimney was tucked away in the attic crawl space of the house and was now the inside wall of the second-floor bathroom. No one had noticed, but the chimney canted about 2 feet toward the front of the house and into the bathroom before it headed toward the roof.

The carpenter suggested tearing out the old, bent chimney and putting in a new cinder-block chimney that would go straight up. We could even salvage the used bricks and use them for the part that shows above the roof. It was a great idea, and I went along with it immediately. The rearranged chimney added a foot and a half to the width of the bathroom, which meant we hadn't needed to raise the peak of the roof to get my head room in the shower after all.

Was raising the roof a mistake? It was a good decision at the time because it gave me head room. My wife tends to believe that, if we had retained an architect, he would have crawled around in the attic, would have made accurate measurements, and would have known about the chimney. He could have solved the problem on paper before we discovered it in real life.

Underestimates by contractors or subcontractors

This issue starts out as the contractor's mistake and problem, but you're inevitably going to become involved in some way. If the contractor has uncovered some previously unanticipated problems, such as rotten floor joists under the bathtub or piping that has to be replaced, he has a right to get additional money for additional work. The contract probably provides for this even if it's a firm bid. If you suspect your contractor gave you an artificially low bid just to get the job and is now trying to stick it to you, however, you have an obligation to your fellow homeowners to give him a very hard time.

One homeowner, departing from his policy of doing it himself, ran into a contractor and asked if he did screened-in porches. The contractor said he did, came around to see the porch, and made a rough estimate of $1,200 including materials—no more than $1,500. He was hired and started doing the work. As the homeowner tells it, "At the end of the week he said, 'Where's my money?' So I gave him $300 on top of the $400 I had already paid him to cover the materials. It was obvious he had never done a screened porch before. When he got to the last $300 or $400, he wanted me to pay him. I pointed out he had not finished. He said, 'You pay me and I'll finish.' I said, 'No. You finish and I'll pay you.' He never came back. I think what happened was the job ended up being more difficult than he thought. When he pulled off, it was at the break-even point. If he finished the job he was going to lose money. Even if I had paid him, I doubt if he would have been back."

Watch Out!
You have to decide for yourself how flexible you want to be in accepting financial responsibility for contractors' underestimates. Some couples prefer to accept occasional increases in the interest of good will. If you end up facing several increases the contractor should have caught, however, you might end up feeling cheated.

Wrong deliveries

Even with all the electronic order-processing gear in use today (or maybe because of it), many of the items that arrive at your house will not be what you ordered. When this happens, you have two clear choices: keep it or send it back. If you're reading this before you remodel, you might feel the obvious answer is to send it back. If you're in the middle of a project, however, you'll understand that timing is an important consideration.

When we discovered that the lumberyard had sent us the wrong color roofing shingles, they were in a pile in the backyard. We sent them back. But what if the crew had already covered half the roof with the wrong shingles? Who would have paid the extra labor of redoing the whole job? Who, in fact, made the mistake? The contractor? The supplier? Or had I been unclear about the color? Fortunately, we never had to find out.

You might find yourself in a similar situation. You can see the time clock running as the debate goes on, and you know the weather report calls for heavy rain tomorrow. Suddenly, the new color might not look so bad after all.

One homeowner ordered kitchen cabinets with polished brass pulls and blind hinges. What he got was antique brass face-mounted 'H' hinges with polished brass knobs that didn't match. His wife surmised that the guy who took her order wrote down the wrong part numbers. Because the cabinets had to be custom-built, the couple had waited 15 weeks and had planned a party to show off the new kitchen. They were already running behind, so they had two choices. They could accept them as they were and have polished brass hinges put on to

Moneysaver
When ordering components and fixtures, double-check to make sure the style numbers are correct. English descriptions tend to get ignored at the plants.

match the pulls, or they could send them back and wait another 16 to 18 weeks. They kept them. Some things you have to just accept.

Judgment calls

The original oak flooring in our living room and front bedroom runs north and south. The oak flooring in the big new room across the back of the house runs east and west. Right up until I wrote this paragraph, I thought it was because the floor joists under the new section went a different direction than those under the rest of the house. I just went downstairs and looked. They run north to south just like the front room joists.

As you will undoubtedly discover, it seems you only get to discuss these problems after the work is done. There is a seam right in the middle of the kitchen countertop, or your deck is a different shape than you thought it would be. Is it a mistake for flooring to run the entire length of a room rather than across it to match the rest of the house? It probably wasn't as much a mistake as it was a surprise. I just assumed it would run the other way. I certainly didn't feel strongly enough about it to have the new floor ripped up and relaid.

Be there when things are installed. You might have a clear picture in your mind of how a window or the floor-tile pattern will look. But if you are not there when it's built or installed, you could be surprised. The builder might have a completely different mental picture. It might even be a prettier picture than yours. The problem is, it's different. Being present during installation will help you avert these situations.

Bright Idea
If the work is different from what you requested and is already done, don't blow up and blast everyone on the job. Take some time, have a glass of wine, and talk it over with your spouse. Then, the next morning, talk it over in a civil manner with your GC. Get some facts on the costs of changing, the additional time and material requirements, and even how the "mistake" happened so you can avoid another one.

It's done right but it looks wrong

You agreed to the plans, you watched it being built, it was done correctly, and now you don't like the way it looks. It could be the location of the front stairs, the placement of a kitchen window, the size of the master bedroom, the color of your living room, or the location of the built-in breakfast nook. This happens a lot, so don't feel bad. The trick is to discover these "mistakes" as early as possible in the building process. It is easier and less expensive to move a stud wall than a wall that has been completely finished. Speak up as soon as you notice something.

You are the one who has to live with your remodeling results. If you aren't happy with it now, you probably won't feel better with time. Stop the work and talk to your GC. Tell him how you feel and what you'd like. He might have some suggestions that will solve your problem. If not, he can tell you how much it will cost to tear out what has been done and to rebuild it to your satisfaction. This requires a change order (a contract within a contract) to cover the cost of tearing out the work, buying new materials, and providing labor to do it over.

In our case, we felt strongly enough about one thing to request a change: the closet doors in the master bedroom. For some reason, the swing direction of the these doors had been a major point of debate from the moment we put them on paper until they were built. Once in place, we learned that a closet might seem large on paper, but when you have clothes poles on three sides and the door opens into the closet, you can barely turn around and half the clothes are blocked by the door. We both opted to have the doors changed to swing out.

How to handle mistakes

Everyone I talked to—architects, home builders, and homeowners—reported that mistakes were made on every job they had ever been involved with. Mistakes will be made on your job, too. Your first inclination might be to scream and point fingers, but that is not the best way to reach a solution to a problem.

Basic mistakes made by consumers

Though many problems can be traced to honest mistakes and misunderstandings, others arise from outright fraud. In such cases, it is usually futile to expect money back or the job done correctly. Homeowners can and should complain to the Better Business Bureau or to their state's consumer protection agency to alert others to the scams.

The following are the most frequently mentioned mistakes homeowners admit to when reporting a remodeler or builder to the consumer protection people:

1. Taking the first bid

2. Taking the lowest bid

3. Not getting a written contract

4. Giving the contractor all the money up front

5. Hiring a contractor with an out-of-state crew who offered a much lower price, took the money, did a terrible job, and disappeared

The best way to avoid being taken advantage of by a contractor is to reread the first four chapters of this book and then do what is recommended. If you follow my recommendations, you won't get just one bid. You'll get three or, even better, four bids. You will know that the lowest bid, or any bid for that

Bright Idea
Reporting a scam or an incompetent contractor doesn't protect you from being taken in by a sharpie, but it might save someone else.

Watch Out!
If you see a crew of roofers, aluminum siding people, replacement window people, driveway toppers, and so on standing in your driveway unsolicited, beware! If their point man tries to convince you that they can do the job immediately "while they are in your neighborhood if you sign up now," try to picture them wearing bandannas over their faces and holding shotguns—they are highway robbers.

matter, can keep a great deal of the necessary work out of the contract and then slip it back in as "unanticipated problems," which get billed at a time-and-materials rate.

There is absolutely no excuse for not getting a written contract, but some people do skip this. You might get away with not having a contract if you keep your money in your pocket until the work is done. Do not let yourself be pressured into signing up today for a "limited" offer. It is illegal not to give you three days to think it over and the option to cancel without any penalty during that time.

A step-by-step approach to confronting problems

Problems occur on every job; it goes with the territory. Dealing with problems, however, is a process where you can exercise some control. Most problems are fairly routine and predictable, and they can be resolved or mitigated with a healthy dose of anticipation, attentiveness, and good documentation. Here's how:

- **Check the agreement.** What do the specifications call for? This is why you want a fairly detailed agreement or contract. If the bid called for 10 electrical outlets and there are only 8, your problem is fairly easy to resolve: Ask your contractor to put in two more outlets. If there are 10 and you want more, be prepared to spend at least an additional $25 each.

- **Keep good records.** Like a spicy meatball dinner, mistakes can return to give you more discomfort unless you keep thorough records of what was wrong, what action was agreed upon, what additional costs were agreed to, and any settlement or compromise you and the builder or supplier agreed to.

A change order is a minicontract negotiated in the middle of a project that adds, subtracts, or changes materials or labor on a job. Your contractor should have a change order form for both of you to sign. Additional costs from changes are one of the biggest causes of disputes between builders and homeowners when it comes time to settle up.

▪ **Find out why it was done the way it was.** Try to make your first reaction to an apparent mistake curiosity rather than anger. Every construction job is a learning experience for everyone concerned: the crew, the contractor, and certainly the homeowners. Before you blow up, find out why something was done the way it was. There might be a very sound, structural reason why it had to be done that way. Your GC should be willing to give you that explanation. If you want something done a specific way, make that very clear before it is begun.

Being clear isn't enough if your plans just aren't feasible. For example, I wanted a laundry chute in our remodeling project. I drew it into the plans for the upstairs bathroom, coming down through the closet. It would have dropped all the clothes behind the furnace, but I thought we could work that out. I hung onto that laundry chute through every revision of the plans. I finally lost it when my GC showed me I was 3 feet off in my calculations between the two floors. I briefly entertained the notion of bringing it down through the bookcase in the living room, but a cooler head prevailed.

▪ **Stay calm and talk with your GC.** A contractor once told me, "Hopefully you haven't stopped

Bright Idea
Use a notebook to track all remodeling agreements and change orders. If you don't keep meticulous records, there will be much confusion when it comes time to settle up and everyone's forgotten what they said or agreed to.

communicating, so when something goes wrong you can figure out how to solve it. If the two parties are mad at each other or don't respect each other, there is no way they are going to be able to talk about what went wrong." Try to determine how a mistake happened and who is responsible. Often you'll find that everyone has contributed a little to the problem by making assumptions rather than communicating clearly. Now is the time to find out what it will cost to correct the mistake and how that cost will be allocated.

■ **Step back and look at the problem.** Ask yourself, "Is it really wrong? Does it look awful or could we live with it?" Like the direction of our oak flooring, some things aren't true mistakes; they are surprises. If it's already done, a good policy is to sleep on it before you make a final decision. Is it something neither of you feels particularly strongly about? If so, maybe you should adapt. If you can nip a problem in the bud, speak up.

■ **Tear it out and do it over, if necessary.** If something is wrong or could be better and it really bothers you, bite the bullet and have the contractor tear it out. It's your house and, as long as you're willing to pay for it, it should look the way you want it to. But try to be decisive. Adding several days of indecision to an awkward situation just runs up the cost and the frustration. It shouldn't influence your decision to rip something out, but try to remember that your carpenter or builder has spent time, effort, and possibly some loving creativity building what you are asking him to tear out. Be diplomatic and considerate in the way you approach the subject.

One builder, Mark Woodward, tells his clients, "One of the things I really dislike is tearing up my work and doing it again." He admitted, "It isn't even the money because I'm going to get paid to tear it up and to redo it. It's a human thing. I know I'm going to make mistakes and the client is going to make mistakes, but it doesn't make it any easier."

▪ **Send it back.** If the problem is with a product or material delivered from the lumberyard, let your GC know you are unhappy and then let him deal with it. If you're like me, you hate to bother people by complaining, and you hate to send things back. I've even kept mail-order shoes that didn't quite fit rather than send them back. I have since gotten over that phase and discovered that mail-order people don't think any less of you if you return something. You don't even have to tell them why.

The point of this short discussion is to emphasize your right to have the correct product delivered. Lumberyards, showrooms, and manufacturers are used to having people return items even when the correct item was delivered. Your effort to return a wrong item should meet little resistance. You will still be considered a nice person.

▪ **Accept it, but negotiate.** The item is wrong, but it's already installed and it took six months to deliver. You've decided that removing the item would be a major hassle. The question you have to ask your GC and, in turn, the supplier of the wrong material is: Should you pay full price? Your poker-playing skills might come in handy here. You are going to have to convince the

Moneysaver
Your contractor is in a better position to negotiate with a lumberyard or supplier because he buys several thousand dollars' worth of materials a year. This buying power can translate to savings for you.

supplier that he can come and take back his product and that you're willing to wait for the right product to be delivered. When he calculates the cost of transportation, the time of his people, and his chances of selling the returned item to someone else, he might offer you a substantial discount or an additional service to keep the already-installed (incorrect item) . . . and you deserve it.

One New York couple who rehabbed a brownstone told me: "We had an architect who insisted on designing the kitchen cabinets. That meant the cabinets had to be specially made at about double the cost of stock cabinets, which we felt looked very similar. The time needed to build those special cabinets was also about double. When they arrived and were hung, we found the cabinet builders had not followed the design submitted by our architect at all. They had simply built us some cabinets from their own stock designs. Our architect had never checked during the building process and did not seem too concerned that they were wrong. We notified the cabinet people to either come and take the cabinets back, rebuild them to the designs we submitted, or negotiate. They decided to negotiate. We are now living with cabinets we don't really like, but we have a large serving island we did not have to pay for. It is not placed correctly in the room—the back door hits it and it is too far from the kitchen countertops—but saving some money helped."

Preventive medicine

If you and your contractor are looking ahead, you have a better chance of catching mistakes early or even before they happen. The most important way to keep mistakes from becoming disasters,

Unofficially . . .
The best way to handle mistakes is to prevent them. The best way to prevent them is to plan thoroughly before you start and think three steps ahead. Have I mentioned this before?

however, is to keep the lines of communication open. Let your GC know if you feel something looks wrong. As one design/builder reported, "We have found if you talk to your clients once in a while before something goes wrong, communication is better. We try to ask our clients at least once a week, 'How are things?' We want to know if anything is bothering them, and more often than not, they will tell us all the good things that have happened."

This builder has found that, if he asks his homeowners about a potential problem, they're usually happy to discuss it with him. If they have to call him and tell him about a mistake, however, the phone might explode in his hands. He reasoned, "The rule is, if you're able to talk about it, you can solve it."

Another way to prevent mistakes is to check out the work each day. Find out from your contractor when major steps in the construction process are going to take place. One couple tried to avoid the inconvenience of living in a remodeling project by taking off for California for two months. They had even more problems, however, when they got back. Their experience offers some examples of additional mistakes you can look out for, and it provides a good case for talking to the people your contractor gives you as references.

The contractor they selected, who seemed to be fairly reliable, was sick for a good part of the job. Making matters worse, his crew that did the work wasn't as skillful. There is a slight ramp into each of the upstairs bathrooms because the floors in the addition don't meet the original floors. When the couple got back, they caught one mistake and made the crew change the strange angle and design of the banister. The pocket door to the bathroom,

Watch Out!
If you want an accurate assessment of a contractor, don't just drive by or quickly walk through homes he's remodeled. You must talk to the homeowners when you check out his references and ask specifically whether they were satisfied with the work.

however, hasn't has worked right since the painter tried to remove the slide mechanism with a crowbar. Their grandchildren tacked a DUCK sign on the new stairs to protect the unwary from the low overhead, which was created because the builder apparently felt a flat floor in an upstairs storage closet was more important than head room on the front stairs. Luckily, their house looks great, and the view of the harbor through the new picture windows is spectacular. Only the owner and his wife know where all the mistakes are.

Mistakes and solutions from experience: the case of the casement windows

My wife and I knew we wanted our windows divided into small panes of glass. We also wanted some increased insulation over a single layer of glass. We toured the building-supply company to see windows. We learned that it was possible to have small-pane Thermopane windows, but that they would be much more expensive and would have to have wide mullions (the wood between the panes). We didn't like the wide mullions, and we didn't like the idea of paying extra for something we didn't like. So we opted for narrow mullions and a form of storm window called *button-on* that is an additional layer of glass insulation. (Incidentally, Thermopane windows that are narrow-mullioned and true divided light—real glass, with real wood mullions, not snap-ins—are now widely available.)

Five people were involved in this decision and order-taking: my wife and I, our builder, my brother (who once represented a window manufacturer and understood all the terms), and the building-supply salesman. It was not a quick process. We didn't see the windows until six weeks later, after they were all in place . . . and wrong.

There are seven crank-out casement windows at the kitchen end of the family room, running from the top of the counters to the ceiling and around a corner. There are three taller casement windows at the living room end. These had the wide wooden mullions we went to so much trouble to avoid. The wooden dividers looked huge as we stood and stared at them. The next morning they didn't look so bad. It was February in Connecticut—the windows were needed. Finally, we accepted them—that is, we didn't say "Take them back."

A week later, the builder called to say the French door unit for the family room had arrived. This was a three-piece unit of floor-to-ceiling windows with a swing door onto the deck. As we drove over, I asked my wife if she was mentally preparing herself for the windows in this unit to be "right." "Oh, no," she said, realizing we had already settled on different windows that now might not match the door. And right they were. They had been able to provide narrow-mullioned, small-paned windows. The unit occupied one-third of the wall space and was between the other windows. Now we stood and stared at the variety of windows. "Can we live with it?" we asked ourselves. Again, we decided we could.

Truthfully, no one has noticed the variety of windows. They all look fine, which speaks well for adapting as a technique for handling mistakes. How should we have handled the problem ideally? I have learned a lot since then and have talked the situation over with other contractors and architects.

We, through our contractor, should have lodged a complaint with the building-supply house. With our four witnesses in tow, we should have met with the window salesman and his manager and checked the order that was sent to the window manufacturer. If this had been a casual decision among many other events on the day we ordered them, we would have no case. We had, however, made a big deal of the final window selection.

Three things could have gone wrong: the order could have been right and the manufacturer built it wrong, the order could have been wrong when it went to the manufacturer (by fault of the salesman), or we ourselves could have ordered the wrong windows. We knew what we wanted. We knew what was possible to make at that time, and we all understood the final selection—the last possibility was unlikely.

If it was the manufacturer's mistake, we could have retained the original windows until the manufacturer could supply the correct ones. We then would have taken the incorrect ones back and possibly negotiated an allowance to cover the contractor's time for replacement. If it was the salesman's mistake, they might have worked something out with the manufacturer and replaced the windows. Failing that, they could have offered us a discount. They should not get their full profit for a mistake, and we should not have been asked to pay full price for the wrong product.

I suspect our contractor should have known about these options and should have pressed our case, but we aren't really unhappy with the results. You have the right to remain silent and the right to speak up. The contractor or subs should point out how they think things should be done; they should explain the advantages of doing it their way and the disadvantages of doing it yours. In the end, however,

Bright Idea
Always keep lines of communication open. A supplier or subcontractor cannot correct a mistake if you don't let him know about it.

you should get what you want. (The contractor could always have you sign a waiver.)

Another contractor brought up some additional points I hadn't even considered. The windows are the kind that can be pulled off their tracks for cleaning. He suggested that new windows could have been made and easily inserted for both types without taking the frames out of the walls. This would have removed the major problem I had with demanding replacements—tearing out all the work and opening up the house to the elements to return the windows.

Insurance

When things go wrong, are you covered? We live in a litigious age. Many people seem to think someone else should pay for our mistakes and our accidents no matter how dumb or careless we have been. Your mortgage holder is aware of this trend and demands that you carry homeowner's insurance at least to the extent of the amount you owe him. When you invite a group of people onto your premises for up to several months to do fairly dangerous work, you open yourself up to possible lawsuits if any of the contractors, subcontractors, delivery people, or even your own sightseeing friends injure themselves.

We have already alerted you to the need to ask for your GC's insurance company, proof of his participation in your state's worker's compensation insurance program, and a performance bond. The problem is that, if just one subcontractor has let his insurance lapse and gets injured, he might sue you for his hospital costs.

While moving the electrical lines on the house of a Pennsylvania couple, a contractor let the line

We tended to forget this was our project, our home, our money, our wishes, our desires. So what if it looks strange to have things kitty-corner or out of balance? If that's what we want, we should have it.

—David Heim, homeowner

Watch Out!
The job site is your property. Check with the insurance agent who carries your homeowner's policy and ask his advice about any additional riders you might need to cover you during your construction period. This is not expensive and will give you peace of mind.

sag too low over the highway in front of the house. At just that moment, a motorcycle went by. As the wife described the scene, "The guy hit the wire just like in the movies." It made the couple realize that one question they hadn't asked at the beginning was whether their contractor was insured and bonded. In that particular part of Pennsylvania, it is legal for anyone with a set of tools and a pickup to call himself a contractor without carrying extra expenses such as insurance.

Fortunately, their contractor was insured and the bike rider was not badly hurt. He did, however, put in a small claim and the insurance company paid it. The couple learned from the experience. When they remodeled their New York apartment, they took out an umbrella liability policy to augment their homeowners insurance because, as they noted, "A contractor could show you he has insurance today, but he might not have it tomorrow."

Try to make a clear distinction between fraud or carelessness and honest misunderstanding. Construction is a very complicated process with lots of room for misinterpretation. If you follow the advice offered for selecting a contractor (see Chapter 1), you should be able to avoid being defrauded. You probably can't avoid mistakes and misunderstandings, however. They are part of the remodeling process. How well you handle them and how objective you are will determine the climate you and your contractor will be working in for the remainder of your project. Look for solutions together, don't become part of the problem.

Just the facts

- Be prepared for the surprises remodeling has in store for you.

- Check out your GC's references and get to know him a little. You are probably dealing with a capable, honest workman, so treat him like one.

- Your construction job will take more time to complete than anyone estimates during the planning phase.

- Make sure you and your spouse do your part on time and don't get carried away in the showrooms.

- When problems come up, stay calm, be objective, listen, and work out a solution that requires everyone to make some concessions.

GET THE SCOOP ON...
The punch list ▪ Handling the last 10 percent ▪
Using callbacks ▪ Last-minute details and paper
work ▪ The Ten Commandments

Wrapping Up the Job

A s your project begins to wind down, you'll need to take care of some final details. In this chapter, I'll give you some advice that can save you time, money, and sanity. I'll explain what a punch list is and how to use it. I'll alert you to some precautions you can take so you'll only have to pay for your project once. I'll also cover appropriate uses of callbacks and some general rules for approaching another remodeling project.

You might feel like your remodeling project will never be finished. After the quick start, which usually involves demolition and rough construction, the work has settled into a regular, if disruptive, routine that shows some progress every day. You've learned to live with the noise, the dust, and the picnics in the living room. You've made a hobby of visiting showrooms. You've made countless decisions.

At this point, you probably feel a certain emotional pride in the fact that you've personally selected every tile, knob, hinge, faucet, nail, and board that has gone into your home. But you're also

135

probably getting very tired of devoting your whole life to the project.

The finish carpenter, who may be working alone, seems to stay in the same room day after day. Your patience and your bank account are running out at the same rate. Hang in there—it's almost over. You just have to address a few last-minute details to ensure that you get the best job possible and to protect your investment.

The punch list

A *punch list* is a list of all the little things the home-owner notices that haven't been done, were done incorrectly, are missing parts or pieces, or don't work correctly. According to one contractor, it's called a punch list because everyone concerned with the job is so frustrated they're ready to punch each other.

The punch list is kind of a litmus test for the whole project. If you and your contractor have been talking to each other along the way, if mistakes have been worked out through compromise, correction, and adjustment, and if you feel you have been treat-ed fairly and honestly, the punch list tour will be a minor event and can even be enjoyable. It gives you and your contractor the chance to review and admire the work that's been done and the opportu-nity to note and take care of any minor glitches to bring the project to perfection.

If the job has not gone smoothly, if you feel you have been taken advantage of, if you think your con-tractor has done sloppy work, and if you've been bottling up your feelings and frustrations, you might be tempted to use the punch list as a weapon to make your contractor really earn that final payment.

Unofficially...
The builder usu-ally has his own list of things that need to be done. There will be mistakes on any job, but a good contractor corrects mistakes without ever being told about them.

One Connecticut couple reported that, at the beginning of their project, they wanted to get along with and trust their GC. They let little mistakes slide by until they finally realized a lot of things were not right. By the time they drew up the punch list, they were so hostile that they criticized not only genuine problems but also insignificant issues.

Who makes out the punch list?

You should definitely take notes about details that aren't quite right as the job winds down, but in the end, your GC should be the one who prepares the punch list with your input. The punch list usually is drawn up during a formal inspection of the project by the GC, the architect (if you have one), and you. The GC is ultimately responsible for clearing up the problems, and he should have a voice in determining what deserves to be on the list. Resolving these problems is the final step in fulfilling the contract. The GC shouldn't be held responsible for work done by people you hired or products you bought.

Most GCs believe the contractor should be keeping a punch list, and the homeowner shouldn't have to concern himself with it. A good contractor has good quality control and catches the mistakes himself. Ideally, you should have faith that your contractor is keeping such a list. You can stir up trouble if you start pestering him about things before the job is over.

What qualifies as a punch list item?

The punch list is usually made up of small items such as installing locks on windows, touching up paint in a bedroom, or replacing trim over the living room window. This is also the place to list any items that have not been installed or are on backorder from the manufacturer. These are items the

Bright Idea
Unless you want to alienate your contractor, don't immediately give him a laundry list of items to be taken care of "or else." Give him a chance to finish his job and to ask you if there is anything you think he overlooked.

contractor will have to install eventually, such as the hardware for the kitchen cabinets or, as in our case, the new living room windows.

What doesn't belong on a punch list?

Certain items should not appear on a punch list. You should be prepared to accept these items as your responsibility. Let's say, for example, that you removed oak cabinet doors and stored them in a damp basement where they became slightly warped. Your builder will not and should not rebuild them. Some basic tasks, such as a new roof or a foundation, are either done or they're not. They don't really belong on a punch list.

Punch list items are more likely to crop up in finish work and detail work. These are what you'll notice first, but you should not demand unreasonable perfection. If the natural wood trim installed by the carpenter doesn't quite match the original wood next to it, you're out of luck. It's very difficult to match 80 years of polishing and aging with a couple coats of stain and lacquer.

Other items you can't put on the punch list are appliances and light fixtures you bought on your own and had the contractor install. Even though he put them in for you, if the dishwasher timer doesn't work, it's your responsibility.

The punch list is a one-shot process. Some items might take some time to correct or deliver, but you should avoid doing what many homeowners do—continuing to add items to the list as they live in the space. There comes a point when you have to accept responsibility for doing your own maintenance work.

How contractors handle a punch list

Some contractors keep a man on their crew who specializes in taking care of punch list items. This person usually is a pretty good carpenter, but he also can handle a paintbrush, change a light switch, install a plumbing fixture, replace a cracked window, and soothe a disgruntled homeowner.

Because the GC is responsible for the entire job, any punch list items caused by subcontractors that worked on the project are still the GC's problem. Sometimes the GC will do little repairs personally and then charge the subcontractor. For major problems, however, the subcontractor is called back to take care of it.

A sample owner's pre-punch list

On the following page is a list of items I noted during the last week of our construction. I listed them as a reminder to myself to make sure the contractor had them on his list. *Remember:* The only official punch list is the one prepared by your builder. If yours is any good, most of the items you list will already appear on the contractor's list.

Homeowners' experiences with punch lists

When I ask homeowners about their builder's punch list performance, I get two completely different reactions. A look of resignation comes over the faces of many homeowners as they recount long stories of frustration and nonperformance. The remainder simply report it as the final step in the process, no big deal. The punch list seems to be like taking a final exam. If you have been keeping up on the homework, you can take the test in stride. If you have been letting things slide, however, and have to cram everything into the last couple nights, it can be a nightmare.

Unofficially...
Your contractor has a stake in the punch list, too. Many contractors hold the punch list in the same regard as having a tooth pulled or being audited by the IRS. As your contractor knows, however, your contract specifies that last-minute details must be completed to get the final payment.

Sample Punch List

1. Lock set missing from upstairs bathroom window.

2. No handles for crank-out windows in kitchen.

3. Missing switch plate in office.

4. Downspout from gutter to the house looks like hell. Can it go around corner and then down? (My builder came back and did this after the job was done.)

5. Painters missed inside door frame in downstairs bath . . . look in the mirror.

6. Need second set of steps off end of deck.

7. Cabinet door in kitchen sticks. (Your builder will probably wait a few weeks until all the doors on cabinets and rooms have expanded. He'll then shave or adjust them all at once.)

8. Popped nail in living room wall.

9. Screens missing for guest-room windows.

10. Could you put labels on the circuit breaker for stove, refrigerator, furnace, hot water heater, and office, etc.

11. I do not have releases from the plumber and electrical contractors.

12. Where are the instruction manuals and warranties for the stove, refrigerator, dishwasher, clothes washer, and dryer?

13. Small crack in vinyl on the island counter in kitchen.

14. Closet door in master bedroom still swings the wrong way. (I realize you have changed this once already.) I will pay for the time to rehang it so it swings into the bedroom from the left.

One homeowner observed, "Correcting items on the punch list was not my builder's strongest point. Because he had gone on to his next job, I had to call him several times. He finally got back to us and everything turned out okay, but I had to nag him. It wasn't that he didn't care; he came back to check out the kitchen several months after it was done to see if everything was okay. He just didn't have the time."

The punch list brings to light many of the misunderstandings of the contract. The homeowner often assumes something is considered part of the job; the contractor assumes it is not.

The next level: callbacks

What do you do when three months after your job is finished a crack appears in a wall, a bedroom door won't close anymore, or the double-hung window in the living room won't open? You can call your contractor and demand that it be fix it.

He would like to ignore you, and sometimes he does. He knows these things are not really his fault, but there is a clause in the standard contract, written or implied, that says he guarantees his work for one year.

Remember you're working in wood

The nature of construction with wood is that things move and shift as the seasons change. This is especially true in areas of the United States where a home goes from summer dampness to winter dryness, thanks to central heating. These wide swings in humidity can wreak havoc on wood paneling and behind the walls of your house.

My own experience illustrates this point. When our remodeling project was complete, one of the

Watch Out!
Use callbacks judiciously. Builders hate them, and the more often you request them, the less likely the builder is to respond.

first things I built in my new woodworking shop was a pine cabinet for my dartboard. When I hung it on the door of my office in August, the cabinet doors barely closed. It was a beautiful fit. By the middle of December, the dryness had made both of the 10-inch doors split from top to bottom, and there was a half-inch gap between the doors. By the following summer, everything had come back together again.

A similar shifting occurs behind the walls of your house. It's not entirely fair to blame your builder because, as many builders have told me, the quality of the lumber available from lumberyards has deteriorated in recent years. Kiln-dried lumber has a higher water content than was previously acceptable, and the grading system for lumber has slipped several notches. Every competent builder allows for some shrinkage and movement, but it's not possible to anticipate the wide range of movement that can take place. Hairline cracks in wallboard or plaster walls are not uncommon, and they are usually beyond the control and responsibility of your contractor.

How builders handle callbacks

Because wood isn't static and unmoving, your builder can't do much about certain imperfections. A hairline crack in a wall could have been caused by wood shrinking or by your new foundation settling or heaving a bit. Because your builder is well aware of the characteristics of wood, he will usually accept responsibility for sticking doors, cabinets, and windows because the work crew should have allowed for that movement when they installed them. As for the walls, the best you can expect is for someone to come and spackle the crack and paint it.

Timesaver
It is best to live in a house for a while and let the shelves, cabinets, drawers, and doors do their initial shifting. Then ask your contractor to come in and adjust everything at once.

If you are entering the humid summer season and you call your contractor about a door sticking, he might try to put you off until later. If one cupboard door sticks now, more will start to stick as humidity increases, and the workers will have to make several trips.

The problem is that your builder has moved on to his next job, and it is probably just as complicated as yours was. One contractor says, "Tell us if it's an emergency. If it is, we will come immediately. If it isn't, let us work it into our schedule." Understand that you are requesting a free service; be pleasant to your builder when you call him back. You might be pleasantly surprised. Just remember, though, that your contractor is probably in the middle of other projects and can't necessarily drop everything and come to you.

A rational approach to the final payment

You can't expect to keep all your money in the bank until the last nail is driven and then write one check to cover it all. As stipulated in the contract, you will be expected to make payments throughout the building process. As the project approaches the final payment, however, more variables are possible and tension can mount.

This tension can create a difficult period for both you and your contractor. Your project is essentially done, and your contractor wants to get paid and move on to the next job, which has probably already started. He doesn't want the last payment to be held up for a twenty-dollar part or while you nitpick about details. You want to get back to a normal way of life, but you might be afraid that, if you release the final payment, the contractor will

> **"**
> Callbacks are a chance to shine because most builders will not do them. If you do them cheerfully and well, you make a very good impression. Frequently, the clients will think of another job they want done or that a friend wants done, and you get some additional business.
>
> —Robert Hanbury, designer/remodeler
> **"**

disappear and all those little items on the punch list will remain undone.

You can both find plenty of evidence to support your concerns. Fortunately, there are ways to break this deadlock. You can specify in your contract that you'll hold back your final payment for a certain number of days—usually between 10 and 60 days, depending on who wins the discussion while writing the contract. During this period, your contractor can create the punch list, and you can issue the final payment when all the items are resolved.

One of my technical advisers has a somewhat different point of view: "It is best to hold onto money until the bitter end. Once you've paid the money, you lose all your power." You'll be the best judge of where you stand with your contractor toward the end of the project. Use your power wisely.

What if you and your contractor can't agree?

You and your contractor can reach an impasse during any part of the remodeling process. Impasses usually occur, however, as the job is winding down and a situation comes up that the two of you simply can't agree on. All it takes is for you to request what you think is a small change and for your contractor to fail to explain how much that "small" change will cost or how much more work it will require before he actually does it. He does it. You refuse to pay for it. You're at an impasse.

You have several options. One of you can give in, you can work out a compromise, or you can take the problem to arbitration.

Giving in

Giving in is a tactic most often used in the early phases of a project to keep peace. It wears thin,

Bright Idea
By the end of a set period of time, if your contractor still hasn't completed a few items on the punch list or if you're waiting for a part to be delivered, retain an amount sufficient to cover that item or part plus the cost of its installation and release the remainder to your contractor.

however, if exercised too often. If the homeowner feels he is being taken advantage of, he will get defensive and resist all further negotiation, even on comparatively minor items.

Calm down and work out a compromise

The best approach is to keep talking, try to understand each other's points of view, and work out a solution that is fair, or even a little unfair, to both. Compromising and giving in are applicable only if the contractor is ethical and honest. If for some reason you decided to go with a fly-by-night outfit, you might as well start protecting your interests early by lining up an arbitrator or your attorney.

Going to arbitration

Going to court is expensive, time consuming, and rarely satisfactory. The arbitration route is fairly simple, and it gives you and your contractor a chance to sit down in an informal setting and tell each side of the argument. There are no attorneys, no jury, and no complicated procedures. You usually get a ruling within a couple days rather than the months involved in a court trial.

Where to find arbitrators

The procedures for requesting an arbitration hearing vary from state to state, but you can usually find an arbitrator through your state contractors' or builders' board. You can also seek assistance from your state attorney general's office, the Better Business Bureau, or the Chamber of Commerce. The American Arbitration Association (AAA) and a surprising number of other groups also can provide arbitrators.

To find an arbitrator in your area, look under American Arbitration Association in your state's

Unofficially...
In most states, an arbitration clause is included in all remodeling contracts (and in all AIA standard contracts).

Business-To-Business directory or check the American Arbitration Association Web page (www.adr.org). Select the directory icon to bring up a map of the United States. Pick your state and you're on your way. The AAA can offer dispute avoidance and dispute resolution including arbitration, mediation, negotiation, fact-finding, mini-trials, and partnering. These processes can be used singly or in combination.

Binding or nonbinding arbitration?

Your contract should specify which form of arbitration you will agree to abide by. If you select non-binding arbitration, you each present your case before a neutral third party who will offer his or her opinion on your case. You can accept the judgment or not. If either party feels badly treated, the case then moves on to the traditional legal approach and a trial.

My recommendation is to go with binding arbitration. This means you each agree that the arbitrator's decision is final, and you each have to act on it. Get the matter over with and get back to work.

Wrapping up the last details

Before you sign that last check, you need to get the following from your contractor: lien releases, certificate of occupancy, warranties, and receipts.

Moneysaver
A single mechanic's lien against your home can hold up a bank loan or kill a sale. Be sure to get a lien release.

Lien releases

The contractor should provide a lien release (a signed release form) from each subcontractor and supplier he used on your project. These forms confirm that each has been paid in full by the contractor for the materials and labor provided. The subcontractors and suppliers relinquish all rights to filing liens against your property. A lien release can save you thousands of dollars. It's simple when it's done correctly and expensive when it's not. Get a lien release from each subcontractor as he finishes his work and presents a bill.

Certificate of occupancy

If your alteration was substantial or if you added new rooms, you will need a final inspection by the local building inspector. During this inspection, he determines whether you and your contractor have complied with all the building requirements of the community. In many communities, in fact, even small jobs need a final inspection.

The inspection and the certificate of occupancy can be applied for by your contractor at the point in construction when the work is substantially complete. In our case, the local building inspector declared our project to be substantially complete even though the painters were still painting, the finish carpenter was still working on the kitchen cabinets, and several doors still had to be hung. The basic systems of the house (heating, electrical, and plumbing), however, were completely installed and working.

Warranties

If you install a new kitchen, heating system, hot tub, or even certain building components, there may be individual manufacturers' warranties on these appliances and products. Your contractor should turn the warranty registration forms over to you, along with any maintenance or operating instruction booklets. These frequently get tossed out with the packing cases they come in, so you might alert the contractor to the fact that you want them.

Watch Out!
If you have been living outside your home during the renovations, you can't move back in until you obtain the certificate of occupancy.

Unofficially . . .
The day your
project is
declared "sub-
stantially com-
plete" marks the
start date for all
warranties except
for those items
that appear on
your punch list.
Those warranties
start the day you
make your final
payment to your
contractor.

Receipts

When your contractor submits his bill for payment, he should attach the receipts for materials he purchased, his subcontractors' bills, and copies of the time cards for his crew. If you haven't been getting them from the very beginning, ask your contractor to supply them. Even if you can't make heads or tails of them now, eventually you will need these receipts when you sell your house. They help to reduce the taxes on the difference between your original purchase price and the new selling price (increased by the remodeling done to improve the property).

You probably won't be in any mental shape to create a detailed filing system during or immediately after a remodeling project, so I recommend that you use my system: Get a box from the local liquor store, label it "House Stuff," and put everything in it. Use this box to store the preliminary sketches you made, all the changes, any magazine pages you tore out, the contract, change orders, meeting notes, and sales receipts. It will be a mess, but it narrows down the search area considerably when you have to find something.

Now that you're done . . .

As you relax in your new Jacuzzi, cradle a steaming mug of coffee in your new kitchen, or crank up the World Series in your new den, take a moment to congratulate yourself on a job well done. Think of everything you've learned since that first day when you decided, "It's time we got started."

You and your partner probably have discovered talents you didn't know you had in planning, decorating, decision-making, human relations, and problem solving. You've learned to function as a team and might even have developed a new level of

---

Stephens' Ten Commandments of Remodelling

THOU SHALT:

1. Spend the money and time to plan thoroughly.

2. Take the time to find skilled, honest craftsmen, get recommendations, and check their references and work.

3. Make sure everyone is bidding on the same plans and specifications.

4. Regard the low bidder with suspicion and negotiate the higher bids.

5. Make sure you have a clear, strong, fair contract.

6. Develop a workable decision-making process with your partner.

7. Visit the site every day and be available for decisions.

8. Talk to your contractor regularly and work out misunderstandings.

9. Pay your bills on time.

10. Keep your sense of humor.

---

respect for each other's abilities. You have weathered a very difficult storm and deserve to enjoy some smooth sailing in your new quarters.

Now you can invite friends and neighbors who watched the destruction and the construction process to come in and see what you've been doing. As you take them on the grand tour, you'll have a humorous story for every room, every fixture, every board, every tile. They might not have seemed funny at the time, but the project's done now, it looks great, and nothing improves your outlook on life like knowing that no one is going to wake you up at dawn with a power saw.

And because reading this book allowed you to approach your first remodeling project as though it were your second, you might be considering another project. (It would be a shame to waste all that experience.) As you start to plan your next project, remember the Stephens' Ten Commandments of Remodeling (see previous page).

In this chapter I have shown you how to exit gracefully from your building project. All loose ends should be tied up, and any painful memories from your construction project should fade as you sit back and appreciate what you have created. Short of that, I hope that you, your spouse, and your contractor are all still speaking and that the bank loaned you enough to pay the bills.

Just the facts

- Use the contractor's punch list appropriately and don't keep adding items to it.

- Don't abuse the final 10 or 15 percent of the project's cost that you still control. Pay the bill.

- Limit callbacks to essentials. Eventually, you will have to learn to run (and repair) your own home.

- Make sure you get lien releases from each of the subcontractors that worked on your home.

- Obey Stephens' Ten Commandments of Remodeling.

Major Remodeling Projects

PART IV

GET THE SCOOP ON...
When to redecorate, remodel, or add rooms ▪
Finding and working with decorators ▪
Adding on by going up ▪ Adding on by going
out ▪ How long it should take ▪ How much it
will cost

Change Your Decor or Change the House

Chapter 7

Creating a new room or additional space, whether within your existing walls or outside the confines of your present house, is the messiest form of remodeling. Wallboard and plaster come down, and carpenters create havoc prior to their reconstruction efforts. Chapters 1 through 6 prepare you for exactly this type of project. If you haven't already read them, go back and follow the suggestions and approaches I've recommended, particularly in the planning phase.

In this chapter, I'll discuss the interim step of hiring a professional decorator, someone who might improve the space you have, before I go into specific approaches to creating new and improved space in your home. I'll suggest places where you can find this extra room or can create new space by building on an addition. I'll also explain how my wife and I created a very satisfying great room by eliminating dividing walls and extending the house to the rear. You'll learn what factors go into the cost of such projects and how much time can elapse.

153

Unofficially...
For various rea-
sons, many fami-
lies spend much
of their spare
time in rooms
originally
designed for
other purposes,
such as spare
bedrooms or
dens.

How you know when to redecorate, remodel, or add rooms

You'll know it's time to change your basic structure and to knock down some walls when you've gone though reams of tracing paper and exhausted all your other alternatives. You can change your home to meet your actual lifestyle rather than the one created for you by the house's original developer.

The original developer didn't know that your kids would be in high school and need room for their computers or that the living room, which used to be called a sitting room, wouldn't be used for either sitting or living. He couldn't have known that it would be there, ready to serve as the backdrop for some as-yet-undefined formal gathering that has never happened. TV sitcom families use their living rooms a lot. Maybe it's because that's where their TV sets are.

Real-life events often make you analyze the look and design of your house. These events can include:

- **Changes in family size.** This could be the birth of a new baby or two, a child leaving home, or an elderly parent or relative moving in with you.

- **Changes in use of space.** Many people now work at home, which creates a need for office space.

- **Changes in lifestyle.** You might have once needed the formal dining room and large living room for entertaining. These days, however, you might be more likely to entertain on the back patio with hamburgers on the grill and a game of bocci.

- **Changes in hobbies.** A toolbox with a hammer, a saw, and a couple of screwdrivers can quickly become a full-fledged woodworking shop. You need room to realize the potential of your new-found craftsmanship.

■ **Changing times.** In the 1800s, kitchens and pantries were isolated from the rest of the house to provide privacy for both the help and the employers. Today, the cook usually is a member of the family and a change in kitchen design is necessary.

■ **Changes in family economics.** Contractors tell me remodeling plans often follow a financial windfall such as a bonus or an inheritance.

Whatever triggers your decision to remodel—even if you're just tired of the way your house looks—once it is in motion, it slowly takes over your life. The kids get involved, you will discuss your plans and ideas with visitors, and you will look at the homes you visit with a newly critical eye. You're well on your way to a remodeling project.

Before you start tearing out walls, adding rooms, or opening up the attic, however, you might look into the possibility of making what you already have look more attractive and exciting. When a woman gets a makeover, she doesn't start with plastic surgery. Her hair color or style changes, she might change to a different color lipstick, and she certainly buys a new outfit or two. You can take the same approach with your home. Just as some women might consult a cosmetologist for expert advice on how to improve their images, a homeowner might consult an interior decorator.

Bright Idea
Make a list of the reasons you want to make changes to your home. If they are primarily aesthetic reasons and not functional, you should consider redecorating as an alternative to structural remodeling.

Bringing in a Professional Decorator

We've all read or heard about movie stars and corporate CEOs who hire famous decorators to come in and redo their company offices, New York apartments, or country homes. You might be under the impression that decorators are just for the rich and famous, but that is not the case. You can probably find a much more low-key local decorator who could come in, give you some good ideas, and help you improve the appearance of your home. Even better, it shouldn't cost you a fortune.

My brother and I recently had the task of selling our mother's condominium in a retirement village in Connecticut. We thought it was beautiful the way it was, but taking down a few pictures convinced us it really needed to be painted. We also noticed the rich green carpet had faded in several areas. Our real estate agent convinced us that refurbishing and adding new appliances would add $15,000 to its value. So we had it done. We were advised by the agent, the painter, and the carpet-laying firm to select off-white walls, off-white carpet, off-white tile in the kitchen, and white appliances. Although this didn't sound particularly creative to us, we had an offer within a week of the work being finished.

When my wife and I remodeled our home 10 years ago, we went with off-white decor as well. In our case, it was Aztec white. (You'd be amazed how many shades of white there are to choose from.) Four years later, we painted the great room yellow and the living room a soft shade of green. This year, we repainted the yellow room tan and went to green in two of the upstairs bedrooms. They look great.

Luckily, we seem to have a good sense of color. Other people, however, admit to having no sense of color or style at all when it comes to putting the finishing personal touches on their home or a specific room. If this applies to you, help is available. Go to your local department store (such as Nordstrom,

Watch Out!
In-store decorators often get paid by commission, so the person you speak to probably will be interested in selling you goods and services provided by the store. This does not necessarily lessen the value of his or her advice, but don't get carried away.

Macy's, or Lord & Taylor) and ask to talk to their decorator. He or she will take you through display rooms where you can see the furniture and fabrics arranged in a homelike setting. There will also be sample books of furniture, fabric swatches, wallpaper, and carpets. The decorator can advise you on the types of patterns, colors, furniture, and accessories that complement each other.

An independent decorator can come to your home and offer advice, but your selections of furniture, fabrics, wallpaper, and accessories will come from the catalogs of the manufacturers. Items in a catalog most likely will be priced higher than those offered in a store, but the quality will probably be better. You just might be getting better value for your money because the decorator buys at wholesale and has lower overhead. You also have the option to have your furniture made to fit your particular needs.

A local decorator will already be familiar with craftsmen capable of building bookcases, making slipcovers, reupholstering furniture, and laying carpet. A decorator will also be able to direct you to lighting, plumbing fixtures, and specialty stores in your area. Because his reputation is on the line with the people he recommends, this can save you the effort of pre-qualifying subcontractors.

The decorators I talked to said they consult with clients to determine both the scope of the project and the budget with which they are comfortable. A good decorator makes an effort to find out what styles you like, what your favorite colors are, and what furniture you have or plan to buy.

Timesaver
Decorators can also serve as arbitrators or referees between spouses who might have widely different ideas of what looks good. Decorators know the right questions to ask and are skilled at helping couples reduce the range of choices to a more manageable number.

How do you locate a reputable decorator?

As with any service you require, the best method of locating and checking out a decorator is by word of mouth. Most decorators advertise in the Yellow Pages, and some probably use your local paper. But the best way is still to ask around. Perhaps your lumberyard or hardware store isn't be the best place to start, but you might check with antique stores, paint stores, or fabric stores for their recommendations. You might also inquire at your state's designers association.

One source for decorating ideas is cable TV—particularly the Discovery Channel or Home and Garden Television (HGTV). These channels have helpful programs that feature decorators who solve home decorating problems. There are also some remodeling and building shows, such as Bob Vila's, that concentrate on upgrading older houses with carpentry or specific furniture projects. They sometimes stay with the remodeling long enough to see what colors the owners put on the new walls. Saturdays in particular feature several how-to shows in a row.

Selecting the decorator for you

After you locate two or three designers, visit them and ask to see their portfolios of past work. You are the best judge of the decorator's skills. This is for your home, and it should be something you like and are comfortable with.

Some designers specialize in their own style and tend to create "signature" works. These are the decorators whose work you often see in magazine spreads.

Decorators, by nature, are independent and creative people. Some have a tendency to dictate what you should have, and some people need that approach. Others make an effort to blend their creativity and taste with what they determine you want. Either way, this is a personal relationship. You should keep looking until you find a decorator with whom you are comfortable.

What an interior decorator or designer will do for you

Decorating or redecorating your home, even if you have impeccable taste, can take months or years as you search antique shops, furniture stores, fabric stores, wallpaper suppliers, and so on. If you make enough money to afford an extensive makeover, you probably don't have enough time to do it all yourself!

This is where an interior decorator comes in. He determines what style, colors, and feeling you prefer and then does the leg work for you. This can involve selecting sample books of furniture, fabrics, wall coverings, paint colors, and lighting fixtures and bringing them to you, usually with some recommendations for your approval.

With the help of your decorator, you can re-create your home, a specific room, or just a problem window in your mind and on paper. The decorator then takes on the more mundane tasks of ordering materials, furniture, and paints, finding the people to put them in place, and overseeing the whole project for you. If you decide you need to do more intense remodeling, your decorator could either oversee the job or recommend skilled and reliable contractors.

Unofficially...
Some decorators tend to convert their client's space into their own personal statement. The client, in turn, gets to brag about his decorator's creation as though it's an original Picasso. You probably are not looking for such an arrangement.

Bright Idea
Delegate, but don't withdraw. Remember, this is your house; you and your partner have to feel comfortable with the way it is decorated. It should reflect your taste, hobbies, and outlook on the world and should fit your budget. Don't just turn the project over to your decorator and walk away.

What will the services of a decorator cost?

This is a little like asking how far is up, but a consulting fee of $75 an hour is pretty standard. Invite two or three decorators to your house. Their first visit should be free while you evaluate them and they see the job. The work can be done on a fee basis or, if you are going to be buying materials, furniture, or accessories through them, they can work on a retail basis. Your decorator's payment then comes as a percentage of the price of the material and furniture you order. If you only need advice, however, the hourly fee should suffice. Decorators also can work on a cost-plus basis, room-by-room, over a period of time.

Remodeling options for making your existing space better

Look carefully at some of the spaces in your house: the basement, the attic, and other obscure corners. You just might find some additional room to work with what you initially might have overlooked.

Finishing your basement

Finishing your basement is a logical option, particularly if you're blessed with a full basement that's not completely filled with essential equipment such as the furnace, the water heater, and the washer and dryer. Basement remodeling also works well for newer homes in which 8 feet of head room is fairly common. It works even better if your home is built on a lot that slopes from front to back, allowing a ground-level exit and even windows on the back wall.

When my family lived in Seattle during World War II, my mother decided that we needed a basement playroom for the numerous teenagers that were hanging around. Unfortunately the basement only provided about 5½ feet of head room (I was already 6'6" at that time). We used sledgehammers, buckets, and a lot of Tom Sawyer–like recruiting skills to dig out and lower the cement floor by 1½ feet. No one should ever do that.

An adult recreation room can take care of your Monday night football addicts nicely, particularly if it includes a bar and a big-screen TV. The basement is also a great place for a workshop or an office. This, of course, assumes you have a basement that doesn't flood frequently or that is so small there's only room for the furnace and laundry gear.

Finishing your attic

If your attic has sufficient head room, you can transform it into an extra bedroom, a home office, or a hobby area. If you are blessed with a set of stairs, the job is fairly straightforward. If not, you might have to sacrifice a closet or two to provide access to the space above. (Remember to build some extra closet space for all the clothes you displaced.)

Don't worry if you have vented dryers or whole-house fans in your attic space. Your contractor can work around these problems by diverting them to the spaces behind the knee walls. You'll have to find another space for your expansion plans, however, if your attic is filled with elaborate roof trusses. Have a talk with your contractor to see if you can work around the trusses, or to see where else to expand.

Nooks and crannies

Mark Alvarez, a neighbor of mine, wrote *The Home Office Book* (Goodwood Press). In it, he describes several seemingly unlikely places that can be developed into an office, a sewing room, or another small

Timesaver
Don't go out of your way to create a separate playroom in the basement for your kids. Many experts believe kids rarely use them.

room: under the front stairs; in a pantry, an extra closet, an enclosed porch; or along a living room or dining room wall. He recommends, however, that the space be screened off when not in use.

All you really need for an office is room for a desk. Your chair can sit out in the passageway when you're using it, and it should fit under your desk (and ideally behind folding doors) when your office is "closed."

If this easy approach is not enough, the layout of rooms has to be changed. Your options include making two small rooms from a larger one or making a bigger room from smaller ones.

Making two small rooms out of one larger one

If you have two children sharing one big bedroom with room for all their toys and a play area, they might like the idea of having rooms of their own, even if the rooms are smaller. As children get older, built-in desks and bookshelves become more important than floor area. You also might put a wall across the end of a large living room to create a cozy library, den, or TV room.

Don't worry about the present location of electrical outlets, ceiling fixtures, or even doors and windows. These can all be changed. The two-from-one rules also hold true when you are trying to create a guest half-bathroom, a powder room somewhere on the first floor, or a master bathroom off your bedroom. You'd be surprised how much you can fit into a 4 × 4–foot space.

Making a bigger room out of two or three small rooms

This option certainly demands that you assess the way you presently use the rooms in question.   One way to get your dream kitchen, for example, might be to take out the wall between the dining room and the small kitchen. You can create the country kitchen you see in decorating magazines. My wife and I did this when we remodeled our ranch house 10 years ago. There was a small kitchen, bath, and bedroom across the back of the house (see figure 7.1). We combined the three rooms into one long great room with 6-foot windows at one end, French doors in the middle, and countertop-to-ceiling windows around the corner in the kitchen area. We also moved the back wall out 4 feet. (The house was only 25 feet deep.) We created some terrific space that is now the heart of the house. When the party gathers in the kitchen, there's room for everyone (see figure 7.2).

Bright Idea
Think carefully about how the space in your home actually is used. You might have purchased the home because it has a separate, formal dining room, for example, but how often do you actually used it for dining rather than as a study hall for the kids' or adults' homework?

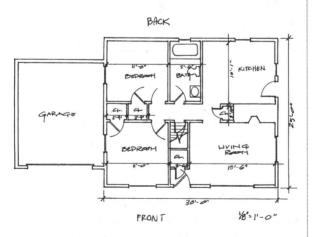

Figure 7.1.
Dimensions of the original 750-square-foot ranch house. Note the three rooms across the back that were made into one great room.

Figure 7.2.
The first floor
plan of the
remodeled ranch
house. Notice the
4 feet added to
the side of the
house.

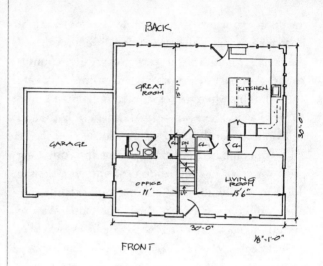

Adding on by going up

Watch Out!
Watch out for
the traffic! Go
over the plans of
your house, com-
bine some of the
spaces, and see
what it looks
like. As you alter
your rooms on
paper, keep in
mind the traffic
flow. You don't
want to create
bottlenecks or
hourglass
passages.

A few other options can keep you on the same foundation yet still create some added space. These
options include gabled or shed dormers and a partial or full second floor.

Gabled dormers

Gabled dormers can help you gain space on the
second floor or even in your attic by building extensions out through the roof. Dormers are simply
windows like those often seen on Cape Cod–style
houses (see figure 7.3). The space created can
furnish enough room for a small bathroom or
simply to bring light into an otherwise dim bedroom. A dormer also is an excellent way to make a
much larger room in your attic. You still have to figure out a way to get up there, but the climb will be
much more rewarding.

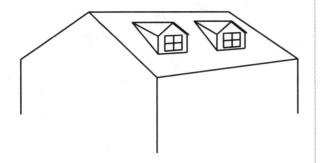

Figure 7.3.
Examples of gabled dormers.

Shed dormers

Shed dormers are also an addition to your existing roof and are used off either the front or back of your house on the second floor. Shed dormers are like running a connection between gabled dormers. They can create a great deal of additional room because they usually run nearly the entire length of your house (see figure 7.4).

If your present bedrooms have slanted ceilings running down to a knee wall, a shed dormer extends the walking-around room right up to the present knee wall. (A knee wall describes the angle of the ceiling to the wall rather than its height. It's usually about 4 feet high with a crawl space behind it.) A shed dormer provides additional space and, with the addition of windows, much more light.

A partial second floor

If you have a long, low ranch house, you could add a second floor over half of it if that is all the extra space you need. If you put your addition over an attached garage of the two-car variety, you can add considerable room without creating undue chaos in the main part of your home. You might have to

Bright Idea
You should keep in mind some design considerations when examining possibilities for additions. You should try to maintain the existing proportions and style of your house. Try to match roof pitches. Use the same construction materials and duplicate the windows of the original building. You owe it to yourselves and to the neighbors who have to look at your addition.

Figure 7.4.
Examples of shed
dormers.

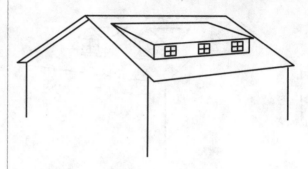

devise a place for stairs from the original house to
the new second floor, but this is not an impossible
assignment. It also offers some opportunity for creativity with open balconies, cathedral ceilings, and
dramatic windows at the far end.

A full second story

You can double the square footage of your home on
the same foundation by adding a full second story.
Your present bedrooms can move upstairs, and the
former first-floor bedrooms can become dens, TV
rooms, or combined into a larger kitchen.

When we invited four contractors to look at our
plans for remodeling our ranch house, only one recommended tearing off the roof and adding a second story. We liked this idea. We added a second
story but retained the "cozy" look in the front of the
house my wife wanted by keeping the single-story
height for the eaves in the front of the house and by
running the roof, unbroken by dormers or windows,
all the way up to the top. To get the room of a second story, we added a shed dormer across the back
of the house. We still had room for three bedrooms
and a full bathroom. We can't see out the front, but
the view of the pond is in back anyway.

Adding on by going out

Up to this point in the book, I have emphasized remodeling that keeps you within your existing house—kitchen, bathroom, changing interior walls, and so on. This is because once you go outside existing walls, the additional space requires excavation, a foundation, and all-new materials. It could also overtax your existing heating system.

This type of remodeling starts to cost serious money. If you decide to expand by going out, however, you have nearly limitless options. Here are a few ideas of what you can add:

- A single-story, T-shaped wing across either end or directly back from the middle of your house (see figures 7.5 and 7.6)

- A single-story, L-shaped wing going back or forward at either end of your house (see figure 7.7)

- Single-story, U-shaped wings going back or forward from the ends of your house (see figure 7.8)

- Symmetrical additions at both ends or both sides of a two-story house (see figure 7.9)

- A single-story addition with a shed roof (see figure 7.10)

Attaching additions to an existing building is a time-honored tradition in all parts of the world—from kings in ancient castles to American farmers. If you live in a rural area, drive around and look at the homes in your town and on its outskirts. Most homes were originally built to meet immediate needs. Then, as more children came or fortunes improved, additional rooms or wings were added.

Watch Out!
When you move outside your existing walls, you are entering the realm of your local zoning regulations, and you might need a building permit. Make sure you are within the building constraints posed by lot or property lines. New construction is often not permitted within 10 or 15 feet of a lot line. (Check with your local zoning administrator.)

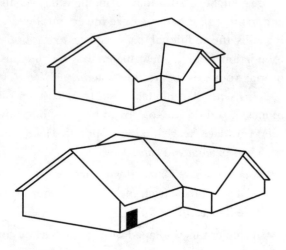

Figures 7.5 and 7.6.
A single-story, T-shaped wing across either end or directly back from the middle of your house.

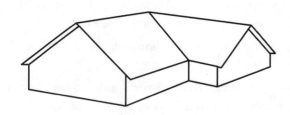

Figure 7.7.
A single-story, L-shaped wing going back or forward at either end of your house.

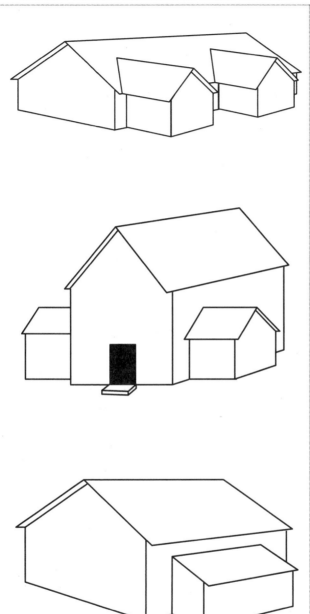

Figure 7.8.
Single-story,
U-shaped wings
going back or
forward from the
ends of your
house.

Figure 7.9.
Symmetrical
additions at both
ends or both
sides of a two-
story house.

Figure 7.10.
A single-story
addition with a
shed roof.

In the suburbs, one common addition was a screened-in breezeway between the house and the garage. These often evolved into finished sunrooms or dens. Because the basic structure was already there, it didn't take much imagination to see what the finished structure would look like.

When contemplating an addition, you should ask yourself how the addition will affect the lighting in the old rooms. When you build an addition, outside walls become inside walls and you lose the windows and natural light. To preserve light in the old room, particularly if the addition is a sunroom or a den with lots of new windows, you can use an open archway or windowed French doors to connect the new wing.

This is a time when you really need an architect or an experienced builder to guide you as you try different approaches. Going through the old laundry room to get to your new two-car garage might be all right, but it would not be a very impressive entrance to your new family room.

The book *How to Plan and Design Additions* (Ortho Books; edited by Kenneth R. Burke; published by Cheveron Chemical Company) provides drawings of 25 kinds of additions. It also contains color pictures of completed additions to get your creative juices flowing.

Other considerations

Regardless of their scope, home improvement projects present risks that typically are not present in everyday life. The following section discusses a few concerns you should be aware of.

Bright Idea
When you are building an addition to your home, don't break through the wall between the new and old space until near the end of the project. That way, you can remain isolated from the noise, dust, and dirt of the construction until the last few days.

Wait for the dust to settle on your remodeling plans

I have tried to prepare you emotionally for the chaos created by virtually any home remodeling project, but some of the mess can be more than an inconvenience—it can be dangerous. The cloud of plaster dust and dirt that mushrooms as a wall comes crashing down is so thick that any sane person will simply get out of the house until it clears or settles.

Unfortunately, this is not the end of it. The dust and dirt will hit the air again as you or your contractor sweeps up. If you didn't covered the registers, it also will haunt you again when the hot-air furnace turns on again in the fall or the air-conditioning system turns on in the spring. (See Chapter 15, "Fire, Fumes, Radon, and Dust Mites," for more information about duct cleaning.)

When using paints, solvents, varnishes, and adhesives, follow the directions on the containers. When they call for "adequate ventilation," have your contractor use an industrial-strength ventilating window fan and open all other windows in the area. Opening just one window is not enough ventilation.

The odor after the application of a product is called *outgas*. How long outgas lasts after the initial application depends on the product. If you are still getting odors a month after a product was applied, something is wrong. Contact your contractor. I suggest using water-based paints and adhesives and nontoxic strippers. Always make sure the containers are tightly sealed after use.

Carpeting is another source of fumes. These fumes can last for several weeks after installation. If you buy 100-percent wool or cotton carpeting with

Watch Out!
Remodeling (tearing out old, dirty, dusty, and mouse-dropping–filled walls) creates a temporary but potentially hazardous pollution problem. Many products you use during remodeling give off odors as they are applied and for some time after. These odors can range from unpleasant to potentially harmful.

no glue on the back, you can avoid most odors. Otherwise, try to get a carpet with a stitched backing, with very little glue, and without any surface treatments such as stain guards. If you're purchasing carpet in a roll, ask the dealer if he would be willing to unroll it for a couple of weeks before it is installed in your home. This allows the fumes to begin to dissipate.

If you can't justify the cost of wool or cotton carpeting or if you want stain guard, you're going to end up with some fumes. Open the windows of the room where the carpeting is installed and create some strong cross-ventilation. Fans can help speed the process, but time is the only cure.

How long should it take?

Only your architect, designer, or contractor can provide an estimate of how long a project will take, and he usually is off by about 50 percent. When we remodeled, for example, my wife and I thought we would get started in November because we were having a warmer-than-average autumn. We encountered an obstacle in the town's Historic District Commission, however, which meets once a month. It needs to run a public announcement of the items to be considered, and it schedules the following month's meeting agenda during the current month's meetings. The Historic District Committee had absolutely no problem with our plans, but it still took two months for the plans to be approved. Instead of tearing off our old roof in an abnormally warm November, we opened it up in a very normal, cold, wet January.

My wife and I were engaged at the time, and we intended to be married on the back lawn of our newly remodeled home. We set a date for the ceremony that seemed far off in the future—July 2. July got closer and our house still looked very much like a work in progress. The back yard lay opened up to receive a new septic tank, two dry-wells, and leaching fields. Our builder guaranteed not only that we would have a completed home but that there would be grass covering the back yard. He made it. The grass didn't last very long, but it was there when we needed it. He was, of course, invited to the wedding.

For those of you keeping track, it took six months from the time the first walls started coming down (not counting all the interview and planning time) to the final "I wills" in the backyard. There is no way we could have lived in the house as it was being torn apart and then rebuilt. I had an apartment in the next town that was actually larger than the original ranch house we started with.

What is it going to cost?

In all the annals of remodeling and building, there are virtually no instances where the final cost was lower than the original estimate. There are just too many places for things to go wrong, changes of mind by the homeowners as the project takes shape, and upgrading of fixtures.

Although you probably won't be able to analyze your project piece by piece or item by item, the total cost should be fairly accurate if you follow the preceding rules. If you stayed within the restraints set by your GC for the to-be-selected items and if there weren't too many changes or surprises, you might come in within 20 percent of the projected cost . . . and it's almost never lower. You'll be in good shape if you remember to increase your construction loan application by 20 percent when you go to the bank initially.

Timesaver
When you add on a new wing, you're dealing with new construction, and so you can probably obtain current figures from your lumberyard or contractor to estimate the average cost per square foot for new work.

In the previous chapters I have taken you through the two most popular and expensive rooms to remodel—the kitchen and the bathrooms. This chapter discussed rearranging the spaces you already have in your home to make it more adaptable to your lifestyle. If what you really need is more space, I've given you some ideas for where to find it. You can stay on the same foundation by venturing into your attic or your basement or by going out through the roof with gabled or shed dormers. If that still doesn't give you the space you need, you must enter the realm of additions . . . where the options become almost limitless.

Just the facts

- Be sure that the rooms, the look, or the space you create suits your lifestyle—not only now, but with an eye to your long-term changing life needs.

- Before you take more drastic measures, investigate the many ways to make your existing space better.

- Evaluate your less costly options carefully before deciding to go up or out for more space.

- Be prepared to spend more time and money than you had planned.

- Listen to a decorator who can add creativity, taste, and the courage to make bold statements you might hesitate to try on your own.

Chapter 8

GET THE SCOOP ON...
Remodeling your kitchen ▪ Available options ▪
The work triangle and other designs ▪ Finding
reputable contractors ▪ When the contractor
arrives . . . ▪ How long it should take

Your Kitchen

If you just want to remodel your kitchen and have turned to this section first, I suggest you back up a bit. Much of what you need to know about planning, finding and interviewing contractors, getting and analyzing bids, and living with a remodeling project has already been covered in Chapters 1 through 7. If you haven't read them, go back and do so now. Virtually everything suggested in those chapters pertains to kitchen remodeling . . . in spades.

The kitchen is the most popular place to start remodeling, and it is the most expensive project (short of building a two-story addition). It is also the heart of your house; you probably spend a lot of your time there. Your parties always wind up in the kitchen, and you are probably tired of making excuses for the way it looks. You're right—it's time to remodel.

This chapter discusses options to help you ease into your project cost-wise and basic rules of kitchen layout to help make your final results more useful.

I'll give you some suggestions from the Kitchen Remodeling Industry Association. You'll learn where to find kitchen contractors and how to spot the ones that might be difficult or dishonest. I'll then take you through the kitchen remodeling process and try to estimate how long you will be camping out in your living room. Throughout the chapter, I'll give hints as to what your project might cost.

How do you know it's time to remodel your kitchen?

As one contractor said when he was telling me how he works with hesitant clients, "The only reason I'm here is because the wife is tired of looking at the old kitchen, and the husband is tired of hearing about it." You might have reached that stage. You've given up the idea of moving to a bigger house, and you've realized that you like your neighborhood. With a little—or possibly a lot of—work, you can make this house work just fine.

A modernized kitchen and bathrooms (see Chapter 9 on bathrooms) are the smartest investments you can make in your home. They return nearly everything you invest dollar-for-dollar in increased value when you sell your home. (The emotional toll, however, cannot be calculated.)

What are your options?

You have three primary options when remodeling your kitchen: a face-lift (minor remodeling), major remodeling in the existing space, or major remodeling including expanding the space. These items are discussed in the following sections.

Unofficially...
Unfortunately, too many homeowners realize it's time to remodel only when they invite a real estate agent to list their home and ask what its value on the market is in its present condition. If your home is obviously outdated and you will be retiring or moving soon, remodel now. You'll get a better price for your home and in the meantime you'll enjoy modern appliances and better working space.

A face-lift

If your kitchen is everything you ever wanted but needs a fresh look, you might consider getting your cabinets refaced. This consists of removing the old doors and drawer fronts and replacing them with new ones. Because your kitchen keeps the same layout, you can put new, same-size appliances in the same locations. You can also install a new sink, laminate countertops in the same basic configuration, replace flooring, and get a new paint job if you want.

In the article "Common-Sense Kitchen Design" in the August 1996 issue of *Popular Mechanics* magazine, Merle Henkenius points out, "Many older homes have site-built cabinets, which are often made of solid pine with pine or birch plywood doors and drawer fronts. Despite the economic lumber, these cabinets are often better built than today's low- to midrange modular units. Moreover, they often include space and shape accommodations and storage features unique to each kitchen." He goes on to suggest that, for $50, you could make a smart choice to paint those cabinets. Add another $50 to $100 for new doorknobs and drawer pulls and you'll be surprised at the results.

In a previous home in Pittsburgh, my wife and I decided to go for a modern kitchen and hired a kitchen design/build firm. We had them pull out all the tall, glass-front wooden cabinets and the butcher-block countertop and put in bottom-of-the-line white metal cabinets and drawers and a Formica countertop. In our case, the new look we wanted also was an inexpensive way to go.

A complete remake of the same kitchen space

A complete remake involves tearing out everything you presently have and starting over with a new

Moneysaver
Just because you're tired of the look of your kitchen doesn't necessarily mean it's a bad look. Try giving it a face-lift or new paint, a new floor, new appliances, or better lighting. You'll achieve a better-looking kitchen at a reasonable price. If you're happy with its present size and can work comfortably in the old layout, this might solve your problem.

kitchen layout. This layout might give you more storage space, more countertop space, a better work triangle (the triangle made from the location of the stove, sink, and refrigerator), new appliances, and so on. A new layout includes all the changes called for in the minor remodeling project, plus it might involve relocating your sink and appliances or installing larger windows, new appliances, or new and more innovative cabinets. You also can try to make room for an island counter and a built-in microwave oven.

If you enlist the aid of an architect or a kitchen design specialist, this remake can give you a beautiful new kitchen with the features you want.

Major remodel with new space

The third option is to create a new and larger kitchen by extending it outside the present walls of your home and onto a deck or an addition. You also can convert other, underutilized rooms into additional kitchen space.

When my wife and I remodeled our home, we combined the former kitchen, bathroom, and a bedroom across the back of the house into one large, kitchen-type great room. We also pushed the back wall of the house out 6 feet, giving us a 15 × 30–foot room. The kitchen (including an eating and cooking island) is at one end, a dining area is in the center, and a TV room is at the other end. We almost never leave this room.

Make sure you plan for multiple overhead lights directly over your work areas in the kitchen. (With a central light, you are continually working in your own shadow.) I recommend putting all the kitchen lights on a dimmer switch so you can turn up the power while you're working and then dim them for a romantic atmosphere when meals are served.

Unofficially... According to *Remodeling* magazine's 1996–97 survey, the approximate cost of what they call a "minor kitchen remodel" is $8,507. The good news is you can get 94 percent of this investment back in increased resale value if you sell within a year. For major kitchen remodeling, the average is $21,262 with a 90 percent return.

Our "remodeling" (some people thought we should call it building a new house) cost $85,000. A recent appraisal of our home put its value at $115,000 over the original purchase price. Obviously, major remodeling can add a great deal of value to your home.

How to approach the task

While doing research for this chapter, I came across an interesting article on the Contractornet Web site (www.contractornet.com/art106), written by Thomas A. Ingle, Certified Kitchen Designer. In addition to giving a rather neat summary of the kitchen remodeling process, Ingle offers some fantastic suggestions about effective kitchen design.

What Constitutes a Good Kitchen Design?

Here are some useful numbers and measurements that have proven their value through the years of kitchens in use. They will keep you from creating kitchen cabinets and drawers that bump into each other when used and will also keep you from designing a kitchen that only you at 4'10" and your 7' spouse can use.

1. At least 32-inch-wide doorways.

2. Walkways at least 36 inches wide.

3. 42-inch work aisles for a one-cook kitchen and 48-inch work aisles for two cooks.

4. Work triangle no more than 26 feet in total length.

5. Kitchens under 150 square feet should have:

- 144 inches of wall cabinet frontage

- 156 inches of base cabinet frontage

- 120 inches of drawer or roll-out storage

- 132 inches of usable countertop frontage

6. Kitchens over 150 square feet should have:

- 186 inches of wall cabinet frontage

- 192 inches of base cabinet frontage

- 165 inches of drawer or roll-out storage

- 198 inches of usable countertop frontage

7. Two waste receptacles—one for garbage and one for recyclables.

8. 30 × 48 inches of clear floor space at the sink, dishwasher, cook-top oven, and refrigerator.

9. 21 inches clear floor space between edge of dishwasher and any object at a right angle to it.

10. Surface cooking appliances should have a vent with a fan rated at 150 CFM.

11. Two work-counter heights: 28 inches to 36 inches high and 36 inches to 45 inches high.

12. At least 24 inches countertop space on one side of the sink and minimum of 18 inches on the other side.

13. 36 inches of continuous countertop space for the prep center and adjacent to water source.

14. No two work centers to be separated by a full height, full-depth tower configuration, such as an oven cabinet.

15. G.F.I. circuits on all receptacles within the kitchen.

Reproduced by permission of the author: Thomas A. Ingle, CKD #101621 of Westchester, PA.

This has been only a guide as to what constitutes a good kitchen design. Consult an NKBA (National Kitchen and Bath Association) professional or a Certified Kitchen Designer (CKD) to determine the best design for you and your family. They will direct you on design trends, what to do or not do, and hold your hand throughout the entire process.

How to find reputable kitchen contractors

First, you must rid yourself of the assumption that, because only one room is involved, you don't need to take a lot of time finding and checking out a contractor. The kitchen is the most costly and most disruptive room you can remodel. You need people who are skilled and experienced in this specialized field.

What type of contractor do you require?

Before starting your search, you have to decide whether your current kitchen space is big enough. If it's not, you need to find a contractor or a kitchen-remodeling firm that is capable of handling general carpentry with structural changes as well as being able to hang cabinets.

When you venture into your neighborhood to find people who have remodeled their kitchens or who have built new homes with kitchens in them, it shouldn't be difficult to locate experienced referral prospects who can either recommend good contractors or steer you away from problem ones. Check the contractors out using the questions from Chapter 1. You can also find an abundance of kitchen-remodeling firms in the Yellow Pages, and they are more apt to use newspaper advertising than most contractors. Don't let the size and slickness of the advertisements dazzle you; be sure to check them out.

The World Wide Web has become a quick and easy resource for finding contractors in various specialties. National associations list the names and numbers of members in your area right on-screen. Tap into the Web or ask a friend to do it for you. The NAHB (www.nahb.com) and NARI (nari.org) are good places to start your search; you can also check out Contractornet (www.contractornet.com). Kitchen designers usually know several good contractors, some of whom could take on a remodeling project.

Contractors or firms to look out for

A lot of money is involved in kitchen-remodeling projects, and any venture with the prospect of big bucks tends to attract shady operators. The following are some specific strategies for weeding out contractor scam artists:

- Your first line of defense is checking out references.

- They can't take your money if you don't give it to them. Keep your down payment low and don't pay for any work that has not been completed or any materials not ordered or on site.

- Make sure the quality level of the cabinets, flooring, and appliances you get is what you expect. Your biggest danger in being ripped off is getting inferior cabinets or other items at premium prices. Check out what you want beforehand by visiting showrooms. Know the prices.

- Don't make the final payment until the work is done and you are satisfied.

Kitchen decisions

The kitchen is the most cost-intensive room to remodel because so much is compressed into a comparatively small space. Also compressed into that space are more decisions per square foot than in any other room in your house.

Style

Style choices are endless, as you probably know if you've leafed through a decorating magazine or strolled through a kitchen showroom lately. You can go for contemporary, traditional, or any of the numerous other available styles. Open shelves and the country look are currently enjoying a comeback. You can also opt for solid doors or for doors with glass fronts. We went with glass fronts containing clip-in pane dividers for a restrained countryish look.

Cabinets

Your kitchen cabinets are the focal point of the room so you want them to look good. They are also your storage facilities so they have to be accessible and practical. You can buy cabinets made to order from numerous manufacturers. Another option is to pick out ready-made cabinets, which are made in enough different sizes to fit most needs. Or you can hire a local carpenter or cabinetmaker to

Unofficially...
I have already alerted you to the scam tactic of being asked for too much money up-front. A large percentage of the cost of kitchen remodeling, however, is made up of items that have to be ordered before the work begins. Don't be alarmed if your first request for payment is around 50 percent of the total cost. Ask to see an itemized bill.

custom-build cabinets for you. Check out your options and their prices. Our contractor calculated an allowance of $3,000 for cabinets, and he could have supplied ready-made cabinets for that price. Instead, we got solid cherry cabinets (listed at $18,000) at a 50 percent discount through a distributor who happened to be a client of mine.

Special designs

Gone are the days when kitchens were simply upper and lower cabinets and drawers. Now, behind those cabinet doors are hidden specialty items: carousel corner racks, slide-out shelves, pull-out garbage cans, tip-down scrub brush racks, and a wide array of specially sized wire storage racks that can be attached to the backs of the doors. There are also so-called "appliance garages"—roll-front countertop storage areas meant to hide a food processor, a microwave, and so on. We chose one to hide our bar area.

Materials

Again, your choices for materials are vast. Wood (solid, laminate, painted, natural, or stained), plastic laminate, and metal are all available. Another option is to have a specialty firm come in and refinish your old cabinets, sometimes called cabinet refacing. These firms can provide a complete facelift or simply new doors. This is less costly than building new cabinets.

Hardware

Hardware includes cabinet knobs, drawer pulls, and hinges. You have to decide whether you want flush doors with invisible hinges or hinges that are part of the decor. The cabinet knobs—and there are hundreds to choose from—might seem like a small item at $5 to $10 each. When you have 40 of them, however (as my wife and I did), it quickly adds up. This was one of our toughest decisions. We made it so late, I had to install them all myself.

Countertops

Countertops are another area where you'll be highly tempted to go overboard. Some beautiful new composites are available as well as the more traditional plastic laminate, ceramic tile, butcher block, and stainless steel. You can also mix surfaces, such as inserting a piece of butcher block into a counter finished in Formica.

Height of countertops

The standard working height for countertops (and all sinks) is 36 inches (3 feet). It hasn't changed since colonial times when the population must have averaged a height of 5 feet. If you (or your partner) are unusually short or tall, test various heights to see whether a variation would be more comfortable for you. Ideally, you should be able to touch the bottom of the sink without bending over. Even if you're 6'9" (like my son), keep in mind that you might want to be able to sell your house to people of average height some day.

General kitchen layout

My wife went through a mental dry run of baking a loaf of banana bread with our proposed kitchen layout in front of her. She reached for pans, mixing bowls, a bread board, flour, spices, butter, the electric mixer, and so on to see how well the kitchen worked. She also tested the direction that the cabinet doors and the refrigerator door opened. She mentally unpacked bags of groceries, unloaded the dishwasher, and cooked a meal. Anticipating and

Moneysaver
Faced with the vast selections and inflated performance claims of various counter-topping materials, it's a good idea to ask your friends what type of countertop material they have, how they like it, and how it has stood up to use.

Bright Idea
Try to visualize
everyday food
preparation,
cleanup, and
storage activities
with your pro-
posed kitchen
design in front of
you.

eliminating potential problems helped us end up
with an excellent layout (though I haven't seen a
loaf of homemade banana bread yet).

Appliances

You might want to pick a new color for your kitchen
appliances. If you're going for all new gear, you'll
have the chance to do this. Otherwise, try to match
the appliances you're keeping. If both gas and electric hookups are available, you can choose either for
cooking. You need to decide between a traditional
range with burners on top and the oven below or a
countertop range and separate wall ovens. Do you
want a built-in microwave oven? Perhaps a deluxe
oven that combines a conventional oven with a
microwave? Other appliances you might need to
choose include a refrigerator, dishwasher, disposal,
and trash compactor.

Location of special storage

Ideally, you already handled the intricacies of food,
dish, and utensil storage while you were laying out
your kitchen. Now you must decide where you're
going to store all the small appliances you've
acquired or intend to buy: coffeemaker, coffee
grinder, food processor, toaster oven, toaster, can
opener, electric mixer, hot plate, crock pot, radio,
and TV. Then you should decide which ones you're
going to leave plugged in on the counter and which
ones will be stored. We put a few appliances out in
full view and stored the rest in big pull-out shelves
behind lower cabinet doors.

Plumbing fixtures

Your major plumbing decision is to choose the sink
or sinks you want. Do you want single, double, or

triple bowls? Do you want a separate bar or veg-
etable sink on the island? Stainless steel or porcelain? If you opt for the latter, you have to choose a
color. Remember that the sink will come with one,
two, three, or four holes drilled in it for various
faucet configurations and a hose. The faucets you
choose have to match the number of holes in the
sink. Now is also a good time to decide whether you
want a water line to your refrigerator for an automatic ice maker.

Watch Out!
It is strongly rec-
ommended that
you do not
install a garbage
disposal unit in
your kitchen sink
if you are on a
septic system.

What you can expect when the contractor comes

Everything I've already told you (and more) about
the life-disruption of a remodeling project holds
true for the kitchen—except you can still sleep in
your own bed and use your own bathroom. There
also are some things you and your contractor can do
to help ease the discomfort somewhat.

Timing

The former builder who appraised my home handed me the following hard-earned wisdom: "Don't
tear out your old cabinets or any other part of the
kitchen until all the new pieces and parts are ready
to assemble in your garage." This includes the new
cabinets (unpacked and inspected), countertop (or
counter materials), floor covering, new sink or
sinks, faucets, and light fixtures. Promised delivery
dates from the manufacturers are not good enough.
Everything should be there, ready to go in. If you're
changing the size of the space or adding new windows and doors, all raw materials (dimensional lumber, plywood, and so on), windows, and doors
should be on hand.

Work scheduling

This might seem similar to timing, but it involves more people. To accomplish a moderately complicated kitchen-remodeling job, you will need (more or less in the order they should appear): a wrecking crew, movers, a carpenter, an electrician, a plumber, Sheetrockers, a carpenter to hang cabinets and countertops, an electrician (again), a plumber to hook up the sink and dishwasher, a floor layer, appliance movers, and a painter. These people won't wait around for your last cupboard to arrive before accepting other jobs. It helps if your GC has sufficient warning of the start date so he can have them pencil in dates. Otherwise, he'll be on the phone every night trying to line up people for the next day or the day after that. (This is not uncommon.)

Family scheduling

Arrange for children to be out of the house or away from the construction as much as possible. Rearrange your social calendar so all gatherings usually held at your home are held elsewhere or are postponed until after the construction is completed. Immediately before construction begins, clear everything out of the kitchen. Empty all your cupboards into boxes and set up camp in your living room. You might want to get sturdy boxes you can stack on their sides with the contents showing like they're on shelves. This will help you find the cereal, bowls, sugar, and spoons when it's time for breakfast.

If the work crew arrives at 7:30 a.m., your job is to have the family up, dressed, fed, and on their way out as the crew comes in. Offer the crew a cup of coffee and a doughnut and talk about the job.

Bright Idea
As the old kitchen is taken apart, have your builder leave the sink, refrigerator, and stove hooked up until the last possible minute. If you can't leave the appliances in the kitchen as it's dismantled, ask your contractor to set up the refrigerator and the stove (or at least a hot plate and a toaster) in your living room.

It's all right to put off some decisions. Some choices just have to be talked over longer. Make sure, however, that you stay ahead of the contractor's timetable. Make sure everything he needs for each subcontractor is selected and on hand when that contractor arrives. You need to be available for on-the-spot decisions as problems are encountered in the construction process. Just hope they are not serious and expensive.

There are some kinder, less costly decisions such as exactly where you want the recessed overhead spotlights to be and which switches you want to be dimmer-controlled.

How long should it take?

The amount of time it takes to complete kitchen remodeling depends on the size and the complexity of what you're planning. It's impossible to say how long your particular project will take. Your contractor undoubtedly should be able to give you some idea. As previously mentioned, however, you should add (at least) half again to the time estimate he gives you. Things just don't go as smoothly in construction as even the most experienced contractors think they will.

Just the facts

- Plan thoroughly and settle on your final layout before you seek out bids. Multiple plans and fuzzy ideas only make the job of comparing bids more difficult.

- Get four bids that include ideas of what your kitchen could look like and inspect jobs each bidder has completed.

- Prepare yourselves to go through a very difficult time while the work is being done and realize

Watch Out!
No matter how uncomfortable he makes your life during the day, insist that your contractor turn the water and electricity back on each evening and definitely for the weekends. If he can't, take the family out to dinner, a movie, and a motel.

that no job in your home will give you more satisfaction and eventual value.

■ Take a long, critical look at the kitchen you have; with some cosmetic surgery, it might still serve your purpose.

GET THE SCOOP ON...
Reasons to add or remodel a bathroom ▪
Finding reputable remodelers ▪ When the
contractor arrives . . . ▪ How long it should
take ▪ How much it will cost

Chapter 9

Remodeling or Adding a Bathroom

Some people spend a lot of time in their bathroom and are sensitive to its aesthetics. For even the most indifferent, however, the time will come when updating becomes either desirable or necessary.

Not only does the overall look of a bathroom and your patience with leaking, running, and dripping water wear thin, the room just wears out over time. Many potential problems in a house are caused by water: leaking roofs, ice dams in the winter, trapped moisture in the walls, flooding in your basement, and so on. In your bathroom, water is imported for everything that flushes, sprays, leaks, and runs over. Problems are bound to arise.

In this chapter, I will discuss some of the equipment and fixtures that can go into your remodeled bathroom. I'll also tell you where to get help, how to check out contractors, and what to look out for in your dealings with plumbers, carpenters, and bathroom-specialty firms.

191

Unofficially...
The bathroom is a room for which we purposefully bring water into our homes. Over time, water can be just as unfriendly in the bathroom as it is in other rooms.

Some reasons for adding or remodeling a bathroom

You probably already have several good reasons for adding or remodeling a bathroom. Even so, there may be other reasons you haven't considered (such as increasing your home's resale value). The following sections discuss some of these possibilities.

You're about to sell your house

As we saw in the case of kitchen remodeling, you might decide to redo the bathroom if you're going to put your house on the market. This can help you get the best price for your home.

Keep guests away from the main bath

Some people are not ready to do major remodeling in their main bathroom, but they still are reluctant to let guests see it in its present form or in its usual state of disarray. You can delay full-scale remodeling by creating a first-floor powder room, which can also solve the problem of simultaneous calls of nature.

Create some adult privacy

Another popular trend is to remove parents from the immediate scene of high morning traffic by creating a bathroom off the master bedroom, which is then referred to as the master bedroom suite.

Other reasons

If you still need other reasons, survey your family members as they line up to use the facilities in the morning. If you happen to have a mixture of teenage boys and girls, I'm surprised you've been able to hold out this long.

What options for equipment and facilities are available?

For a relatively small room, you will have to make many decisions. You will need help designing your new bathroom, particularly if you're trying to squeeze a powder room under the stairs or into a closet. Water needs to be brought into the room and then taken away. Air can get in by itself but must be exhausted through a fan and a vent stack.

Before you invite an architect or a bathroom-design specialist to take part, you and the members of your household should answer the following questions to help you sort through the many options available:

- How many people will be using the facility? Is one bathroom enough or do you need two full bathrooms?

- Should you add a family bathroom or can you swing a master bath?

- What is the traffic pattern in the morning? Is everyone on the same schedule? Would a dual sink arrangement ease the problem? Should you have a separate closet for the toilet?

- What are the family's bathing preferences? Do you have dedicated tub bathers or is the shower preferred?

- If you're considering a second bathroom, could you make do with just a shower stall without a tub? Would you prefer a whirlpool bath?

- Do you have adequate storage? Make a list of all the things you need to store. Don't forget all the cleaning and cosmetic supplies.

- What different parts of the bathroom can help store all these things (in the shower, under the sink, in drawers, on shelves)?

- Have you considered the European approach to bathrooms—creating a separate room for the toilet and bath? This enables simultaneous use of the various facilities.

Moneysaver
When I visit people who have installed a whirlpool bathtub or have purchased a home that has one, they always point it out on their house tour. I ask when they last used it, and the response invariably is "several months ago" or "never." Survey your family before putting one in.

- Have you considered the lighting in your bath? (Lighting over the sink(s) is essential.)
- Have you considered newer, water-saving fixtures such as a low-flow shower head or a low-water toilet? You can still obtain a water-rich environment with water-saving features.

After you discuss how your family uses its present facilities and what you would like to change, the number of hard choices you have to make is astounding. Adding to this difficulty is the urge, when confronted with great-looking and expensive alternatives, to indulge in overspending. Be forewarned, it is very easy to be swept into a big cost overrun.

After you answer the preceding questions to your own satisfaction, it's time to ask for help. You need to decide whether to hire an architect, a bathroom-design specialist, and/or a general contractor. You also have the option to serve as your own general contractor and to hire all the mechanical people as you need them.

How to find a reputable contractor for your bathroom project

Ask friends and neighbors for names of bathroom contractors whose work and ethics they can vouch for, and walk through model homes. Use the techniques discussed in Chapter 1 to search, check out, and evaluate each potential contractor.

If you decide to hire a design/build firm or a bathroom-specialty firm, you may have the added advantage of seeing various plans and layouts in three dimensions on their computer-aided design (CAD) computer systems.

If you decide to start a full-scale bathroom remodel, review the sample proposal/contract in Chapter 2 and reread the explanations. The contract covers remodeling a bathroom for a sum of $16,905. With my translation of the stipulations—owner-purchased items and assumptions of workable plumbing, solid subflooring, reusable trim—if any of the fairly predictable surprises crop up, the owners' final outlay could easily double.

As I mentioned in Chapter 2, this contract was given to me as an example by a reputable firm and is not meant to be a sample of deviousness. Contractors have learned that, if they include the cost of every potential problem in their quotes, they could never win the bidding contests.

Bathroom decisions

Bathrooms have become the latest status symbol. People are spending thousands of dollars on raised whirlpool jet tubs overlooking panoramic views. If you think you'll really use this exotic equipment, by all means go for it. Just remember that these special tubs are costly to buy, install, and operate, and they are very costly to repair.

Here are some of the areas where your opinions will be needed and some of the options available:

- **Plumbing fixtures.** Bathtubs vary from the traditional cast-iron tub on claw feet to nearly Olympic-sized swimming pools. Your choice of tub dictates whether you want a shower in the tub or in a separate stall. You also need to select a sink or two and the toilet and its seat.

- **Cabinets.** Bathroom vanities offer many of the same design, style, and material options as kitchen cabinets. You might consider a vanity

Timesaver
You can be your own designer. If you have a computer, you can purchase a CAD program to play with your own ideas. In 1998, Macintosh-compatible programs could be purchased for about $20.

Moneysaver
Visit lots of showrooms and displays. Attend home shows in your area. Price the fixtures and materials you want. This will help you more accurately calculate the final cost. You will also know whether the contractor's allowances for your cabinets, faucets, shower heads, toilets, and so on are enough.

with room for two sinks. It also is handy to have cabinet storage for towels.

- **Plumbing fittings.** Be sure to tell your plumber how high you want the shower head before he drills the hole. (In our home, we had it installed 7 feet high to accommodate my height.) In addition to the shower heads, you also need a set of faucets for the sink(s) and the tub.

Bright Idea
Be sure to measure the distance between the outlet holes on both your sink and your tub so you can buy faucets to fit. If you selected the faucets first, buy sinks and a tub to match.

- **Urinal.** Another bathroom fixture you might consider, especially if you have young men in the family, is a urinal. A urinal lessens the need for accuracy and uses less water per flush. Another option is a bidet, which is common in Europe. A bidet permits personal washing and is beneficial for people with pain or inflammation such as hemorrhoids.

- **Miscellaneous.** You also need to choose towel bars, hooks, toilet-paper holders, medicine cabinets, toothbrush holders, soap dishes, mirrors, exhaust fans, and perhaps an auxiliary heater and sun lamp. Now that you have this nice new room, you also might want new towels, mats, and rugs, a new shower curtain, and new window curtains (or shades or blinds).

Questions for the bathroom: what to keep?

When looking at your bathroom, ask yourself the following questions: What do I like about it now? What do I want to change? For people with older homes, other questions top the list. What is historically appropriate? What works for a modern household? These questions are the beginning framework for your reconstruction. After you decide which resources from the past will remain in your space, you can begin to fill in what reasonably can be salvaged, what can be purchased used, and what can be blended into the new space.

You are fortunate; many manufacturers of new products now combine the ambiance of old-style fixtures with today's technology. Old faucets might look romantic, for example, but they also can be nearly impossible to refurbish. On a happier note, some people recommend that you rebuild your old toilet if at all possible. Few new toilets, even those that are supposed to be reproduction size, truly fit into an older bathroom. The dimensions of the new tank are often not quite right, so the aesthetics do not work.

When I brought in GCs to evaluate my 100-year-old mill in Vermont, one of the contractor lines that used to infuriate me was, "It would be a lot easier and cheaper to tear this thing down and start over." I've been a little guilty of that same philosophy as I talk about your new bathroom, so let me back up a little. If you have an attractive old or even antique bathroom, don't be a hurry to tear it out and modernize. Just think of all the clawfoot tubs and Thomas Crapper flush toilets (yes, he was the inventor) people wish they could get back.

It is wise to have a list of questions and issues to be addressed before starting work on your bathroom. Wall and floor repair and restoration come first with one exception: shower or tub valves in the wall. It is important to evaluate the life expectancy of the valves before retiling the walls in front of the valves. Many times, the tub and shower valves are no longer in good working condition but the tile work is exquisite. In this case, check to see whether you can access the valves through a wall on the other side. It is easier to repair lath and plaster than to cut out tiles.

Bright Idea
Save the toilet. The toilet tends to be the easiest to restore or to get salvaged. An old toilet can sometimes be transformed into a work of art with just a thorough cleaning and a new seat. After the toilet is finished, it's easy to get excited about the rest of the space.

If tile repair is necessary for other reasons, you should seriously consider how much life is left in the in-wall fixtures. Tile repair and replacement is expensive and time consuming. So make the decision whether to replace the fixtures before any tile work is done.

Resurfacing old tubs and sinks

Many times, the tub in the bathroom cannot be replaced with a tub that has the same look. You might try to rescue the original tub by resurfacing it. Before you resurface a fixture, you need to understand the quality of the process and material. The resurfacing material is either an epoxy resin or a polymer with properties similar to fiberglass. The durability of the finish depends on the surface preparation before application and the care taken after it is in place. When completed, the surface of the entire tub or sink looks new. Most professional resurfacing companies offer a five-year warranty for their work. In all likelihood, the surface will hold up for close to 10 years before it needs to be resurfaced again.

Adding a hand shower to a footed tub is a nice feature. You can rinse your hair and can wash the dog better than in a regular shower. A hand shower requires a vacuum breaker added between the hose and the hand set. Having space for a walk-in tile shower is, of course, the best of all worlds. Otherwise, it is possible to have a stationary shower arrangement for a footed tub. A number of shower-rod systems are available for this purpose.

Pedestal basin preservation

Today's pedestal basins generally are made of vitreous china (the same material used to make toilets). Older pedestal basins were made from either cast

Moneysaver
Keep as many fixtures as possible. Replacement parts are available for toilets. The tub and the sink can be resurfaced if they are worn and stained. The biggest problem often is the condition of the faucets, but they can usually be replaced.

iron and porcelain or china. Older china basins were usually more expensive, not to mention more elaborate in design and therefore difficult to refit.

When retrofitting an existing pedestal basin, some measures can be taken to help keep frustration to a minimum. If possible, bring the sink top along. If this is not possible, bring photographs and measured drawings. If purchasing an older basin, see whether it has an overflow. Unless you can determine that the drain system is all there, you might not want to get involved with it.

What to expect when the contractor arrives

I have the same advice for remodeling the bathroom that I did for the kitchen: Don't let your contractor start tearing apart this vital part of your daily life until all the new major components are resting on your garage floor and have been checked. You and your family will not be happy if you have to find alternate toilet and bathing facilities while you wait for a delayed or reordered tub, shower stall, vanity, or toilet.

Anticipating the scope of the project

You can count on the fact that the mess created will extend throughout the house, especially if the removal of old wallboard is involved (as is likely). You should be aware of the extent of the work to be done from your talks with the contractors who bid on your job and from the proposal and contract you received. If you're in a house that's more than 40 years old, there's a good chance your old pipes will have to be replaced with copper ones. And since your walls are opened up, you also could probably use some new wiring.

Watch Out!
If you have older sinks manufactured by Crane, be alert. Crane Company made many beautiful pedestal basins, but they are also incompatible with those of any other manufacturer. This can prove to be a problem, especially if the drain assembly is not intact.

Bright Idea
If you're getting a new tub or a hot tub, make sure you move it into the space while the doors are being rebuilt or while there are stud partitions instead of solid walls. These items often do not fit through standard doorways.

For bathroom remodeling, the subcontractors you will probably see are (in approximate order): wreckers, a carpenter, a plumber, an electrician, Sheetrockers, the plumber again, the electrician again, a floor layer, movers, a tile installer, a finish carpenter, a painter, and maybe the electrician again (depending on the versatility of your painter).

Note that several of the subcontractors appear on the scene more than once. The electrician, for example, works when the room is open with only the studs showing. He can drill holes and run wires from the circuit panel to each lighting fixture spot or outlet and can install the outlets. After the Sheetrockers are finished, he returns to cut holes in the Sheetrock to find his boxes (if they did not pull the wires through for him) and to install the plugs and light fixtures. (He will probably leave the faceplates off for the painter.)

The plumber, too, makes several calls. First, he replaces all that needs to be replaced in and behind the walls and runs new lines to any new locations for sinks, tubs, toilets, and so on. He also must come through the flooring, and finally he has to hook up the fixtures to the water and waste lines.

Your bathroom is going to be out of commission for hours if not days at a time. You can brush your teeth in the kitchen, but you need to have some bathroom privileges lined up with a neighbor or a friend. Most contractors will try to keep the vital equipment available for the family each night and, hopefully, every weekend.

Securely cover up your furniture and bookcases with plastic. Drape plastic sheets over the open doors of the bathroom. Try to isolate the dust and the plaster. No matter what precautions you take, however, the rest of the house is going to show some wear and tear.

You should consider two other things for your new bathroom:

- While the walls are open, you might want to install a new phone line on the wall near the toilet. (Stephens' Law: Placing weight on a toilet seat causes the telephone to ring.)

- You might want to build an emergency drain in the floor for tub and toilet overruns.

How long should it take and what will it cost?

If all the parts are available, the job itself should move pretty quickly. As previously mentioned, however, you should add 50 percent to your contractor's time estimate to be on the safe side. For this question, I'll refer to *Remodeling* magazine's 1996–97 study of national averages. The average bathroom addition, which involves adding a second bath to a house with one or one-and-a-half baths (the half-bath being a powder room with no bathing facilities)—including ceramic tile and a linen closet—costs an average of $11,645. It also, however, adds an average of $10,593—or 91 percent of the remodeling cost—to the sale price of your home if you sell with one year. In some regions, you can expect to recover more than 100 percent of the cost.

You should weigh the additional pleasure and convenience of a new or modernized bathroom against the likelihood of being able to recoup your outlay when you sell the house.

In summary, this chapter examines the adventure of designing and remodeling your bathroom and provides some reasons to do it. You now should have enough options to keep you busy until next

Unofficially . . .
Even remodeling costs can be largely recouped. The average bathroom remodeling, involving updating an existing bathroom with a new tub, toilet, medicine cabinet, lighting, and ceramic tile, costs $8,423 and returns 77 percent—or $6,480—of your investment on a resale.

building season. Just be aware that it will only get worse when you and your spouse visit the bath showrooms.

Just the facts

- Step back and look closely at your present bathroom; you might have the equipment that the rest of world is searching antique shops to purchase.

- Follow the rules for finding a reputable contractor: locate four, get bids, check references, read the contract, and talk to the contractor regularly.

- Control your urges in the plumbing fixture and bath showrooms; they can cause a serious leak in your bathroom budget.

Systems Repair and Replacement

GET THE SCOOP ON...
Avoiding getting burned by furnace repair ▪
Staying cool when repairing your air-
conditioning system ▪ What to do when you get
the cold shoulder in the shower

PART V

Staying Warm and Maintaining Your Cool: Heating and Air-Conditioning Systems

The major supply systems in your home tend to go unnoticed when they are working properly. If any of them break down, however, life as you know it comes to a halt. If your air conditioner or furnace begins to deteriorate, it might take a while for you to notice, because the house will just gradually change temperature toward the uncomfortable. Similarly, you might not realize you don't have a hot-water system for some time because you still have some 80 gallons of comfort left. When it's gone, however, you will definitely notice and will have to take some action.

Heating, ventilation, and air-conditioning (HVAC)

The heating and air-conditioning systems are the parts of your house that have probably been there as

Unofficially . . .
According to *Consumer Reports* magazine, three out of four new homes come equipped with central air. Though it adds little to the overall cost of new construction, it can enhance the resale value of the home.

long as or longer than you have. The system you consider the most basic to your comfort depends on what part of the country you live in. In the north, for example, heating is the primary need. Air-conditioning is more likely to be regarded as a luxury—one or two air-conditioning units or fans might get you through the few hot nights. In parts of the south and southwest, however, central air-conditioning is often regarded as a necessity.

Many remodeling projects require at least some modification of the heating, ventilation, and air-conditioning (HVAC) systems or installation of new HVAC equipment. This chapter covers some ways to reduce your utility bills and offers some insight into higher-efficiency equipment. You'll learn how to select an HVAC contractor and how to avoid being taken advantage of. Finally, I'll give you a rough idea of the time and costs involved.

Depending on your present systems' efficiency, your heating and cooling costs can be reduced by up to 50 percent by installing new, high-efficiency equipment. By installing this new equipment (and perhaps by enhancing your insulation to reduce air leakage throughout the house), it's possible to prevent an increase in your utility bills even when major additions are built. Moreover, comfort can be improved by better dehumidification resulting from properly sized air conditioners and heat pumps.

How to know when it's time to replace your furnace

A furnace burns natural gas, propane, or oil to heat air, water, or steam, which then is circulated throughout your home. No furnace can reach 100-percent efficiency. Some of the heat must go up the chimney and into the area surrounding the furnace.

Ten years ago, my wife and I bought a small ranch house built in 1946. We then proceeded to double the number of floors and to more than double the size. Our contractor figured we would need to replace the old, oil-fired furnace. The original furnace installer, however, had oversized the unit enough that our HVAC subcontractor simply added additional ductwork and saved us the cost of a new furnace—for a while.

This past summer, in an unplanned effort to field test every chapter in this book, I replaced our oil furnace (along with replacing the hot-water heater and the gutters, cleaning the ducts, repainting the entire house interior and the outside trim, and re-sealing the deck). How did I know it was time to make the switch? I learned by watching the oil company serviceman as he gave the system its annual cleaning. The amount of soot build-up in the flue, the amount of oily gunk inside the fire box, and the increasing monthly fuel bills finally convinced me to listen to the advice of several successive servicemen.

If your furnace is running comparatively well, can be tuned up to over 65 percent efficiency during its annual inspection, and is not a source of danger (such as carbon monoxide gas), it probably isn't cost-effective to replace it. It takes years to recover the cost of a new furnace when only a 10 to 15 percent improvement in fuel economy is gained. Our particular antique was over 50 years old and couldn't hold a tune-up. At the end of this section, I'll give you some other tips for extending the life of your current furnace.

How to know when it's time to buy or replace your central air conditioner

It's safe to say that, if your air conditioner stops working and a repair service can't get it to run, it's

Moneysaver
According to *Consumer Reports* magazine, if the furnace in your home is more than 20 years old, chances are it wastes more than a third of the fuel it burns. New furnaces are much more efficient and, therefore, are much cheaper to run.

time to buy a new one. When replacing an air conditioner or a heat pump, strongly consider replacing both the indoor and outdoor coils/units. These units are matched to provide the rated efficiency. Without this match, the equipment does not operate at the rated efficiency you're paying to achieve.

In addition to the usual desire to be cool on a hot day, some people need a central air conditioner for health reasons to filter out airborne particles such as dust, lint, and, with more sophisticated filters, microscopic pollutants.

I learned that my new furnace could be adapted to take a central air conditioner. I opted not to do it, but my installer assured me that I can add an outdoor cooling unit and hook it into my new hot-air system in the future.

How to locate a reputable HVAC contractor

You most likely already have a furnace and/or an air conditioner in your home (which I hope you have been getting serviced regularly), so you should know at least one company to call. Don't let this traditional relationship keep you from getting at least two other firms to come in, talk to you, and provide estimates and bids for salvaging your old unit or for new equipment. Let each firm know you are talking to others in order to keep them in a competitive mood and to filter out some of the more outrageous claims. The following are sources for reputable HVAC contractors:

- The logical first choice is your fuel dealer. Dealers frequently augment their delivery services to include selling, installing, and servicing new HVAC equipment. Many oil companies offer an annual service contract to their customers. Under this service contract, they answer

Watch Out!
Just as you are advised not to go grocery shopping when you are hungry, you shouldn't make a hasty air-conditioning decision on only the second 90-degree day of the summer. Give yourself some time to make a cool-headed decision, so to speak. It is also all right to run out and buy a couple of window fans, however. Moving air has amazing cooling effects.

any emergency calls and conduct an annual inspection and cleaning. The same company probably services whatever equipment you purchase. If you have been satisfied with the company's performance in the past, it's a good omen for the future. Go for two more contractors anyway.

- If you've been happy with your furnace over the years and your oil dealer doesn't carry that particular brand, by all means call the local distributor for the brand you want. Check out the prices and follow-up services available from your distributor. If they don't compare with your oil dealer's service, you probably won't have any trouble getting your oil-delivery firm to adopt your new furnace with a service contract.

- Visit your neighbors and friends for names of dealers and contractors with favorable reputations. You can probably view some of the latest equipment plus cut-away display models at an HVAC display room or a home show. Visit a few and educate yourself.

- Read the purchase and installation contract carefully.

Determine exactly what is included with the equipment and what is covered by the warranties from both the manufacturer and the installer. *Consumer Reports* magazine checked the warranties of 25 manufacturers and found that they varied widely. Many had important exclusions. Most covered the heat exchanger for a lifetime, but parts were covered from one to six years. Most warranties did not cover the cost of labor, which can be sizable.

Some warranties were not transferable to any new owners of the house. *Consumer Reports* recommends buying a service contract.

What to look out for in an HVAC contractor

Whether you are buying a new furnace through your GC because of the larger house you've created or replacing an outmoded, inefficient, old unit, do not rely too heavily on the size and capacity of your old unit when ordering your new one. The science of heating has advanced in both measuring need and equipment efficiency. You might not need as large a unit as your original. On the other hand, your new addition might have increased your heating demands beyond your old furnace's capabilities. A heating engineer can advise you.

If a dealer sells you a larger unit than you need, your unit not only will cost more to purchase, it will cost you more in fuel over the years to come.

In addition to considering purchase price and energy costs when looking at high-efficiency furnaces, you should also be aware of potential problems. Until recently, such furnaces caused the equivalent of acid rain within the units. Water vapor condensed on the heat exchanger, eating holes through which carbon monoxide could escape into the house. Manufacturers have been working on the problem, but these units might still require more frequent repair.

When it comes to central AC units, get references from at least three contractors. Be forewarned, central air-conditioning is an expensive type of cooling. If your dealer sells you a unit with too much cooling capacity (measured in tons of cooling, in which 1 ton equals 12,000 BTUs per hour), your unit not only will cost more to purchase,

Watch Out!
Closely weigh the advantages and disadvantages before buying a new high-efficiency furnace. It costs about $1,300 more but saves you only about $140 on your annual heating bill. Therefore, it will take you nine years to recover the additional expense.

it will cycle on and off frequently, cost more to run, and dehumidify inefficiently. It's better to undersize your unit than to oversize it.

Variety of heating options available

When you're looking at new furnaces, be sure to consider the federally required annual fuel-utilization efficiency rating (AFUE), the yellow tag or decal on the furnace. You should look for an AFUE of at least 78 percent. Your 20-year-old gas-fired furnace probably has an AFUE of 65 percent; an old oil furnace might be slightly higher. New furnaces typically rate around 85 percent. Various heating options include:

- **Oil-fired heating equipment.** Current oil-fired heating equipment is available in the 78 to 87 percent AFUE range. The best of these units use *flame-retention head oil burners* (FRHOBs), which are more efficient than the standard, gun-type burners. Newer units also eliminate barometric draft control by using a fan or a high-pressure burner. Eliminating this control results in a savings of approximately 10 percent over an FRHOB with this control.

- **Gas-fired heating equipment.** For gas-fired heating equipment, AFUE values can again be used to compare units. Currently available efficiencies range from about 78 to 97 percent. Gas-fired furnaces with efficiencies of 90 percent and higher are commonly called *condensing furnaces* because water vapor in the combustion gases cools to the point of condensation. The average AFUE of gas furnaces installed in the 1970s was about 63 percent. Many of these are probably still in use because some furnaces, especially older ones, can last 30 years or more.

Unofficially...
Here is a comforting piece of information: Design improvements have made newer gas- and oil-fired heating equipment potentially safer because the products of combustion are either exhausted mechanically or completely sealed from the air in your house.

- **Air-source heat pumps.** If you are planning to install a new air-conditioning unit and your heat currently is provided by electric-baseboard or electric-resistance-forced air units, you should strongly consider installing an air-source or geothermal heat pump instead.

   The heating season performance factor (HSPF) is used to compare the efficiency of heat pumps in the heating mode. Currently available air-source heat pumps have HSPFs in the range of 6.8 to 10.0. Depending on weather conditions and the HSPF, heat pumps use one-half to one-third as much electricity as electric-baseboard heaters and electric-resistance furnaces. As with air conditioners, seasonal energy efficiency ratings (SEER) are used to compare the efficiency of heat pumps in the cooling mode. SEER ratings in the range of 10 to 14 are currently available. Different heat pumps have different combinations of HSPF and SEER ratings.

- **Geothermal heat pumps.** These units are similar to conventional heat pumps in that they transfer heat from inside to outside or vice versa. Instead of using air as the heat source/sink, however, they use water or soil. To achieve this heat transfer, a loop of pipe is placed in the ground or the water (a well or pond). These units are generally more efficient than air-source heat pumps due to the more moderate temperatures of water or soil compared to air. This results in up to double the efficiency of air-source heat pumps.

   These units also have some comfort benefits because they produce warmer supply temperatures than air-source heat pumps. The requirement for exterior underground piping for these systems makes them significantly more expensive to install than conventional heat pumps. Payback can often be realized, however, well within the life of the equipment.

In addition to geothermal heat pumps, other new options include:

- **Scroll compressors.** Generally are more efficient, longer lasting, and able to produce higher supply-air temperatures than traditional compressors.

- **Variable- and dual-speed fans.** Use less energy to operate by selecting the most efficient speed to move the air as needed. Add to overall comfort of the homeowner.

- **Variable- and dual-speed compressors.** Use less energy to operate than single-speed blowers. Might improve comfort by reducing the speed of delivered air and providing better dehumidification.

Variety of air-conditioning systems available

Air-conditioning units sold in the early 1980s (many of which are still in use) had an average SEER of about 8. Because high-efficiency units generally do not dehumidify as well, proper sizing of these units is critical. A variable-speed blower, which also saves energy compared to a standard single-speed blower, also improves dehumidification for these units. Options for cooling your home include attic fans, ceiling fans, room air conditioners, and central air-conditioning.

- **Central air conditioners.** A necessity in the southern U.S., they are frequently built-in the way heating is in the north. If your home is

Moneysaver
When selecting among air conditioners, use the posted SEER values to compare the efficiency of one unit to another. SEER ratings in the range of 10 to 17 are currently available.

heated by hot air, the necessary ductwork is already in place for central air-conditioning and a cooling unit can be added on.

Bright Idea
When autumn comes, don't forget to pack some insulation over your attic fan or you'll siphon off a considerable amount of your expensive warm air. Then, when the time comes, don't forget to take it off in the summer.

- Although not technically an air system, a **whole-house attic fan** is an economical alternative to a central air conditioner. If the outside air temperature drops from 85 degrees to a more comfortable 75 degrees, it takes about four hours to affect your home. An attic fan can change the air in your house in about two minutes and can bring its temperature down to 75 in about two hours. You'll also get a cooling breeze.

A whole-house fan can ventilate your whole house on the electricity used by a single room air conditioner. This costs three to five cents an hour. Attic fans come in sizes from 24 to 36 inches. They require cutting and framing a hole in your top-floor ceiling (usually over the stairwell) and have automatic shutters that open with the force of the fan and close when you shut it off.

- **Ceiling fans** became popular in the United States during the energy crunch of the 1970s. People began to realize their value as a cheap way to cool a house and to push warm air down from a cathedral ceiling in winter.

Ceiling fans should be mounted so that the blades are at least 7 feet above the floor, for obvious reasons. (You don't want to scalp your taller guests and family members.) Serviceable fans start at $60; fancier ones can cost over $500.

- **Room air conditioners** are also a good option for cooling. I may have sounded slightly condescending to those living in the North and Northeast who feel that they need air-conditioning. I must confess that, although I only run it a few days a year, I have a room air conditioner in my home office here in Connecticut. (I tell people it's not for me, it's for the computer.) When the temperature rises over 90 degrees, I tend to shut down; unfortunately, my clients don't.

In the evenings, when I'm usually in the TV area, I place a fan in the door of my office and push the cool air from it into the next room. When the outside temperature cools sufficiently, I shut down the little air conditioner, open the windows in the TV room, turn on the attic fan, and pull the cooler air in with a nice breeze.

Dozens of room air-conditioning models are offered by dozens of manufacturers with various levels of energy conservation and cooling capacities. Small models start at around 5,000 BTU of cooling per hour, which is sufficient for a small room or a bedroom. Window AC units can range as high as 11,000 and 14,000 BTU and can cool one large room or two small ones.

Pick the room you want to cool, measure its floor area, go to the HVAC department of a home store or a plumbing supply house, and look for the yellow EnergyGuide label. The higher the EnergyGuide energy rating (EER), the lower the unit's operating cost. You can expect to pay between $300 and $600 for a room air conditioner, depending on its size and features. The reliability of room air conditioners is surprisingly good and long lasting.

Other than the numerous manufacturers and models available, the major variable is the size (in tons) of the unit your home requires. Contractors frequently use rules of thumb such as 1 ton per

1,000 square feet in a well-insulated house (400 square feet in a poorly insulated house). Your requirements can also be affected by the number of east- and west-facing window are as you have and the efficiency of your ductwork system. Get help from the resident engineer at your local HVAC contractor to calculate your particular needs. The best time to consider central air-conditioning is during major remodeling, when selling of your home, or during new construction.

Air-source and geothermal heat pumps can also cool your home. When the season changes, a heat pump becomes a cooling unit.

How to get the most out of any heating or air-conditioning system

The following methods can help you create an efficient HVAC system:

- **Insulate walls and ductwork.** The first thing your central air conditioner or furnace installer will look at is the tightness of your house's outside walls and windows (known as the *envelope*).

- **Check the condition of your heating ductwork.** These conduits are used to move the cool air from your unit to your rooms. (For more technical information about ductwork, refer to Appendix E.)

- **Evaluate the size of the equipment.** Do not assume your currently installed equipment is properly sized. HVAC equipment should be sized using the ACCA Manual-J or a similar method for air-conditioning. The same warning holds true for your furnace.

- **Carefully choose ductwork routes.** It is preferable to locate ducts within the building envelope. Try to avoid running them through

Moneysaver
Investing time and money in your home's envelope and making ductwork improvements (insulation, air sealing, and so on) often enables you to install smaller-capacity (and lower-cost) equipment. If you have a highly efficient building and duct system, buying only moderately efficient cooling equipment often makes sense financially.

unheated or uncooled areas such as attached
garages, crawl spaces, or attics. This option is
not always possible, however, even with new
work. In this case, ducts should be sealed with
mastic and perhaps should be better insulated.

- **Calculate your building's needs.** Don't blindly
  accept rules of thumb such as, "1 ton of cooling
  capacity per 500 square feet of floor area."
  Check inputs for air-leakage rates, design (maximum) outdoor and indoor temperatures, insulation values, and assumed distribution system
  (usually duct system) losses.

- **Reconsider buying a new furnace.** Currently
  installed oil-fired units can be improved by
  reducing the nozzle size. Making the improvements and repairs to your home's envelope and
  tightening up your duct system can enable you
  to continue using your old unit even with a
  remodeling enlargement.

- **Consider zoning.** It is possible to zone forced-air
  systems with sensors or thermostats in each
  room and an air-moving fan at the furnace end
  of the room's ductwork. With single-room heating and/or cooling equipment, you get the
  same effect as zoning if the units are equipped
  with an automatic thermostat. Zoning can lower
  operating costs by allowing thermostat setbacks
  in unoccupied areas while maintaining comfortable temperatures in occupied areas.
  (Heated or cooled air is delivered only to certain desired areas.)

- **Look into programmable thermostats.**
  Programmable thermostats can help you save
  money on fuel bills. Assuming a five-degree

setback for eight hours at night, you can both wake up to a warm house and save 5 to 9 percent on heating bills when using a gas furnace and as much as 12 percent when using a heat pump. Heat pumps, however, require thermostats specifically designed to provide setback without unnecessarily using electric resistance.

Additional savings can be achieved by using a daytime setback as well. In the case of gas- or oil-fired furnaces, you might want to install a unit that is up to 40 percent oversized to enable faster warm-up of the house when thermostat setback is used. On the cooling side, savings of around 11 percent are likely when using a setup of five degrees for eight hours per day.

What you can expect when the HVAC contractor shows up

Assuming your ductwork and insulated envelope are in good shape (a major assumption), surprisingly little time is required to take out your old furnace and to install a new one. Mine arrived in the morning with two men in a truck, and they were done by noon.

When it comes to a new central air conditioner, the quality of the installation can greatly affect the ultimate efficiency of the system. Refrigerant lines should be properly evacuated and confirmed with a micron gauge. Proper charging with refrigerant is critical. Contractors should use equipment that can accurately measure the amount of refrigerant so that it corresponds with manufacturer recommendations. Proper air flow across the indoor coil should be confirmed. Block register boots during construction and vacuum them out before air handler operation. Air-conditioning coils and heat exchangers should be cleaned and filters should be replaced before turning on a new system or connecting to an existing system.

An attic or whole-house fan requires some carpentry in your attic. With the right tools, an ability to measure accurately, and the self-confidence to cut a hole in the ceiling, it is not a complicated job. You'd be better off getting your HVAC people to handle it, however, because it also requires a control switch you can get to and an electrical outlet in the attic near the fan.

How long should it take?

The changing of a furnace or an air conditioner is not terribly disruptive to your home and only takes a few hours. Installation of a new furnace or central air conditioner, room air conditioners, or whole-house fans can be measured in hours rather than days. If you are getting a geothermal heat pump, however, a lot of ground work is required. Your particular project should be discussed with your contractor.

You can install ceiling fans yourself if you are blessed with a ceiling electrical outlet where you want to install your fan. Read the directions and keep the total weight of the fan within the load limits of your receptacle.

How much should it cost?

Our particular furnace came to about $1,600, including installation. Central air conditioner costs vary by region, but you can expect to pay between $3,000 and $4,000 for a package that includes equipment and installation. Room air conditioners cost between $300 and $600. Try to get the installation included. Ceiling fans cost between $45 and $600.

Bright Idea
Room air conditioners are really too big for one person to handle. If you can do so, get the store you buy it from to install it.

Both heating and air-conditioning can be installed by the same contractors and use the same distribution system throughout your house. Heating and air-conditioning energy efficiency can be increased from 20 to 30 percent by tightening the insulation in your home's envelope, by taping leaky joints, and by insulating your ductwork.

Locating a trustworthy HVAC contractor might simply involve contacting your present fuel oil dealer. Even if you are happy with his service, be sure to get bids from two others as well. You can obtain additional technical information from fact sheets prepared by the NAHB Research Center (400 Prince George's Boulevard, Upper Marlboro, MD 20774; 800-638-8556). The fact sheets also are available at the NAHB Web site (www.nahb.com).

Getting the most out of your water heater

Unofficially...
When your water heater needs repairs or replacement, you'll feel it immediately. Water heating can account for 15 to 25 percent of the energy used in your home.

After it breaks, repairing or replacing your water heater is not something you can put off for long. It's an important part of your home that greatly increases your comfort level.

The rest of this chapter covers how to increase your water heater's efficiency and what improvements to look for when you are forced to purchase a new water heater. You'll learn some alternative ways to heat water and how to avoid shower discomfort when someone else in the house turns on water, either hot or cold. I'll also offer tips to help you find a good contractor, and I'll tell you how much time and money are involved in installing your new water heater.

How do you know it's time to replace your water heater?

It's fairly easy to recognize when you need a new water heater—there's water on the floor around your heater. If there's just a little water, you might simply have a loose pipe connection or a leaky faucet washer. If there's a lot of water, however, the chances are good your old heater bit the dust.

The most common problem is in the lining of your tank, and this is not a repairable item. You'll need to buy a new one. The average life expectancy of a hot-water heater is about 15 years.

How to locate a reputable supplier and contractor

The same situation exists for water-heater contractors as for your furnace or whole-house air conditioner. If you're happy with the service you've been receiving, the firm presently supplying your fuel—or even your utility company—is your best source for a new water heater. They will either have an HVAC division, will have a subcontractor with whom they work, or will be able to recommend one to you.

If you go directly to an HVAC dealer to replace your electric hot-water heater, they probably will sell you an electric replacement. I went to our oil dealer and received information about switching to an oil-fired hot-water heater. With the high cost of electricity in the northeast, it seemed to make sense to switch, especially when they predicted that I would recover the cost of the new tank over five years with the money I'd save on electricity bills. You should investigate your options, get some additional price quotes, and make some comparisons.

Consider the following factors when comparing water heaters:

Moneysaver
If you are trying to sell your house and your prospective buyer contracts a home inspection, the age of the water heater will be one of the items listed on the report. If it's at or near 10 years old, replacement or an allowance for a new one might become part of the sales contract. You are not required to go along with the request, however.

Timesaver
The cost of oper-
ation or efficien-
cy of various
water heaters
can best be
judged by com-
paring the infor-
mation on the
EnergyGuide
label, the yellow
tag found on
new water
heaters.

■ **Energy costs.** Water heating typically accounts
for 15 to 25 percent of the energy used in a
home. Consequently, improvements in water-
heating efficiency offer good opportunities to
save money.

■ **Hot-water usage.** A growing family or the addition of an aging parent can lead to an increase
in water use (more people or bathrooms) and
higher water-heating costs. In this case, the cost
of a more efficient water heater would be recovered quickly.

■ **Size.** When replacing a water heater, don't
select the new one based on the size of the old
one. Smaller tanks are inherently more efficient
than similar bigger units. You should consider,
however, whether you usually have sufficient hot
water and how your water needs might change
as a result of remodeling. An added bathroom,
for example, might necessitate a larger tank.

■ **Location.** Generally speaking, in the northern
part of the country it is preferable to place water
heaters within heated spaces (not in garages or
enclosed storage areas, for example). In warmer
climates, where heat loss from the tank is an
unwelcome addition to the air-conditioning
load, a garage or shed might be the best location. The 90-degree days actually help heat the
water.

Water heater types available and the advantages of each

Unlike your furnace, which you can continue to use
even after it has passed its prime, a dead water
heater needs to be replaced immediately. You do
have options, however, when you select its replacement. You can change the method of heating—gas,

electric, oil, and so on—depending on which is less expensive or more available in your part of the country. You can also adjust the capacity.

In an effort to make it easier for the public to compare water heaters, the government has devised a numerical system to measure energy efficiency— the Energy Factor (EF). I can't explain all the numbers and measurements that go into this rating; all you really need to know is that a lower number is better.

Another method of comparison is the estimated range of annual cost. Using national averages for the cost of the various fuels and the average usage by the average-sized family, a number (or range of numbers) for the average annual cost is derived. Various types of water heaters include:

- **Electric tank-type water heaters, standard type.** Energy Factors (EFs) range from .86 to .95 for a standard 50-gallon tank. The estimated range of annual cost, using an electricity price of $0.08 per kilowatt-hour (kWh), is $370 to $408.

- **Natural gas tank-type water heaters, standard type.** EFs range from .54 to .63 for a standard 40-gallon tank. The estimated range of annual cost, using a gas price of $0.55 per therm, is $128 to $152. (A therm is a measure of heat quantity like BTU.)

- **Oil-fired hot-water heater.** This is the type my oil company sold me last spring. It has a 32-gallon tank, an EF of .66, and a first-hour rating of 134 gallons. The benefit that convinced me to buy it was a recovery rate 3 times faster than gas and 10 times faster than electric. The estimated annual cost of oil for this unit (residing in Connecticut) is $178.

Unofficially... You probably won't have time to take on an exhaustive search for the perfect contractor/ installer. After all, your family won't stand for cold showers while you do the research. The installation time is minimal because your new unit probably comes in a crate, fully assembled and ready to hook up.

- **Heat pump water heaters.** EFs range from 2.1 to 2.5 for an 80-gallon tank. The estimated range of annual cost, using electricity price of $0.08 per kWh, is $141 to $167.

- **Geothermal heat pumps.** These can be equipped with desuperheaters, providing hot water when in the cooling mode. They also can provide dedicated water heating that operates on demand.

- **Tankless (or instantaneous) water heaters.** These heaters are more common in Europe, but they are slowly catching on here. Cold water is heated as it flows through the unit. No storage of hot water is necessary, and the unit is only on when you turn on the hot-water tap. They can be either gas or electric and are most useful for small loads, in remote locations of your house, or in a newly remodeled area. In these situations, running pipes from the central water heater might be difficult, expensive, or waste too much water.

- **Solar water heaters.** Various types are available. They can provide some water heating during all seasons, often 100 percent in the summer. Solar water heaters can be elaborate piping and storage units laid out under glass on the roof, or they can be as simple as a rain barrel full of water from the downspouts, warmed by the sun and dipped out to water plants.

Energy-saving steps

Even if you are not in immediate need of a new hot-water heater, some conservation steps can improve the efficiency of your hot-water system:

- **Tank insulation.** Wrapping your tank in an insulated blanket is one way to conserve heat loss

Moneysaver
Raising the temperature of the water that enters your hot-water heater saves energy. Tapping a storage tank in the attic to hold water that has run through coils on the roof is free heat. If you can run your water heater's feed line through coils in your furnace, you can make double use of the furnace heat.

and, consequently, energy usage. Older tanks might have R-3 insulation; newer tanks have built-in insulation available in the R-4 to R-20 range. The extra cost of an insulated tank will likely be recovered by energy savings within one year in most cases.

- **Pipe insulation.** Easy, inexpensive, and cost-effective to install, insulation should be added to all pipes from the tank for at least the first 6 feet.

- **Heat traps.** Traps prevent heated water in the tank from mixing with water in the pipes. Easy, inexpensive, and cost-effective to install, heat traps can be added as a retrofit or to new tanks that lack them. Some new water heaters have built-in heat traps.

- **Flue dampers.** Dampers are installed on naturally drafted gas water heaters to seal off the flue when not in use. The damper opens automatically when the water heater turns on.

- **Timers.** Used on electric water heaters, timers shut off the heaters for a certain time period (typically during the hours when you're at work). Timers might be unnecessary if the tank is well insulated or if you need hot water during the day.

- **Load-management devices.** These are typically installed by the electric utility for free at your option. They enable your utility to remotely turn off your water heater in times of heavy electrical demand. Utilities typically give a credit of around $5 per month if you install this option.

- **Water temperature.** Set the temperature to around 120 degrees Fahrenheit unless your

Watch Out!
I used to set my water temperature to about 140 degrees under the assumption that, with hotter water, I would use less by mixing in more cold. I might even have been right for the time spent in the shower, but the heater had to keep the water at that higher temperature all day. Not a good idea.

dishwasher does not have a separate water-temperature booster or if you consistently have insufficient hot water. Temperatures above 120 degrees are dangerous, especially for children and the elderly.

- **Water use.** Installing low-flow shower heads and faucet aerators can reduce water use significantly. Some people find that a low-flow shower head is like bathing in a mist, but some newer models have adjustable flow control.

How much will it cost?

The cost of a water heater depends on its size and type. You can look forward to an outlay between $900 and $1,500. This includes installation and adjustments. Your warranty on the tank will probably be five years, and you'll probably have a limited warranty of one year on parts and workmanship.

The cost of my particular oil-fired heater replacement was $1,600 in the spring of 1997. I can't say my electric bill has dropped, however, because a teenager moved in with us at about the same time. Our oil bill, however, has not increased appreciably.

Pulling it all together

The following is a quick summary of items to consider and check. Everything in your home connected with heating or cooling is a source of energy usage. The water heater falls just behind the furnace in total use and, consequently, is worthy of attention. For existing and new water heaters:

- Insulate the tank
- Insulate the pipes
- Consider heat traps
- Consider timers

- Consider a flue damper
- Consider supplementary solar heating
- Adjust the temperature setting

For new water heaters:

- Select a high-efficiency model
- Consider the annual cost
- Determine the proper size
- Determine the required first-hour rating
- Consider the location

Much of the information in this chapter was based on fact sheets prepared by NAHB Research Center with support from the U.S. Department of Energy and the National Renewable Energy Laboratory. You can obtain more information about this and many more remodeling subjects at www.nahbrc.org.

Just the facts

- Don't put off upgrading your furnace or water heater because you expect to sell your house in a few years. You might have to replace it prior to a sale, and you might as well get some pleasure out of it yourself.

- Don't rely on the specifications of your old furnace when ordering a new one; measurements of need are more sophisticated now.

- To save on your energy bill, throw a thermal blanket around your water heater, insulate your pipes, and install a timer.

GET THE SCOOP ON...
What to do when your electrical system goes
haywire ▪ How to replace old wiring ▪
How to insulate yourself ▪ Saving money with
improved energy efficiency

The Electrical System and Insulation

Chapter 11

Sooner or later, every house has electrical problems. Likewise, many of us have accumulated electronic gadgets that were not anticipated when our homes' electrical systems were designed and installed. A neighborhood-wide outage is no reason to call in your electrician, but many older homes experience their own blackouts on a regular basis. Of course these seem to come at the worst times. You're in the middle of preparing the Thanksgiving turkey, you've just plugged in all the Christmas-tree lights, or you're sawing parts for a workshop project when a fuse blows.

Your electrical system

Like fire, electricity has the capacity to harm as well as to contribute to our well-being. For this reason, it's best to err on the conservative side when confronted with electrical problems.

Bright Idea
If you work on a computer, use programs that automatically save your work every several minutes. This can help you avoid lost work during power losses.

How do you know you need an electrical contractor?

If you still have a fuse box, you're due for an upgrade. Even homes with circuit breakers, however, can have a power loss when a circuit gets overloaded. This is a sign you need more power in your home.

For some people, a power loss is a mild inconvenience; for others, such as computer users, it can be a disaster.

Even with obvious signs of need, the most common time for an electrical upgrade is prior to the sale of a home. It is common for prospective buyers to request and pay for a home inspection as part of a sales offer. If you want to get your asking price, call in an electrical contractor to bring your service up-to-date and up to code.

The second most common time for an electrical upgrade is when you're doing any remodeling that requires a visit from and the approval of your local building inspector. Of course, that inspection can be triggered by more mundane problems such as the need for a new hot-water heater or furnace. Upgrading in these situations is not an option. If you want approval to continue to live in the house, you need a certificate of occupancy. To get it, you have to meet the existing codes.

Other reasons for calling in your local electrician usually involve something not working, such as the electricity being off or repeatedly shutting off without you knowing why. Any malfunction in your fuse box could be a fire hazard, particularly if you are using several extension cords to make up for too few outlets. Additionally, when adding a workshop or putting in an attic fan or air conditioner, you might discover there's no more room in your present circuit panel. Or perhaps you want to add a dedicated circuit for your computer.

You don't have to take on a whole remodeling project to upgrade the wiring and circuits in an older home. Electricians have a near-magic ability to snake new wires throughout your house—inside the walls and even down to your basement—without tearing out any existing walls.

What you can expect from an electrician

According to an electrician friend of mine, when you call in an electrician to solve a problem or to fix something, you should expect that the problem will be solved by the time he leaves. In this day of specialization, however, there might be times when an electrician will have to coordinate his work with another contractor. An electrician will hook up the power portion of your new water heater, for example, but a plumber is required to install the water heater and to hook up the water.

In construction, scheduling an electrician is critical because most jobs require at least two and frequently more visits to your home. In a remodeling job, he is often among the first and the last contractors on the scene. First, when your new room's walls are just studs, he runs the wires and installs the outlets and switch boxes that will be behind the wallboard. This is also when you get your new panel board with its circuit breakers. The electrician then must come back after the walls are up (and possibly painted) to wire the switches and plugs into the boxes; to put on the faceplates; to install the lights, lamps, and fans; and, finally, to turn on the power and make sure everything works.

Moneysaver
When installing a new panel board, buy one with a few more circuit breaker slots than you currently need. This will make adding new circuits and service upgrades much easier and less expensive.

How to locate a reputable electrician

Electricians are usually hired by GCs as subcontractors for new construction and for remodeling projects. The GC has located capable firms through trial and error and is willing to vouch for their capabilities and their work. If you ask a neighbor who has recently remodeled for the name of his electrician, he probably won't know who it was. If you are looking for an electrician for a specific task in your home, you can probably find one in the Yellow Pages. Don't settle for just one, however; invite two or three to offer suggestions and to bid on your project.

66

Some remodeling firms use unqualified apprentice electricians on their jobs. There is a lot more skill and training involved in this profession than simply avoiding getting a shock.

—Stephen Pryor, electrical contractor

99

All electricians must be licensed by the state(s) in which they practice. Ask to see their license. Their license number must appear on their stationery and contracts, and most states require that the number be painted on their trucks. They must also carry liability insurance and workers' compensation insurance. Ask to see their insurance policies and, if you have any doubts, call the insurance company to check.

To be a qualified electrician, a person must go through a five-year apprentice program. An apprentice gets half-pay during the first year and works up to 85 percent of the basic pay rate during the fifth year. He then becomes a journeyman electrician. Apprentices usually work as helpers or with a qualified electrician on larger projects and new construction.

How to spot a scam artist

The first clue that an electrician might be a scam artist is if he comes to you unsolicited. Another clue is if he lacks a state license. You also should be wary if he asks for a large payment in advance. A reputable firm bills you upon completion of the work. You should put on the brakes if you are getting a hard sell such as, "I can only offer you this price if you sign up now." If you hear any of this, invite in some other firms.

Here's another suggestion from a reputable electrician: "It doesn't matter how long an electrician has been working on your problem. If it isn't fixed, don't pay him." This particular electrician also pointed out that some firms raise their prices when they are busy, sometimes even doubling them. It is worthwhile to try to hire electricians when they are less busy. Finally, a good contractor returns your calls promptly, particularly in this age of cellular phones.

Signs of a reputable firm

One electrician I interviewed invariably talks with the homeowners about the job to find out what they want done and how long they plan to keep the house. Usually this information presents some options from which to choose. If you want a new service, it can be top-of-the-line with metal conduit pipe and copper wire, or plastic pipe and copper wire, or you can use the less expensive plastic conduit and aluminum wire.

Household electrical wiring is like water-supply lines. If you want more water or a heavier flow, put in water pipes with a larger diameter. The same is true of electricity. If you have a heavy electrical draw from the appliances in your kitchen, you can increase your amperage with new, larger wiring that can carry 100 or 200 amps. This increased capacity also goes back through your circuit breaker panel to the lines from the pole to your house.

The following are some general cost and time guidelines:

- Your electrician probably charges about $40 an hour.

- It takes about two hours to hook up a new water heater.

- It takes about a day to change or upgrade your service. (With two guys, it takes about six hours.)

- A 100-amp service upgrade costs between $700 and $1,000.

- A 200-amp service upgrade costs between $900 and $1,200.

Nine years after we remodeled our house, I finally decided it was time to upgrade the electrical system in the garage. For some reason, we ignored it when we did the rest of the house. Several things that made me realize I needed help:

- The fluorescent lights shut off on their own, especially in hot weather. In time, they also turned themselves back on.

- I kept tripping the circuit breakers whenever I tried to use my table saw or my radial-arm saw. This also shut off all the lights.

- I had extension cords running all over the garage to the various pieces of equipment. I had even more cords running from the single outlet in the ceiling to clip-on lamps and to the fluorescent lights.

I retained a local HVAC contracting company, which also has electricians on the payroll, to bring the wiring up-to-date. I now have a 200-amp dedicated line for the extension reel, into which I plug my power saws. The entire electrical service into the shop has been beefed up. I got some larger, used, fluorescent tube lights and they now plug into an outlet in the ceiling that is controlled by the old light switch. I have electrical outlets every 4 feet along the wall at the back of my workbench and on two sides of the garage.

I tell you this, not to sell you on the idea of creating your own workshop, but to show you that it *is* possible to upgrade the electrical portion of your home or any individual room without going thorough a major renovation.

Electrical work can be divided into the parts that are hidden beneath and behind the surfaces and the parts that show and glow. Your electrician can upgrade your power from 100 amps to 200 amps to handle the greater electrical draw of dishwashers, ranges, freezers, dryers, and other appliances. This is done by running heftier lines into install your circuit board's panels.

Electricians can install task lights over work areas or even a dining room chandelier. They also can set it up so you can turn on all the table and floor lights in your living room from one wall switch.

The best time to do electrical work is during the construction phase of your project when the walls are opened up. It's also possible just to upgrade the electrical systems without disturbing your basic structure. Electrical work is one of the few jobs done in your home by contractors that is considered dangerous. Electricity can cause serious injury and even death. Consequently, most homeowners and other subcontractors leave the electrical parts of a job to the electricians.

Moneysaver
Even today's modern kitchens often have electrical outlets every few feet on the wall above the countertop connected by a commercial-style metal conduit. This saves having to break into the walls and snake wires, and it gives your kitchen the new industrial or commercial look.

Unofficially...
You can take up the battle of energy efficiency at any time in the life of a house. When you take on a remodeling project, however, you have a unique opportunity to make cost-effective energy improvements.

Insulation: the sun screen and wind breaker for your home

Houses are complex systems that are affected by air flow, moisture, heat gain and loss, construction, climate, and occupant behavior. These items interact and ultimately influence energy use, comfort, health, and building durability.

Heat can be lost or gained through ceilings, floors, walls, doors, and windows. Air and moisture move into and out of your home through openings in the building. Sunlight bounces in through glass areas and absorbs into solid surfaces, dissipating later as heat.

Your house is a battleground for nature's elements—an arena for which you have purchased a four-season ticket and yet, with any luck, will never witness any of the daily, monthly, and seasonal contests. To carry this analogy even further, you may also fill the role of water boy (when the roof springs a leak or the tub overflows), groundskeeper, the coach (responsible for directing the offense and able to call up skilled players to shore up your defense) and, of course, the owner who has to pay all the expenses.

The basic principle you as a homeowner are fighting is the tendency for warm air to flow from a warm place to a cool place. For people in northern climates, this means the air you are paying to heat is trying to escape outdoors. For people in southern climates, it means the air you are paying to cool is being invaded by the warm air outside. As anyone who has experienced a cold draft blowing down his neck can attest, however, cold air tries to get into warm spaces as well. The more you can slow this great escape, the more comfortable you'll be, the healthier you'll be, and the more money you'll save in your heating and cooling bills.

When and where to insulate

If your outside walls are getting new siding, they can be easily insulated before you add the siding. If you're upgrading your furnace or cooling system, old air ducts can be sealed or upgraded and might even save you the cost of your new equipment. Energy savings can be made in three main categories:

- **The building's envelope.** Wall, floor, and ceiling insulation, air sealing, and improved windows.

- **Equipment.** Heating, cooling, water-heating equipment, appliances, and lighting.

- **Daily operation and maintenance.** Thermostat settings and water use.

How do you know you need better insulation?

You probably already know. If you live in a house built in the past few years, you are probably in good shape. The older your house is, however, the less likely it is to be as well insulated as it could be. In addition, if you're spending a lot more for oil, electricity, or gas than your neighbors with comparable homes, you probably need help.

The benefits of better insulation

Saving energy and money is an obvious benefit, but better insulation also provides other benefits such as lower maintenance, improved property resale value, and reduced environmental impact. You probably understand the role of insulation regarding warm and cold air, but it also affects moisture in the form of condensation—a major problem.

Moneysaver
The best way to determine whether you are sufficiently insulated is to call your local utility company and ask for an energy audit. Oddly, it is to their benefit to have you use less electricity, because they will not have to build new electrical generation capacity if they can get present users to be more efficient.

Bright Idea
A rule of thumb to remember when installing insulation is that the plastic-like vapor barriers and the foil or paper backing on rolled insulation should face the warm or air-conditioned area.

Creating a barrier against vapor

The water on the inside of a single-paned window on a cold day is the most obvious example of condensation. If your insulation does not have a vapor barrier, condensation also occurs inside your walls and on the surface of the pipes running through your walls and your basement. Water in your walls or ceilings is not good—it will eventually cost you money in repairs. Warm, moist air travels from the warm side until it reaches a barrier and moisture forms on the cooler surface. If, for example, you install paper-backed insulation in your basement ceiling with the paper showing in the basement, all the insulation above it will be saturated with moisture as the water works its way from the warm side to the cool side. With the paper against the first floor, however, the moisture forms just under the floor, leaving the insulation dry and effective.

Lower demand for heating and cooling

Another benefit associated with reducing air infiltration, adding insulation, and installing better windows is the possibility of being able to install a smaller-capacity heating and cooling equipment when it's time to replace your furnace or air conditioner. Smaller-capacity equipment is less expensive to purchase and, in the case of heat pumps and air conditioners, provides more efficient operation.

Improved resale value for your home

Some home buyers ask to see the seller's heating bills for the past year. Your work toward energy efficiency can help improve your home's sales appeal. In addition, some mortgage companies request estimates of anticipated expenses in the buyer's home. Lower fuel bills might give your buyer more purchasing leverage.

Some basic questions to consider when insulating

Because insulation is something we consider only when we feel a draft or receive an outrageous power bill, our thoughts on the subject tend to be superficial. For a more informed perspective, ponder the following questions.

How much insulation is enough?

Insulation is measured and rated in R values. An R value is the amount of resistance to infiltration provided by 1 inch of the material being measured. A higher R value indicates greater insulation and protection. If you live in the northern or northeastern part of the United States or anywhere in Canada, it's recommended that you have enough insulation to provide R-19 in your outside walls and R-38 to R-40 in the ceilings below ventilated attics. In milder climates, R-11 in the walls and R-19 in the ceiling is sufficient. For more specific information, see Appendix E.

What improvements need to be made?

Before deciding on upgrades, consider your budget, the payback periods, your comfort, other potential benefits, and the estimated useful lives of alternatives. Remember that spending a little more money initially for an energy-efficient product or system often improves your comfort and makes financial sense in the long run.

An action plan for improving your home's insulation

When signals such as strong drafts appear, you'll know you have an insulation problem. How to confront the problem, however, is not always so obvious.

Moneysaver
Insulating your attic with 10 inches of fiberglass insulation cuts an estimated 30 percent off your fuel bill. (Heat rises, you know.)

A job where you can start at the top

First you should venture into your attic, into the space up through the trap door in your closet, or out through the small door in the knee-wall of your second floor bedrooms. If you don't see any insulation lying between the floor joists, get on the phone.

What to look for . . . bring a ruler

If you see something yellow or pink, that's good! To find out how much insulation you have, however, stick a ruler down between the insulation and a joist and measure the thickness of the insulation. To reach R-40, the fiberglass or rock-wool battens should come to the top of your 10-inch joists. If you have less than 10 inches, add enough new insulation to bring it up to 10.

Insulating an attic room

Timesaver
If you are adding fiberglass or rock wool to existing insulation in the attic, to achieve 10 inches of insulation, buy the type without any paper vapor barrier on either side. Your attic insulation already has a vapor barrier on the bottom side against the warmth of your house. You are now just adding to its insulation value by adding inches.

If your uninsulated attic has been finished off as extra living space and if you are doing your own installation, be sure to insulate the walls, the space between joists in the ceiling, and between the roof rafters for the slanted part of the ceiling. Make sure you leave room for ventilation between your new insulation and the roof. Don't block the air passage from the eaves to the roof ridge (the beam that runs the length of the house at the top).

If your attic is unfinished and needs new or additional insulation, you can probably do it yourself. If it is more complicated than you anticipated with new walls or a ceiling you can't get on top of, get help or buy a book designed for do-it-yourselfers.

Insulation in the walls of your home

Insulation in the outside walls is important. If you live in an older home with no insulation, however, it might not be worth the trouble and expense. Make an extra effort to seal all the cracks and seams around your doors, windows, baseboards, and electrical outlets and get some storm windows. Try to stop the direct inflow of air from the outside.

There are a couple of things you can do to improve your outside wall insulation.

- **Insulation opportunities during remodeling.** If you're tearing off wallboard during a remodeling project, insulating is a breeze, so to speak, and is undoubtedly part of your contractor's plans.

- **Insulating walls as they stand.** This can best be done by a blown-in or loose-fill insulation (see the upcoming section "Types of Insulation Available"). This method can be difficult and expensive, but in a very cold climate, it's worth it. You can also attack the problem from the outside. If you are re-siding your house, a vapor barrier and rigid insulation can be applied to the outside before the new siding goes on.

The cost-payback check

Insulating your walls can save 16 to 20 percent off your fuel bill. Figure out what 20 percent of your current heating cost is. Next figure how long that savings will take to repay the cost of the insulation, based on your contractor's estimates. Then decide whether it makes sense to pursue it.

Types of insulation available

Insulation falls into six basic categories (with some overlap): batts and blankets, loose-fill, blown-in, foamed, rigid-core, and reflective.

Batts and blanket insulation

Batts and blankets are the insulation type seen most frequently today. They are also the easiest for the

Unofficially...
A fact to consider when insulating walls: Homes constructed using 2 × 4 studs (the norm in all older homes as well as some new ones) can never achieve insulation values higher than R-9. Homes constructed using 2 × 6 studs allow a sufficient thickness of insulation to reach R-19.

homeowner to install. The insulating material is usually either fiberglass or rock-wool fibers. Batts come in precut strips; blankets are in continuous rolls from which you cut lengths to fit.

Both forms can be simply fitted into the space or stapled to the wood. In your basement ceiling (another good place to insulate), the paper or foil side should face toward the heated or conditioned space. It is common to hold the insulation in place with wire hangers or a length of stiff wire a little longer than the space between the joists. Bend it slightly to insert it; it will hold the batts or blankets in place.

Batts and blanket insulation is affordable, can be installed easily, and is available at most building-supply stores. A utility knife is the best tool for cutting insulation. Wear gloves and long sleeves, especially when working with fiberglass. It won't kill you, but it does itch.

Loose-fill insulation

Loose-fill insulation is designed to be poured, blown in, or stuffed in place. It can be made from several different materials: fiberglass, rock wool, cellulosic fiber, expanded vermiculite (made from mica ore), and perlite (made from volcanic rock). Loose-fill materials come in bags or bales and work well in accessible attics or to fill wall cavities, including cinder-block walls.

Cellulosic insulation

Cellulosic insulation, a variety of loose-fill, is made from recycled newspapers and wood fiber treated with a fire retardant. It can be used in both walls and attics. It does not need vapor barriers because it is a moisture-storage material and can accept and release moisture freely.

Timesaver
Be sure to measure the space between your rafters or wall studs before buying insulation. Both forms of insulation come in widths of 15 and 23 inches to fit various construction methods; you won't have to trim them to fit.

Blown-in loose-fill insulation

Blown-in insulation, as the name implies, is blown into wall cavities using special pneumatic equipment best run by professionals. In its early days, cross-members between wall studs and settling would leave uninsulated voids. An expert installer and some adhesive additives solve these problems. The materials used for blowing can be cellulose, loose mineral fibers, fiber pellets, or fibers coated with adhesive.

Foamed or sprayed-in-place insulation

Foamed or sprayed-in-place insulation usually is polyurethane and should be installed by professionals. It provides a high R value, doesn't shrink or settle after application, and does a good job of getting into all the odd spaces to block drafts. It is a barrier to moisture. Foams and sprays are best used in new construction around foundations, in walls, and on beamed ceilings. It is comparatively expensive, however.

Rigid-board insulation

Rigid-board insulation is made from various materials: polystyrene, polyurethane, polyisocyanurate, and asphalt-impregnated fiber board. Rigid panels can be used as roof insulation under shingles, wall sheathing under siding, or around foundations.

According to code, polyurethane insulation must not be left exposed because of its potential combustibility. It is usually covered with a half-inch of wallboard or drywall. Rigid panels are usually covered on one or both sides with foil facing to increase the R value.

Reflective insulation

Reflective insulation is made from aluminum foil and is most effective in hot regions because it blocks

Bright Idea
New and better products and ideas for insulation appear on the market every day. Talk to your insulation contractors for a solution that best fits your needs.

radiant heat. As flat sheets, it simply blocks heat transfer through roofs. In multiple layers with air spaces, it becomes a barrier for reducing heat gain through roofs, ceilings, floors, and walls.

TABLE 11.1: THE RELATIVE R VALUES OF INSULATION MATERIALS

Material	Inch Thickness
Fiberglass batt and blanket	3.27 to 4
Rock-wool batt and blanket	3.2 to 3.7
Fiberglass loose-fill, blown	2.2 to 3.3
Rock-wool loose-fill, blown	2.9 to 3.6
Cellulose loose-fill, blown	3.6 to 3.8
Vermiculite loose, poured	2.27
Perlite fill, poured	2.2
Sprayed-on polyurethane	6 to 7.3
Fiberboard sheathing	1.32
Expanded polystyrene Extruded	5
Molded	3.85 to 4.35
Polyisocyanurate board Unfaced	5.8 to 6.2
Faced	7.1 to 8.7

R values, properties, and uses of various insulation materials

Batt or blanket insulation

- Used for crawl spaces or basement ceilings and walls

- Typically made from fiberglass, also available in mineral or rock, wool, cotton, and some new types of fiberglass

- R-3.1 to R-4.3 per inch

- Available in R-11, R-13, R-15, R-19, R-21, R-30, and R-38

- 2×4 cavity can be up to R-15, 2×6 cavity can be up to R-21, 2×8 cavity can be up to R-21, 2×10 cavity can be up to R-38.

- Available with or without a vapor barrier

Blown insulation: wet spray fiberglass and cellulose

- Made from fiberglass fibers or treated cellulose (recycled newspapers)

- Mixed with a small amount of adhesive, which allows materials to stick to vertical wall surfaces

- R-3.0 to R-4.0 per inch

- 2×4 walls (cavity) can be R-10.5 to R-14, 2×6 walls (cavity) can be R-16.5 to R-22

- No inherent resistance to moisture transmission

- Can provide very good resistance to air leakage

Blown insulation: spray foams

- Used for crawl spaces or basement ceilings and walls as well as for air sealing of holes and cracks

- Made from various types of foam

- R-3.6 to R-6.2 per inch

- 2×4 walls (cavity) can be R-12.6 to R-21.7, 2×6 walls (cavity) can be R-19.8 to R-34.1

- Most provide good inherent resistance to moisture transmission

- Provides very good resistance to air leakage

Foam sheathing

- Used for slab perimeter, basement or crawl-space walls, and air sealing of large holes

- Common types: expanded polystyrene or EPS (white, beaded appearance), R-4.0 to R-4.5 per inch; extruded polystyrene or XPS (various colors, smooth surface), R-5.0 per inch; ure-thanes and isocyanurates (yellowish, often foil-faced), R-6 to R-7 per inch

- Can be applied on top of roof rafters (for cathedral ceilings) and between layers of sheathing

- Available in thicknesses starting at one-half inch

- Provides more consistent insulation because fewer interruptions are made for framing members

- Material itself provides good to very good resistance to moisture transmission

Polyethylene sheeting

- Used over bare earth in crawl spaces and at the exterior of basement walls

- Sometimes applied directly behind drywall (appropriate in northern climates only)

- Provides very good resistance to air leakage, if installed properly

- Provides very good resistance to moisture movement, if installed properly

- Used primarily (with foam/caulk) to seal off cracks and to keep out air, does not possess much of an R rating

Spray foam/caulk

- Used to seal small cracks and holes, such as around chimneys, pipes, ducts, and wires

- Provides very good resistance to air leakage

- Provides very good resistance to moisture movement

Savings

The following information indicates the estimated annual heating and cooling savings (per 100 square feet of wall) that can be expected from upgrading a basement wall with no insulation to the new insulating value.

- R-7 continuous, draped blanket $13.70
- R-11 within 2 ¥ 4 framed wall $14.55
- R-11 continuous, draped blanket $15.20
- R-13 within 2 ¥ 4 framed wall $15.50

(Based on a house with an 80-percent AFUE furnace and a 6.5 SEER air conditioner in the climate of Baltimore, MD. Fuel prices are $0.08 per kilowatt-hour and $0.55 per therm.)

This fact sheet was prepared by NAHB Research Center (400 Prince George's Boulevard, Upper Marlboro, MD 20774; 800-638-8556) with support from the U.S. Department of Energy and the National Renewable Energy Laboratory.

Other ways to improve your home's energy efficiency

Since you're insulating to improve your home's use of energy, you might go the additional mile and consider some of the actions discussed in the following sections.

Thermostat settings

If you have a setback thermostat, you should use it. If you have one of the newer, more sophisticated models, you can set up multiple setback schedules for workdays and weekends. This enables you to lower energy usage while maintaining comfort and convenience. For the most part, you should be able to forget about the thermostat after it's set. Even if you don't have a setback thermostat, you can still realize savings. It just takes the additional effort of changing the temperature manually.

Better insulation around new windows

Spray low-expansion foam between the window frame and the wall framing (instead of stuffing insulation, as is commonly done).

Window location and size

New dual-pane windows might not show a dramatic improvement in your energy usage, but you should be aware that windows can provide a net energy gain by allowing the sun's rays to fall on the glass during the winter (when the sun is lower) and by blocking the rays with shading in the summer (when the sun is higher). When planning your remodeling project, try to reduce the area of windows facing east and west to avoid summer heat gain. Try to properly shade windows with overhangs and awnings, and take advantage of any trees on your property as a shield against summer's hotter sun.

Watch Out!
The installation of new skylights is not necessarily a good idea. They almost always let in more heat in the summer and drain heat in the winter. Also, the morning sun shining in on the bed can be an unwelcome wake-up call for light sleepers.

Don't get too carried away with insulating

According to the recommended minimum air-exchange rate, at least a third of the air in a house should be exchanged every hour. Many older homes replace all the air every hour. Some energy-efficient houses built today, however, have leakage rates as low as 0.05 natural air changes per hour. This is too tight and calls for the use of controlled mechanical ventilation to ensure occupant health and comfort. It *is* possible to have too much of a good thing.

Use of hot water

To use less water and energy, consider low-flow shower heads and aerators for other faucets. (This, in my opinion, takes much of the pleasure out of showering, but you should be aware of the advantages.) Water and energy can also be saved by running washing machines and dishwashers only when full. In the case of washing machines, cold water can be used for virtually all loads. Although this does not save water, using cold water instead of hot saves energy. When buying a new washing machine or any electrical appliance, look for the most energy-efficient models. The new front-loading washing machines are the most efficient because they use much less water than top-loading models. (They also are gentler on your clothes and can handle larger loads.)

In the kitchen

Energy can be saved by air-drying dishes in the dishwasher rather than using the heated dry cycle. Cleaning the coils at the back of your refrigerator can help reduce energy use and can extend the life of the refrigerator, and periodic defrosting of your freezer unit will increase its efficiency. When cooking, use a microwave whenever possible. Not only do microwaves use less energy than conventional ovens or stoves to achieve the same result, they contribute less to the heat that must be removed by air-conditioning in the summer (and you thought they were just for re-heating your coffee!).

Lighting

You should look into installing compact fluorescent lights (CFLs). Although they are more expensive than the incandescent bulbs normally used, they have a much longer life and use less energy. These fluorescent bulbs now fit in most lamps and overhead light fixtures, and they turn on instantly. Remember, one of the best ways to save energy used for lighting is to turn off lights when they're not needed. (This is a rule you can enforce more effectively after your kids have moved out.)

Moneysaver
If you keep an old refrigerator in the basement for extra cold storage, consider whether it really is needed. Refrigerators are often the biggest energy users in the house. If you need the extra food-storage space, buy a larger refrigerator when remodeling or put a new chest-type freezer in the basement.

Where to get help with your insulation

If you live in an older home that is in obvious need of additional insulation, it can be tough to know where to begin. Here are a few sources for advice:

- **Your contractor.** If you are already doing a home improvement project, much of your new insulation will be installed by the contractors you have already hired for your remodeling, new roof, new windows, or new siding jobs.

- **Your utility company.** If you decide to tackle insulation as a project in itself, you can get help and advice from your electric-utility company. Your fuel-delivery company might offer a service or know of someone else who does. They might also be able to recommend firms that can do the work.

- **Specialists.** For blown-in and foam insulation, you need professional help. Professional firms should be listed in your Yellow Pages, or you can contact their associations.

- **An infrared portrait of your home.** This service involves taking an infrared photo of the outside of your house on a cold winter day. All the escaping heat shows up as red blobs on a negative. Our house looked like one big blob—this alerted us to a big need.

Just the facts

- You don't have to wait for a big remodeling project to upgrade your electrical system; it can be done one room at a time without major interruption.

- Stop the inflow of cold air from the outside (or warm air during the hotter seasons) by caulking around windows and doors.

- Improve the efficiency of your heating or cooling equipment.

- Insulate your home so the air on the inside is not adversely affected by the air on the outside.

- Remember that basic insulation rules call for R-17 to R-19 in the side walls and R-30 or better in the attic; the higher you can raise the R values, the better your insulation will be.

Things That Need Fixing

PART VI

GET THE SCOOP ON...
How long appliances should last ▪ Whether
appliance fixing is still an option ▪
When you should fix it yourself ▪ When and
where to get it fixed ▪ Service—what to look
out for and how to protect yourself ▪
Warranties—what they cover and for how long

When Appliances Quit: Fix or Replace?

Chapter 12

We keep an amazing number of gadgets around our homes, each with the potential of breaking. These gadgets range from pencil sharpeners, can openers, and heating pads to microwave ovens, TV and stereo consoles, refrigerators, and stoves.

The good thing about home appliances (as opposed to your car) is that, when an appliance breaks down, you are usually warm and comfortable. You don't have to walk anywhere in the rain. Granted, timing is important. An oven that quits on Thanksgiving morning with a 24-pound bird in its craw and 30 relatives about to descend may outweigh a dead battery at 2 a.m. at a suburban train station. By and large, however, appliance breakdowns are more of a nuisance than a real inconvenience. You have time to consider your options for getting your appliance back on its feet.

This chapter will help you decide whether to fix it yourself, get it fixed, or get a new one. It also covers manufacturers' warranties and the value of extended warranties.

How long appliances should last

Chances are, you and your spouse are actually the major reason you replace appliances in your house. These decisions are often made not because your present equipment has broken but because you want some refined feature or convenience available only on new models. For instance, your present point-and-shoot 35-mm camera might work just fine, but you want a zoom lens. Your coffee maker is still perking along perfectly, but you want your coffee on a timer so it is waiting for you when you come downstairs in the morning.

The table on the following page appears in the *Consumer Reports Buying Guide* for 1998. Consumer Reports used *Appliance* magazine, a Dana Chase publication, as its source. A product's useful life depends on its actual durability and intangibles such as your own desire for some attribute or convenience available only on a newer model. These estimates are from manufacturers and trade associations.

Should you fix it yourself?

The first question to ask yourself is, "Do I want this item fixed or am I tired of it?" Some modern products never die completely; only parts or pieces of them die. The oven timer doesn't work anymore, but you've learned to watch the clock. Your stereo system doesn't play tapes anymore, but it still has a fine FM radio.

We tend to forget exactly how long we have owned an appliance and how different its replacement is going to be. The one obsolete item you are most likely aware of is your computer. When you

Moneysaver
New construction methods and the use of circuit boards instead of wires and tubes have reduced the cost of many household products to the point where it is simpler to throw away the old and buy new than to repair.

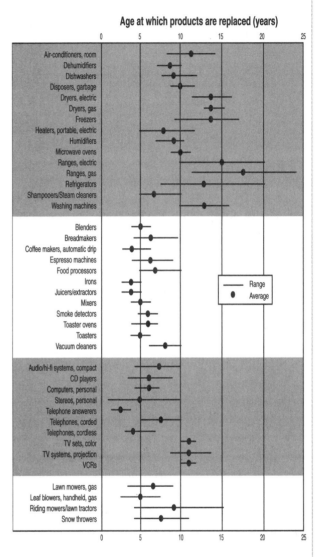

Age at which products are replaced (years)

How long things last. (*Appliance* magazine)

bought it five years ago, the amount of memory on your hard drive or the speed of your modem was more than you thought you'd ever use. Now you hesitate even to offer it to your kids for their homework and games.

If a personal-grooming product such as a hair dryer or an electric toothbrush stops, your first reaction might be to try to fix it yourself. Don't. (If I have to tell you to make sure you unplug it first, you shouldn't be doing this sort of thing.) Throw it away and get a new one. Even if you have some mechanical abilities, you probably will find there is no way for you to apply them. With the advent of molded plastic bodies and crimped or welded connections instead of screws, nuts, and bolts, you can't even get to the parts without breaking and entering.

I also recommend that you never try to fix your own TV set or stereo equipment. Some appliances, however, such as your washer and dryer, can be taken apart with a screwdriver or the right hex-nut tool so you can get to the inside where a broken fan belt awaits your attention. Often, the manuals that come with the equipment can guide you through simple repairs. If you get stuck, you can call the manufacturer or the store where you originally bought the appliance for advice. The manufacturer will either send you a new part or tell you where you can find one.

Fortunately, some of the most expensive appliances—washing machines, dryers, and stoves—still have some mechanical innards that can be repaired by the average home mechanic. The following are some sources for guidance:

- Go to the owner's manual that came with the appliance. If you're lucky, it will be complete enough to take you through some simple repairs and to tell you how to order parts.

- There are many books offering general fix-it-yourself advice, such as Consumer Reports Books, Time-Life Books, and Readers' Digest Books. One amazing book by J. T. Adams titled, *How to Buy, Repair, and Maintain Home Systems and Appliances* (Arco Publishing, 1981) is over 1,000 pages long with 800 illustrations. Pick up any one of these at your library or bookstore and follow the directions offered.

- Go back to where you bought the appliance. Radio Shack and Sears, among others, have service departments that offer advice, sell parts, and take over when you give up. If your appliance is at home when you go to the repair department or call in, make sure you know the model number, the serial number, and the date of purchase. With both Sears and Radio Shack, you usually don't need to have your sales receipt in hand. You'll already be in their computer along with the item you purchased, its warranty period, the model number, and so on.

- Mass-marketers such as KMart usually carry some replacement parts such as carafes that go with various coffee makers.

- Call the manufacturer and ask for repair help. Most have a 24-hour customer-service line designed just for you.

Bright Idea
Designate one drawer in your house as the owner's-manual-and-warranty drawer and use it to hold all the paperwork that comes with each new appliance. Don't put off starting such a collection until you have time to get organized; it won't happen.

When and where to get it fixed

I once came home to a loud, annoying buzzing from the kitchen. After checking the various smoke alarms, I narrowed the problem down to the clock on the electric stove. I jiggled the knobs and managed to change the tone of the buzz but not stop it. I lifted the stove top and determined that the clock had no back panel. I endured the noise for half a day then went to the Yellow Pages to find a local appliance-repair company. Within two hours, an appliance repairman and I were standing together looking at and listening to my clock.

He didn't know how to get to the inside of the clock either. He did, however, come up with the brilliant idea of sending me down to the circuit breaker panel to switch the range's breaker off. This created a much more pleasant atmosphere for further discussion of what to do next. I learned several things:

- Although the appliance repair shop had a local listing, it actually was located several towns away and served most of the state. People tend to call local tradesmen for home service, so many shops make an effort to appear local.

- There is a house-call fee ($40 in my case) that must be paid whether or not any further repairs are necessary. If you decide to either purchase a new appliance or go ahead with the repairs, however, the $40 goes toward paying the bill.

- The repairman carried a price and labor guidebook with him and was able to tell me that replacing the clock on my stove would cost $249 and would take a couple of weeks to deliver. This price included a new clock and the labor to install it. I asked whether there was a way to disable the clock, thinking we could live without the timed-baking feature if we didn't have the noise. He said he couldn't do that but didn't tell me why. I assumed it was company policy.

The next step was to report all this activity to my wife, who felt it was ridiculous that he couldn't unhook the clock and sent me back for further negotiations. I called another local appliance dealer and discussed my problem with him. He asked whether the oven had a self-cleaning feature. I said it did. He said he would not disconnect the clock either because, if we used the self-cleaning feature in the future and forgot that the clock was disconnected, the oven would continue to heat and would not shut off, potentially causing a fire.

We discussed new stoves, or ranges, as they like to call them. I could buy a new range without the self-cleaning feature for a little over $500, and it could be delivered within a couple weeks. That settled the fix-the-clock issue; for the price of two clocks, we could have a new stove. Then, on one of my trips up from the basement after turning on the stove, I noticed that the grinding buzz wasn't there. I proceeded to set the clock and the buzz returned. The next time it stopped buzzing, I didn't fool around with the clock and it's still quiet. We got the reprieve that the repairman predicted could happen.

Basically, three types of service are available:

- **Factory service** is provided by some manufacturing companies, who maintain their own service centers or service fleets.

- **Authorized service** includes privately run repair shops accredited by manufacturers to fix their brands. Sometimes the store that sold you the equipment acts as an authorized repair service.

- **Independents** set up their own shops and have their own rules. Some retailers offer repairs in this category.

You should be aware of the following facts of appliance repair life:

Bright Idea
Examine the design of the controls on any appliance you buy. Do they make sense? In the 10 years we've used our stove, we've never gotten comfortable with the arrangement of the top burner controls. They are all on one side of the control panel, and the two outside controls operate the two front burners. We still turn on the wrong burners unless we really concentrate.

- It will cost anywhere from $25 to $80 to find out whether your appliance can or should be fixed. This is sometimes called a *bench cost*—what a repairman charges just to investigate. If you decide to go ahead with the repair, that amount is credited to your bill. Even if you decide to toss the item, you still pay the basic fee.

- Be familiar with the cost to replace the appliance before you agree to repair the old one. Spending $30 to repair a coffee maker when a new one is only $25 doesn't make financial sense.

- Know what your warranty period is. Sometimes the hassle of locating an authorized repair facility, getting your proof of purchase together, and getting your equipment to the dealer is just not worth the effort. Warranty work must be done by an authorized dealer or it voids your warranty.

- Be prepared to make at least two trips. Nothing can be fixed while you wait. The two trips might be as much as a month apart, although two weeks for a repair is normal.

In January 1994, *Consumer Reports* magazine published their survey of approximately 7,000 readers who reported on nearly 18,000 large and small products they had had repaired between 1987 and 1992.

Three-quarters of the readers, when asked about recently broken items, reported that they simply threw them away if they were comparatively inexpensive items—blenders, blow dryers, portable stereos, telephones, and so on. One-third of the more expensive items—washing machines, televisions, vacuum cleaners, and so on—also went unfixed.

Moneysaver
When you take your appliance to a repair facility, let them know you want all the replaced parts returned to you. This cuts down on the odds of being cheated.

When asked what they did with the products they didn't fix, the readers responded as follows:

- More than 50 percent of the readers reported throwing away the cheaper items.

- About a quarter of the readers reported selling or giving away personal computers, lawnmowers, clothes dryers, color TVs, washing machines, refrigerators, microwave ovens, and vacuum cleaners.

- I was heartened to find a third category of which I am a member—people who keep the items and never use them. More than 50 percent of the respondents who had a broken camcorder or 35-mm SLR camera couldn't bring themselves to throw them away. The percentages of keepers went from 50 percent down to 30 percent for point-and-shoot cameras, tape decks, stereo equipment, personal computers, cordless phones, food processors, VCRs, answering machines, and electric razors.

Fixing an appliance yourself, however, seems to be the way to get more satisfactory service. About 78 percent of the readers who repaired their own equipment were satisfied with the results; only 70 percent of readers who paid for the service were satisfied. Respondents who did their own work had fewer problems thereafter than those who had others do the repairs. They also spent less, saving over $50 on average.

If you want to follow the trends, clothes dryers were the most self-repaired items, followed by lawn mowers, vacuum cleaners, ranges, washing machines, personal computers, dishwashers, and refrigerators. Don't be hesitant about calling the manufacturer of your appliance. Armed with your product's model number, serial number, and all the supporting instruction manuals, you can frequently get the help you need over the phone. You can also order parts this way.

Protecting yourself from scams

To get an idea of what goes on behind the counter in your local small or large appliance-repair shop, *Consumer Reports* had their engineers "spike" a few vacuum cleaners, VCRs, and washing machines. Their staff members then took them in for repairs in the New York, Chicago, and Los Angeles areas. The results were reported in the January 1994 issue.

The vacuum cleaner repair shops seemed to be where a person should be the most on guard. With only a frayed power cord to repair, three shops fixed the cord, added a $2 belt, and charged an average of $26. One took three weeks to do the work. Other vacuum-repair shops fixed the cord but also claimed to have replaced motor parts or bearings. No parts were actually replaced, and the bills came to $59 and $68.

The VCR-repair business can cost you even more. The nature of the repairs made on a "popped belt" problem actually could be the result of the technician looking for the cause. Some shops charge a bench fee simply to open the case (one was $20, another was $50). Two of the shops did the repair correctly, but one charged $50 and the other charged $90. Other shops were more creative and added parts for between $70 and $124.

The washing machine repair business seems to be in pretty good shape with both factory-authorized and independent repairers coming to your home and solving the simple problems simply. Costs for the calls ranged from $40 to $82, and the length of the wait for a service call ranged from a couple of days to three weeks. The independent repairman charged $60, which was less than the factory-authorized agent's $82.

You should ask the following questions before requesting a house call:

- Is there a trip charge? This is normal for nonwarranty work; it involves travel to your home plus a minimum labor fee. The basic house call usually is between $30 and $45. Find out ahead of time.

- Is the labor charge a flat fee or an hourly rate? If hourly, find out whether the repairmen work in 15-minute increments.

- If you have a large appliance such as a huge TV or an air conditioner, find out whether there is an extra charge if it has to go back to the shop.

- Find out what type of warranty the repair shop offers on its work. A 90-day warranty on parts and labor is not uncommon, but it can vary from shop to shop.

- Ask to receive all the replaced parts. This lets everyone know you are interested in what goes on and in your equipment (and in the shop).

Get the people who sell and deliver your new appliance to take the old one away even if you have a pick-up truck and four strong sons.

You should do the following before leaving your machinery at the repair shop:

- Get an estimate. Find out whether the service includes cleaning the equipment's innards.

- Find out how long the shop estimates the job will take. *Consumer Reports* found that slow service was the biggest complaint of its surveyed readers.

Bright Idea
Make removing and disposing of your old appliance part of the agreement to buy the new one. If a dealer does not agree to this, move on to one of his competitors. This is not a big deal for them, but it can be a major pain (literally) for you.

- Again, ask for the replaced parts.

- Get a claim check with a description of your item, its serial number, model number, and brand name. Have the clerk sign the claim check.

- Keep all receipts pertaining to work and service calls for your equipment. Get a written copy of the warranty and any extensions offered by the repairer.

One way to avoid the high cost and uncertainty of repairing large and small appliances is to buy appliances with a history of low maintenance and repair costs. *Consumer Reports* magazine publishes a buying guide at the beginning of each year. The guide summarizes all product and service studies done over the past year or two by the magazine and provides the results in concise, easy-to-read charts and lists. If you're contemplating the purchase of a new refrigerator, stove, or dishwasher, pick up a copy.

Manufacturers' warranties

The manufacturer's warranty is your best back-up for service in case a product breaks down early. The average warranty is about 90 days for parts and labor; some go up to a year for manufacturing defects. If your purchases seem to hold up beautifully until the 91st day and you want additional protection at no or little additional cost, just purchase your equipment with an American Express card, some standard Visas or MasterCards, or any gold or platinum card. These double the manufacturer's warranty period for up to one year.

Major appliance warranties

The manufacturers' warranties that come with major appliances vary, but a "full-year warranty to repair, without charge, a defect or malfunction occurring during the first year after date of purchase by the original consumer-owner" (quoted from Frigidaire) is pretty standard. Frigidaire also guarantees the refrigerating system for a full four-year term from the second through fifth years.

The range warranty from Frigidaire is for one year from the date of purchase. In comparison, Sears Roebuck offers a limited two-year warranty on its Craftsman Power Lawn Mower. This warranty covers workmanship and material defects if you have taken proper care of your mower.

Extended warranties: worth the cost?

If you have shopped for any big-ticket power tools, appliances, or electronics lately, you have probably noticed that, immediately after buying the product, you are asked to buy an extended warranty on the item you just bought. *Consumer Reports* recommends that you don't buy these extended warranties because most problems with new purchases (especially electronic equipment) will show up almost immediately. After they pass the initial 90-day period, they may well run for years.

I do, however, recommend buying an extended warranty for power lawn mowers. The chances of running over tree roots, rocks, and small garden tools are high enough to justify some additional protection.

When to replace appliances

Fixing appliances and all the electronic gear around your house can be a time-consuming, frustrating,

Unofficially...
Warranty statements are surprisingly short. They usually state that the manufacturing company will fix anything caused by a defect in workmanship or materials. They also specify how long the warranty is valid: 60 days, 90 days, one year, two years, and so on.

and costly task. Fortunately, the cost of many replacement appliances has dropped over the past few years. It now makes little sense to repair a phone, an answering machine (particularly if it isn't digital), or even CD players and TVs if they are between 5 and 10 years old.

Maybe you're happy with 13 channels on your snowy TV, and you don't see anything difficult about getting up to change the channel or to turn up the volume. I'll bet, however, that you could adjust as fast as the rest of us to the magic and power a TV remote bestows on its possessor. You might have to face the fact that you or your spouse wants new gear while the old gear still works. You might not live long enough to wear out your old Canon 35-mm camera, but do you really want to miss out on auto-focus, panoramic pictures, or the new digital cameras?

If it bothers you to throw something away before it breaks down completely, you might be able to donate it to your local high school, church, or Salvation Army branch (although they seem to be getting a little picky these days). Go out and get some good stuff.

Just the facts

- Save the warranties and instruction manuals in one place.

- No appliance lasts forever, as the chart at the beginning of the chapter shows. Most of the products in our home have a life expectancy.

- The best chance you have of being happy with a product and having it serve you long and well is by buying smart to begin with.

- Research any item you want to purchase with *Consumer Reports* or one of the many specialty magazines. They may already have run exhaustive tests on the product you are considering. Most libraries have back issues of these magazines.

- When something eventually breaks, the question is whether to fix it yourself, get it fixed, or buy a new one. It's perfectly acceptable to give up and replace an appliance.

GET THE SCOOP ON...
Facing up to an interior face-lift ▪ Fast-buck
artists ▪ Painting and papering options ▪
Lead-based paint

Refurbishing Inside Your Home: Paint and Wallpaper

Chapter 13

Painting the walls and woodwork inside a house is something most people think they can do themselves. The necessary tools are either somewhere in the basement or are inexpensive to replace. And everyone knows how to paint. Right?

I had a long talk with the owners of a paint store. A hardware store also can pass along secrets for getting a paint or papering job done, whether you do it yourself or hire someone. I also learned what we lost when lead disappeared from the paint scene.

This chapter shows you how to find a good painter or papering contractor and how to recognize tactics used by some to get a little more income from the job than they deserve. I won't tell you what colors to use, but I can introduce you to the differences between water-based paints and oil-based paints and between a $23 gallon of paint and $12 gallon (besides the price). I'll also try to give you some idea of what to expect when a painter or a wall-papering contractor arrives, and I'll share a nice compromise I discovered between a professional job and doing it myself. Finally, in the unlikely event you discover that the paint on your walls contains lead, I'll give you some advice on how to handle it.

How do you know you need an interior wall face-lift?

If you're male, chances are you'll never notice the need for new paint or wallpaper. Women seem to have a lower tolerance for faded, soiled, chipped, and peeling walls than men.

I was able to fend off the inevitable for a few months with concerns about the cost, and a vague promise to do it myself when I got the time. I had, after all, done the first repainting five years earlier with yellow walls in the great room and a nice green in the living room. I had not, however, bothered with the woodwork or ceilings. I knew crunch time had arrived when my wife started looking up painting contractors in the phone book. For three weeks last August, I researched interior painting for this book by painting. When it was done, I had to admit that the house looked a lot better. It really had been time to repaint.

How the removal of lead affected paint

We've heard a lot lately about the harm leaded paint can cause to adults and especially to children. There's no question that it was a wise decision to get rid of lead in paint, but I never knew how its removal affected paint's durability.

We are paying a price for safety. Paint with lead would last between 5 and 10 years on the outside of

Unofficially...
One change brought about by new paint standards is the loss of paint that can be applied at 32 degrees. The current recommended temperature for painting is now at least 50 degrees air temperature and 50 degrees surface temperature.

a house before repainting was necessary. The life expectancy of a paint job now is between three and five years. The next round of protection, which came into effect in 1998, is an effort to make paint more environmentally safe. It is an effort to make paint more Volatile Organic Compounds (VOC) compatible.

The owner of a Benjamin Moore paint store pointed out that his company dropped lead as an ingredient in paint over 17 years ago and was already working on new formulas to meet the new standards.

Hiring a painting contractor

Most people know how to wield a paintbrush, and many have painted a room or two. Sometimes, however, our limited painting experience causes us to underestimate the skill of a professional painting contractor. Painting is about more than slinging paint. It involves doing prep work, understanding surfaces, selecting the right paint, paying attention to detail, and getting the job done right with the least disruption. While you might hire your neighbor's teenage son to save you the trouble of mowing the lawn, you wouldn't consider hiring him to put on a new roof. Don't confuse your painting project with mowing the lawn. In all but the simplest cases, your painting needs are best left to the pros. In all likelihood, you and a professional painter are about as similar as a two-finger typist and Vladimir Horowitz.

How do you locate good painters?

Once again, ask your neighbors and friends for recommendations. In addition, you can add your local paint specialty stores to your list. A paint store

Bright Idea
Even paint store owners who are willing to give you names of painters will advise you to check their references by talking to past clients. You also should look for someone with at least five years of experience in the painting business.

manager will know most of the painters in your area and can probably give you four or five names.

The lead time necessary to start a painting job is much less than the lead time required by most contractors in construction. There are no elaborate drawings, no town approvals, and no waiting for delivery of materials or components. Work can start whenever you want, depending on your painter's availability. In the middle of summer, this could prove to be a problem. The better the painter is, the longer you might have to wait.

You still need a proposal or a contract in which your painter should outline what he will do, when he will do it, how long the job should take, and how much the labor and paint will cost.

How to spot the less-than-honorable contractors

There are some well-meaning but incompetent or simply inexperienced painters in the business. You shouldn't have to pay for on-your-job training. There also are techniques for ripping off homeowners.

One such technique is to charge the client for a high-quality paint and then buy the least expensive brand. One paint store owner described a scene in which a lady who was getting her home painted came in for an additional gallon of paint for her painter. The owner charged her $12, and she questioned whether he had made a mistake on the cost. Her painter had been charging her $24 a gallon for the same paint.

There's also another level in this scam. Painters have been known to buy $12 paint with their contractor's discount and then charge the client $24 plus a 15 percent commission. Always go to the store and find out the price of the exact paint you want.

What you should expect when the painter comes

If your only experience with interior painting is doing it yourself, you'll be surprised how long it takes for your professional painter to actually open a can of paint.

The following is a list, more or less in order, of the steps involved in painting one room of your house:

1. The painter, possibly with a partner, moves all your furniture into the middle of the room and covers the pile with a drop cloth. (If your home has a lot of delicate knickknacks or antiques, you might have to do your own moving for liability reasons.)

2. He then lays drop cloths on the floor around the walls.

3. Next he removes all the light-switch and electrical-outlet faceplates and takes down the ceiling and wall light fixtures. All the doorknobs are removed as well as all the locks on your windows and all the curtain-rod hardware, towel bars, and clothes hooks.

4. Finally, he gets to the surface of the walls and the woodwork, but not with a paintbrush or roller. He now starts his prep work.

5. Prep work begins with spackling (applying a putty-like plaster compound to) all the nail holes, cracks, dents, and gaps in the walls and the woodwork. Your painter also should hammer in any popped nails and fill the resulting dents. He makes your carpenter look good by filling any gaps left by wood shrinkage or mistakes made by the finish carpenters.

6. Then he uses sandpaper on all the rough surfaces he has created and any hardened drips

Unofficially...
My son introduced me to a phrase that carpenters often use amongst themselves when they cut a miter a little off-line. "Don't worry. The painters will fix it."

and runs left by previous painting. He cleans the accumulated grease, grime, smoking residue (cigarette or fireplace), cobwebs, and dust from the surface.

7. The last step in the prep process is to caulk around every door and window frame and along the baseboard. Now your painter is ready to open a can of paint.

8. The next step is to apply a primer coat of paint to the walls and the ceiling. (There is even special paint for ceilings.) If you are moving from a darker color to a lighter color, you probably need a heavy primer, which is more opaque.

9. Finally, your painter gets to the part you thought you hired him for—painting your room. Invariably, two coats of paint are necessary. (One is never enough.)

Having a room painted puts the room out of commission for the duration of the job. Having two or more rooms painted at the same time is just as disruptive to your daily life as any remodeling project.

A good painter cleans his brushes, rollers, and paint pans at the end of each day. The room(s) itself, however, stays in a state of disrepair until the job is done.

Watch Out!
No matter how much time you spend in the paint store matching color cards to pictures in decorating magazines, the paint that shows up on *your* wall will look different.

It is impossible to pick a color with complete accuracy. So make sure you're home when the first coat goes on the wall . . . and after it dries. There's a chance you will be happy with the actual color and will be able to adjust. If you aren't and you can't, talk with your painter. The paint dealer can make subtle adjustments to lighten or darken the unused cans of paint.

Other considerations

Finding a contractor is only the first step on the road to a successful paint job. Dozens of decisions need to be made in terms of how you want the room to look. The following pointers can help you narrow your choices before you bring a professional into the mix.

What are your painting options?

Picking colors is only the first of many decisions you will make. The following are some of your options:

- **The amount of the shine in your paint.** The list of shine types is long, and varies among manufacturers, but it runs roughly from flat through matte, low-gloss, semi-gloss, and medium-gloss to high-gloss.

- **Water-based latex or acrylic paints.** These are the formulas of choice for most do-it-yourselfers because they go on fairly easily and dry quickly. Brushes and equipment can be cleaned in the kitchen sink.

- **Oil-based paint.** My paint dealer recommends oil-based paint for interior woodwork because it levels better and doesn't show brush marks. With the right cleaning agents, cleaning up brushes and equipment is not much more difficult than with water-based paints. He suggests using a roller on walls, whether using oil- or water-based paint, and a brush for woodwork.

- **High-end paint versus low-cost paint.** You can realize immediate savings by buying cheap; high-cost paint is at least twice the price of its lesser brother.

  The better paint doesn't have much in it that's different; it just has more of the good stuff such

Bright Idea
With the fast drying time of acrylic paints, two coats can be applied in the same day and missed spots can be touched up immediately. Oil-based paint should dry overnight before the second coat is applied.

as more and better titanium. You get less splatter and better coverage with good paint, and it stands up to repeated washings better. Talk this point over with your painter and factor in the length of time you plan to remain in your home.

- **Spray painting.** Water-based and oil-based paints can be applied with a spray gun and a compressor. This is now the method of choice in new construction and in commercial buildings; it is something best left to the professionals. The advantage is that the painting goes much faster. The disadvantage is that the coats are thinner. The final product is not quite as smooth as with rolling or brushing, but you probably won't notice the difference. You still need a primer coat and two finish coats. It also involves completely covering windows, the floor, and all woodwork with plastic.

A do-it-yourself compromise

If you're torn between doing it yourself to save money and an understandable reluctance to take on the responsibility, consider a compromise—painting your house with a professional or semi-professional. I did this last summer with a neighbor; together we painted 80 percent of my house.

The advantages are:

1. As a semi-professional painter, he showed up at 8 a.m. every morning, got us started, and worked until 4 p.m. with a half-hour off for lunch.

2. He did all the prep-work with the thoroughness it requires.

3. We divided up the jobs. I did the ceilings because, at 6'6" tall, I had a natural advantage. I

also did most of the walls. He did the skill jobs such as cutting-in the delicate area where the walls meet the ceiling and around windows and doors. He also did all the woodwork around the windows, doors, and baseboards.

4. He was able to spot the areas I missed. He also did the stairwell walls and ceilings from a ladder, saving me from likely injury.

5. This approach gave us two people to move the heavy bookcases, beds, and furniture out of the way. We also provided each other with company.

6. I think I saved a good percentage of the cost, and we did in three weeks what could have taken me months alone.

The following are a few clever and workable labor-saving devices for painting:

- **Paint pads** should replace rollers for walls and trim.

- **Paint pads with edge wheels** provide guides for edging (an essential painting tool).

- **The paint stick** sucks paint directly from the bucket into the handle. Paint is then fed into a roller by pushing down the plunger in the handle (another essential tool).

- **Foam paintbrushes** are cheap, hold more paint, and make neater, straight lines.

How long should it take and what will it cost?

How long it takes to paint depends on the size of the room(s), the condition of the walls, how many painters show up, the type of paint used, and the speed of the painters. Your painter, who will know most of these variables, can give you the best time estimate. Regarding costs, your painting contractor can take several different approaches.

- He can offer a flat rate (or firm) bid based on his estimate of the paint quality you want, the time estimated for the job, and the going local rate.

- He can charge based on time and materials. This is probably the fairest approach, with workers' time billed hourly plus the cost of the paint.

- He can use a different approach to the same method. Some painters, according to my paint dealer, buy the paint and pass on their contractor's discount to the client. Others take their discount and charge the customer the retail price, thus providing themselves a little extra profit.

Now you know enough to check with your painting contractor and his paint store before you sign the contract.

Dealing with the possibility of lead paint

If you recently bought an old house and don't know when it was last painted, or if you have somehow managed to avoid repainting your own house for the last 20 years, there might be lead-based paint on the walls.

Ninety percent of homes built before 1940 contain lead paint. It was more durable than other paint of the day and was usually used on hard working surfaces such as kitchen cabinets, door and window trim, exterior siding, and porch floors. It was used less frequently on interior walls and ceilings. Some lead paint was still being sold in the late 1970s, so if your house was built before then, there's a chance it was used.

Don't panic if you find or suspect lead paint. First, find out if you really have lead paint. If you are about to buy a pre-1978 house and you have young children, you might consider hiring a service to conduct a lead-hazard assessment. This involves using an x-ray fluorescence device that produces instant results. This service costs between $200 and $400 for an average-sized house.

Another way to check for lead is to send paint chips to a lab listed by the U.S. Environmental Protection Agency. You can also check lead levels with a home-testing kit. Make sure you sand or scrape a small area to get through several layers of paint. A drop of a solution on the exposed surface gives you results within five minutes. There are also some mail-in kits.

The best kits, as sampled and reported in the July 1995 issue of *Consumer Reports* magazine, are Acc-U-Test ($7) or The Lead Detective ($30) for light-colored paint and Know Lead ($15) or LeadCheck ($18) for dark-colored paint.

In the same article, *Consumer Reports* suggested that, if the lead paint is in good shape, simply covering it with wallpaper, paneling, or a thick coat of new paint can control the problem, probably even better than trying to remove it. The dust is far more dangerous than the paint.

Wallpapering for a design change

In the 1800s, virtually every wall of every home was wallpapered. Some papers were ornate and beautiful; many were cheap and ugly by today's standards. New homeowners of older homes often are confronted with layer after layer of wallpaper that must be laboriously removed before they can paint the walls. When these homeowners decide to remodel, it takes more effort to bring their look into the twentieth century.

Unofficially...
In the 1970s, when lead was at the top of the EPA hit list, crews attacked many run-down apartments with power sanders, scrapers, and heat guns, raising clouds of lead-laden dust that often did more harm to children than before the abatement efforts.

The use of wallpaper slowed over the years, but it managed to retain a pretty firm hold on certain rooms such as kitchens, nurseries, children's rooms, and bathrooms. Now it has moved back into consideration for any room in the house.

Like painting, wallpaper-hanging seems to be something everyone thinks they can do themselves. Some homeowners actually can manage, through luck or through mechanical skills, to do their own papering. Others start and then have to call a contractor to rescue them.

How do you know when and where to wallpaper?

The first clue is an overpowering urge to change the way your home looks. This feeling strikes many people—usually in the spring. This urge boosts the sales of decorating magazines and increases the number of visits to paint stores, home shows, and building supply warehouses. Now, I suggest you should broaden your search to include the wallpaper sections.

If your walls (and ceilings, for that matter) are in good shape—free of cracks, water stains, dirt, and grime—you're an immediate candidate. If your surfaces are not perfect or if they have old wallpaper already on them, new wallpaper is still a viable option; it'll just take more preparation.

Selecting your wallpaper

Upon entering the wallpaper department, you probably will first notice that, although most people still call it wallpaper, the term now covers wallcovering materials made from paper, fabric, vinyl, canvas, and other materials. The industry now refers to any material pasted on walls or ceilings as *wallcovering* rather than wallpaper.

Wallcoverings are priced in units called a *roll* or a *single roll*, but they only come packaged in multiple-roll bolts—double-roll or triple-roll bolts. A single roll contains about 36 square feet of material. Allowing for pattern-matching waste, however, you'll probably only get between 30 and 32 square feet of usable material out of each single roll.

To figure out the number of rolls you need, measure the width of each wall. Add all the wall widths together to calculate the perimeter of the room. Then multiply this number by the height of the walls (assuming all are the same height). It is recommended that you do not subtract for windows, doors, fireplaces, and so on. Measure as though all the wall surfaces are solid. Then divide the total by 30 to compute the number of single rolls you need; subtract one single roll for two average-sized windows or doors.

Bright Idea
Rather than figuring all these subtractions yourself, it is simpler to take your measurements to a dealer and let him compute the number of wallcovering rolls you need.

Should you hire a wallpaper contractor?

As I describe preparing your walls, matching the pattern, and actually removing and hanging wallpaper or wallcovering, you might have second thoughts about doing it yourself. If you are determined to give it try, however, there are some basic rules you can use to temper your enthusiasm. According to the people in my local hardware store, you might consider a contractor if:

- The room you plan to paper is too big and would take you too long to finish.

- It is a small room with many corners, angles, doors, or windows such as a bathroom, a powder room, or a breakfast nook.

- You have selected a wallcovering with a large repeating pattern such as big cabbage roses.

Wallpaper patterns usually repeat every 24 inches, but some go up to 30 inches. If you start in the wrong place, you can waste half your paper just trying to match it up.

What a wallcovering contractor will do for you

A contractor goes through the following steps as he takes on your wallcovering job. Remember, these are steps *you* must accomplish should you decide to do it yourself.

1. **Accurately measure the space.** First your contractor takes all the measurements of the room(s) to be done. He then goes with you to the supplier and advises you on the complications or appropriateness of your choice of wallcovering. He also helps you place the order.

2. **Prepare the walls.** Your wallcovering contractor starts by removing, unhooking, and unscrewing all the same items a painting contractor has to remove before he starts work. This includes light switches, wall plugs, and wall lamps. He leaves door handles and window fixtures in place, however.

   Preparing a wall for wallcovering means first filling all the cracks and holes, cleaning out water-damaged spots, and filling the gaps with spackling compound. You then need to smooth or sand any rough spots.

3. **Cover the old wallpaper.** If your wall currently is covered with old wallpaper, you might be able to leave it on and put new paper directly over it. This only holds true, however, if the old wallpaper was actually made of paper.

4. **Remove old wallcoverings.** Your contractor will
have to remove the old wallcovering if it is
chipped, coming loose at the edges, or too dark
or highly patterned to hide easily. If the walls
are covered with a vinyl or fabric wallcovering,
removal is not too difficult. Just work a corner
loose and start peeling it off. This technique
also works with strippable wallpaper or if a special strippable paste was used when it was originally hung. If you have an old house, however,
don't count on this.

Wallcovering removal techniques

With regular wallpaper, removal is not so easy. The
contractor has to soak the paper and then scrape it
off by hand. (He will know this at the start of the
project, so you can expect the estimate for the job to
include the extra time necessary.)

1. The quickest way to remove wallpaper is to use
a steamer that wets and loosens the paper so
it can be scraped off. These machines can be
rented from your wallpaper dealer or from a
tool-rental agency. The steamer looks like something from the Dark Ages, a miniature
kerosene-fired or electric boiler that makes
steam and sends it out through a hose to a flat,
perforated metal pan. When you hold this pan
against the wall, steam comes out through the
holes and saturates the paper so you can scrape
it off with a putty knife. (Use a wide-bladed
knife or you'll be there forever.)

2. Your contractor will also know how to remove
wallpaper without a steamer. There are special
wallpaper-removing liquids that you can mix
with water. They can be applied with a large

Watch Out!
Canvas or vinyl
wallcoverings
should never be
hung over old
wallpaper. If you
are unsure of the
proper procedure,
check the manu-
facturer's instruc-
tions that come
with the new
material.

sponge, a brush, or even a garden-type sprayer. Saturate the papered surface. Let it soak for a few minutes and then scrape. The liquid softens and penetrates better than plain water and makes it easier and quicker to remove the old paper.

3. You might encounter some special problems. If your wallpaper has been painted over or protected with a plastic coating, none of the preceding methods of removal will work because the water or steam cannot penetrate the surface. The way around this is to scratch the surface with coarse floor-sanding sandpaper. Rub it back and forth over the surface so water can penetrate.

4. After the old paper has been removed (and my advisers tell me that anything can be removed), the wall should be thoroughly scrubbed with hot water and detergent to remove any remnants of old paste or adhesive. Allow the wall to dry and apply sizing, a form of sealer, before hanging the new wallcovering.

Preparing the new surface

You are about to install a new wallcovering that is perfect and beautiful. The time will probably come, however, when you or someone in the family will tire of this covering. You will get some new furniture that just doesn't fit the old decor, and you will want to do the room over. Now that you have discovered how difficult it can be to remove old wallcoverings, make sure your contractor takes precautions with the products he uses to apply this new wallcovering.

When you get down to the bare wall, you might find that it was painted dark brown prior to the

Bright Idea
A new tool on the market, the Paper Tiger, looks like a palm sander but has a series of rotating burred wheels inside. These wheels penetrate the coatings on your wallpaper, making water penetration possible. The only power required is you or your contractor.

application of the wallpaper you just had so much trouble removing. Now is a good time for you to learn that most wall coverings are not opaque—whatever is under them can show through. This is particularly a problem with deep earth-tone colors such as brown and red.

Your previous owner's cabbage roses or scotch-plaid wallpaper might haunt you if you simply paper over it. Your contractor should prime the old surface with something akin to Wall Prep, a primer-like product which is brushed on, and which includes sizing. Wall Prep can even be tinted to match the color of the new wallcovering. Here's one more bit of hiding lore you might need: Don't count on anything yellow (paint or wallpaper) to hide anything under it.

What are some of your wallcovering options?

It wouldn't surprise me if wallcovering stores have lower heating or cooling bills than average because of the tons of wallcovering sample books that line their walls. The selection at wallcovering stores is endless, and many homeowners spend days, weeks, even months thumbing through samples, trying to make the perfect selection. Some wallcovering stores even provide coffee and snacks to keep their long-selecting customers awake and nourished.

Your contractor or the store's personnel can explain the basic categories of wallcoverings. They include:

- **Paper wallcoverings.** You already know about these. They include pre-pasted coverings that you simply dip in water.

- **Vinyl wallcoverings.** A good choice for your bathroom, a young child's room, the kitchen, and dirty-handed traffic areas.

Timesaver
Make your next wallcovering removal a breeze. Have your contractor apply a coat of sizing to the bare wall. Use special strippable paste and a strippable wallcovering, if it comes in a pattern you like.

Bright Idea
If your walls are a real mess or you have wood paneling you want to change, look into wall liners. They go on like wallpaper but act like a thin coat of new plaster to smooth walls with cracks, holes, and imperfections. A single roll is 19 inches wide and 30 feet long. It would take about 8 rolls to do a 12 × 12–foot room.

- **Textured wallcoverings with embossed designs.** Offer subtle, three-dimensional effects in a variety of designs.

- **Printable wallcoverings.** For people who want to create their own designs with paint and stencils, sponge prints, rubber stamps, rag prints, rolled-rag prints, or balled-up newspaper prints. Don't laugh. There are contractors (or perhaps we should call them artists) who do this type of work. It makes it possible to exactly match difficult-to-find shades in your rug or other room features.

- **Wall murals.** You can feature historic or rural scenes in your living room or numerous children's scenes containing favorite cartoons or story-book characters in a child's room.

- **Flocked and fabric wallcoverings.** These are available in rich colors and designs.

How do you locate a capable wallcovering contractor?

In addition to collecting recommendations from people you know, you can broaden your search by including painters. Many wallcovering contractors also are painting contractors, although not every painter takes on wallcover hanging.

Wallcovering contractors do not need to be licensed in most states; consequently, it is easy for anyone to set himself up in the business. It is a demanding trade; there is always a steady flow of people getting into and out of the business. This can make it difficult for your local wallpaper or hardware store personnel to recommend contractors.

What are the possible scams or shortcuts you might encounter?

It's possible to wind up with someone who is incompetent, but with wallcovering, this is easy to spot quickly. The easiest way for a contractor to short-change you is to charge you for high-priced material and then buy it more cheaply. I suggest you have your contractor help you select at least the type of wallcovering you use; you might as well check out the price and manufacturer while you're there. Your selection probably has to be ordered. Stores keep lots of pattern books, but they try not to carry too many rolls of wallpaper on site.

Your contractor might have a trade discount at the store. I suggest you let him have the percentage he can make on the transaction. It helps pay for the time he has spent holding your hand and estimating the job. He may or may not offer to share it with you.

You probably have to buy the wallcovering up front, but don't pay a lot in advance for the job. If it's a long job, some interim payments might be all right, but make sure enough of the cost—let's say 25 percent—remains to be paid upon completion so it will be worth his time to finish.

What can you expect to pay for a wallcover-hanging contractor?

As was the case with other types of contractors, the many variables make it impossible for me to give you a hard and fast price range. There are, however, some guidelines you can use. Cost variables include the following:

- The cost of the wallcovering is the most wide-ranging number in your calculations. A single roll can cost anywhere from $13 to $65 or more.

- A ballpark figure for the hourly wage of a wall-covering contractor is between $20 and $30.

- Methods of bidding on jobs can vary. Contractors might charge a certain cost per hour or a cost per square foot of covering. You might get the square-foot cost for a large, fairly square room and the hourly cost for a small, many-angled bathroom.

- Another variable is the pattern you select. Some intricate patterns can be a challenge to match up; others are simple. Some create a lot of waste if not started properly and even then can be costly. (If your contractor is there when you make the final selection, he should be able to alert you to this problem.)

What warranties can you expect?

Your contractor might warranty his work for up to a year to protect against your wallcovering coming loose, peeling, bulging, or wrinkling. Some wall-covering manufacturers warrant their products—particularly the prepasted type—against peeling, edge-lifting, and design flaws. Ask about both types of warranty.

When asked for a summary of his hints to potential homeowners who want to install wallcovering, Chris Wolf of Ken's Hardware advised, "Make sure you measure correctly, have patience, and recognize when a job is beyond your capability."

I am indebted to the Consumers Union edition of *The Complete Guide to Home Repair and Maintenance* by Bernard Gladstone for some of the information in this chapter about preparing walls for and removing wallcoverings. I have not gone into the intricate details of how to actually hang wallcoverings because this is, after all, a book about hiring contractors. If you decide to do your own hanging, Gladstone's book offers detailed, step-by-step instructions and many illustrations showing this fine and demanding art.

Just the facts

- The most essential part of both painting and papering is thoroughly preparing the walls before you start.

- Know the cost of the paint or wallcovering you select; this helps your contractor avoid the temptation to switch qualities or costs on you.

- Apply your wall coverings with the assumption that you will be the one removing them someday—use strippable paste and strippable wallcoverings.

GET THE SCOOP ON...
When to demand new flooring ▪ Locating
reputable contractors ▪ The basics of flooring ▪
Matching intended use to flooring materials

Repairing or Replacing Flooring and Floor Coverings

Chapter 14

Virtually all remodeling projects require some attention to flooring. New kitchens and bathrooms obviously need new floor coverings and, even if you are blessed with wood flooring, it probably needs some refinishing. Flooring consists of many choices as you move from the kitchen to the bathroom to the dining area and living spaces. This chapter covers the qualities of various flooring surfaces and discusses where each can be utilized to its best advantage. You can even change the color or tone of the stain on a wood floor to match new decor.

Some of your floors might not be as bad as you think. This chapter discusses ways to bring your wood, vinyl, and ceramic floors back to life when you might have given up on them. It also goes over some of the work your contractor will be doing as he removes old floor coverings and prepares the base for your new coverings. You'll also learn what you can do to prepare for his visit.

How to know you need new flooring

You've probably been slowly wearing down your wood and vinyl floors for years by tracking mud and dirt in and not cleaning it up until after a few people have ground it in. The Japanese have hit upon the simple solution: They remove their street shoes when entering a home. Most Americans, however, have not adopted this custom.

In addition to not taking good care of our floors, Americans also differ from the Japanese in thinking that floors are disposable. In most situations, aesthetic considerations come into play long before the floor actually wears out. Ponder the following:

Moneysaver
You might not need new wood flooring or have to cover up the one you have. Wood is a very forgiving material. It can be sanded (repeatedly) to a smooth, scratch-free surface and then stained, oiled, or waxed back to its original beauty or a new shade.

- Flooring wears out its welcome before it wears out. According to manufacturers, a vinyl floor will last nine years or longer. The average actual life is seven years, however, because people get tired of the old look and want a change.

- When your floor is really worn out, you'll notice that the undercoating of vinyl or linoleum is beginning to show through—for example, in front of the kitchen sink.

- The most likely time to make a change to your flooring is when you're remodeling. Kitchen and bath remodeling almost certainly includes new flooring. You also probably don't want to leave the same old carpet in your newly redone den or bedroom.

When drawing up a budget for your remodeling project, you should be aware that the rooms and decorations around the project are soon going to look worse by comparison. You might be wise to allow some money for buying new carpeting, drapes, furniture, and perhaps a new bed for the master suite. (And the kids are going to clamor for new beds and furniture, too.)

Locating reputable and skilled contractors

Finding a reputable, skilled contractor to address your flooring needs is a matter of networking, perseverance, and checking references.

- **Right on the job.** One of the advantages of having a GC handle your project is that it's up to him to locate the various subcontractors needed on the job. Occasionally, someone on his own crew can remove and lay new vinyl flooring. His crew is certainly the ones to put down the underlayment. Our contractor was a skilled tile man who thoroughly enjoyed doing this demanding job. He did the tile work around the upstairs bathtub/shower and around the downstairs stall shower and floor.

- **Asking around.** If you have to find your own contractor for a small job or if new flooring is all you want, ask for recommendations at the tile display room. You also can get recommendations from friends and neighbors and can check the Yellow Pages.

- **Checking references.** When you find someone you think you want to work with, check his references. In addition to getting estimates, try to see some of your tile prospect's past work.

- **Making sure the installer will be available.** Because subcontractors sometimes accept a job long before they are free to start it, you should also ask how soon the job could be started. The

Timesaver
One contractor told me that many contractors use take-out coffee places and Dunkin' Donuts shops as landmarks when they give each other driving directions. Early-morning coffee is a universal contractor requirement. An hour spent in your local coffee shop might furnish you with enough leads to fill all your subcontractor needs.

timing of the tiler's arrival on the job site is not as critical as some other subcontractors, however, because flooring is invariably the final step and can be delayed.

The basics of flooring

Your floor starts with joists (2 × 10 boards set on edge) that run across your building from the front or sides and meet at the center supporting beam. Joists are usually 16 inches apart and offer a good base for your flooring. Over this is laid ¾-inch-thick, 4 × 8–foot sheets of plywood for subflooring. This subflooring is laid before any interior walls are constructed. If you tear out an interior wall during remodeling, you'll find subflooring under it. There won't be any vinyl or wood-finished flooring under interior walls, however, because that is installed after the walls are up. (The gaps in your finished flooring can be patched.)

Wood flooring is sometimes laid down on this subflooring. It is usually nailed down, but it also can be installed with adhesives just as vinyl can. An additional layer of underlayment is usually needed under vinyl or ceramic tiles.

Which flooring in which rooms

In the beginning, floors were wood or dirt. Brick was used in kitchens, but the kitchens were often in an attached shed and the bricks were simply laid on the dirt. We still prize the wide-board pine floors in our oldest homes. People today frequently try to re-create them with old boards, but this method is expensive.

As linoleum and vinyl became available, they replaced wood in the "wet" or high-traffic areas of homes, mainly kitchens and bathrooms. Wood does

Watch Out!
It is vital that the subflooring and/or underlayment be level, dry, clean, and have no protruding nails. Test the floor's rigidity by walking around on it. If it moves up and down, you need another layer of subflooring or more supports from below.

not react well to water. Wall-to-wall carpeting became the covering of choice in other areas of the house—such as the living room, dining room, and bedrooms—because people discovered they could have carpeting for about the same cost as hardwood. The carpeting was installed right on the subflooring.

If you bought a house with wall-to-wall carpeting, you might already have hardwood floors underneath. Pry up a corner of your carpet and take a look. Wood flooring can be used wherever you want including kitchens, bathrooms, and high-traffic areas. Although wood is still affected adversely by water, with the advent of polyurethane, urethane, and acrylic finishes, your wood floor can withstand as much punishment as a vinyl floor can.

Qualities, benefits, installation, and maintenance of common flooring options

There are many flooring options, and when you make one decision there will be three further options to complicate the process. Just keep in mind your objectives and the kind of traffic and appearances you expect.

Wood

If you already have wood floors but don't like their condition, do the work necessary to revive them. They're worth it. Bring in a wood-refinishing contractor and get them sanded. After they are smooth and stain-free, have them coated with at least three coats of a high-grade protective coating.

Protective coatings are clear and do not add any color to your floor. If you want your floors to have more character, pick one of the dozens of

Bright Idea
Before you begin staining your wood floor, test your choice of stain on scrap wood of the same species and finish before you do the whole floor. Like paint, you also should wait until it dries to judge the color.

wood-stain tones available and apply it before you add any protective coatings.

The following are your choices in protective coatings:

- **Oil-modified polyurethanes** are the most common protective coatings. They can produce a high-gloss, semigloss, or matte finish. (Scratches are less noticeable with the matte finish.) These coatings are easy to apply but they dry slowly, which means a longer wait to get your house back to normal. Also, it can be difficult to repair damaged areas. Prices are moderate.

- **Moisture-cured urethane** dries very quickly. Don't try it yourself; get a professional. Three coats are recommended, and it emits a strong odor while being applied. It too is difficult to use in repairing damaged areas. Prices are moderate to expensive.

- **Water-based acrylics** are quick-drying and produce a low-gloss finish. They are easy to apply and emit only mild odors. They are fairly durable and are easy to repair. Three coats are necessary. Prices are moderate to expensive.

- **Water-based urethanes** dry quickly, are very expensive, and are difficult to apply. They are highly durable, however, and are easy to repair. Four coats are required, and they produce a satin to low-gloss finish.

- **Penetrating stain and wax combinations** soak into the pores of the wood and harden to form a protective seal. The wax gives a low-gloss satin sheen that wears only as the wood wears. It will not chip or scratch and generally is maintained with additional thin applications of wax. Wax finishes usually are applied more often than surface finishes. Only solvent-based (never water-based) waxes, buffing pastes, or cleaning liquids specifically made for wood floors should be used.

■ **Prefinished** wood flooring is available from some manufacturers. The wood comes to you already impregnated with acrylic. This saves on-site work and time, but you cannot sand it off and refinish it later, should the mood strike you.

To maintain a wood floor, keep it free from dirt and grit by vacuuming and dry-mopping it frequently.

Whether you're remodeling or building, have your wood flooring delivered to your home several days before it will be installed. This gives the moisture content time to adapt to your environment. Otherwise, shrinkage and warping could occur.

The cost of wood flooring, which runs between $5 and $10 per square foot, is augmented by the cost of the labor to install it and the materials and labor to stain and protect it. Get bids and compare.

Vinyl

Vinyl flooring is a popular choice for kitchens and bathrooms. No other type of flooring offers such a wide variety of uses and options. Better yet, it's generally priced more economically than other flooring options. If you think vinyl flooring is just for the kitchen, think again. It's perfect for any area of your home that receives heavy traffic and use—bathrooms, utility rooms, work rooms, playrooms, patios, entryways, and more. Vinyl flooring is exceptionally moisture-resistant, and its easy care and maintenance will be appreciated for years to come.

Unofficially...
Solvent-based coatings are prohibited in some towns on the East and West coasts and in Phoenix and Fort Worth. Your local building codes can tell you whether any coatings are prohibited in your town.

Modern advances in vinyl-floor production have created an incredible variety of styles, colors, and types from which to choose. Whether you prefer traditional colors and styles, a high-end wood floor look, natural stone, or a marble finish, you can find high-quality tile or sheet vinyl to provide almost any look you desire.

If you already have a vinyl floor you're basically happy with except for some squares that are missing, badly stained, or broken, consider getting them removed and replaced. If you were clever enough to save some extra tiles when the floor was installed (and if you can still find them), the task will be easier. Unfortunately, even if you saved extra tiles, they still might not match. You might consider replacing several squares with a contrasting color or design to go for a dramatic effect.

Although many manufacturers claim to have largely achieved carefree products, most homeowners notice a loss of luster over time. Various products on the market claim to regain the shine, but once started, the treatment will have to be continued. The best maintenance works with all surfaces: Dry-mop or vacuum loose dirt and grime before you grind it in and scratch the surface.

The cost of vinyl—still the least expensive alternative—runs the gamut from $1 to $10 per square or more; patterned antiques can go for as much as $75 per tile. You also have to remember that labor, underlayment, adhesive, and grout can more than double the cost of the basic materials. You can expect the installed cost to run somewhere between $6 and $30 per square yard.

Ceramic tile

Ceramic tile, in this country, has long been relegated to the walls and floors of the bathroom. In recent

Moneysaver
A new vinyl floor can be installed over your old vinyl floor if the old one is in good repair, is level and clean, is not cushioned, and hasn't been waxed. Adhesives won't stick to wax, so make sure you strip it off. In addition, your floor will be a little higher; you should consider planing off close-clearing doors.

years, however, it has moved to countertops in the kitchen and can be used in high-traffic areas including the kitchen floor (if the correct tile is selected).

If you thought there were too many options in the plumbing or kitchen-cabinet showrooms, wait until you enter the world of ceramic tile. Even after you agonize over selecting two contrasting colors of tile for a floor, you still have to decide which pattern to lay it in.

Ceramic tile is made of clay and is pressed or shaped into form and then fired in a kiln at a high temperature. The higher the temperature and the more times it is fired, the stronger and less porous the resulting tile will be. After the first firing, color and glazing are added and the tile is returned to the kiln. The glaze can be textured, smooth, matte, or high-gloss. Tile can be made by hand or by machine. Machine-made tile lends itself to more precise patterns and more uniform installation. The choices of basic tiles include:

- **Paver tile—glazed or unglazed.** The unglazed tile is considered better for kitchens and bathrooms because it offers more traction. Pavers are made of either clay or porcelain and, being dense and hard, they are easy to maintain. They come in 6-inch, 8-inch, and 10-inch sizes.

- **Quarry tile.** This tile has a slightly textured surface, making it less slippery. It comes in deep red, tan, or a dark natural hue. It can be finished with a sealer for added stain resistance.

- **Ceramic mosaics.** These come in a wide variety of shapes, colors, and sizes as small as one inch. This gives you virtually unlimited variety when laying out designs and patterns. Some manufacturers offer stock patterns that can give you a custom look at an uncustomized cost.

Bright Idea
Have your dealer deliver your vinyl flooring a few days before you intend to have it installed. Like wood, it needs time to adjust to the conditions of your home.

Watch Out!
Not all tile is the
same. Don't put
glazed wall tile
or decorative,
thin wall tile on
your floors. They
are not strong
enough.

Installing ceramic tile can be a tricky business. Don't try it unless you have watched someone who knew what he was doing. The basic requirement is the same as for all floor coverings: You need a smooth, level, clean subflooring and possibly an underlayment.

Tile should not be installed over wood floors laid on concrete (common in high-rise apartments). Remove the wood and pour and smooth another ⅜-inch layer of cement before starting the tiling process.

You should also consult an engineer to determine whether your floors can support the considerable added weight of tile. This is not a problem in most bathrooms or even kitchens, but if you are tiling a long hallway or a large room, your new floor could wind up in the basement. Your tile installer should be aware of the weight problem and should be able to advise you. You also might be faced with additional floor height (as much as 1 to 1½ inches, if you use the thick-mortar method).

You have one more selection to make—the color and glaze of the grout. *Grout* is the material that goes between the tiles; it definitely becomes part of your pattern. It can be almost invisible, or you can highlight your design with a contrasting color.

- **Cement grout** is the most common type of grout. It comes in a powder that is then mixed with water. It has good water retention and is fairly flexible.

- **Latex cement grout** has to be mixed with liquid latex before being applied.

- **Mastic grouts** are sold in paste form. They tend to be more flexible and stain resistant than cement-based grouts.

- **Epoxy grouts** are the most water resistant and create the strongest bond, but they are tricky to work with. The room's temperature is critical, and cleanup can be difficult if not done immediately. Epoxy grouts are among the most expensive; in return, however, you get a long-lasting job even in high-traffic areas.

- **Silicone-rubber grout** comes ready to squeeze out of a tube and is best used around bathtubs and sinks. It is not generally recommend for laying floor tile because it's too soft even after it sets.

Carpeting

Carpeting has been a favorite floor covering in Europe ever since Crusaders brought Oriental carpets back to their countries from Asia and the Middle East. These carpets were hand-woven, pure-wool carpeting, and they are still considered the best carpets in the world. They are also among the most expensive, costing from hundreds of dollars to many thousands. The cost depends on the materials, workmanship, and place of origin.

- Wool is still regarded as the best carpeting material, but less expensive carpeting materials—many of them synthetic—have brought carpeting prices down and are a vailable to virtually everyone.

- Other carpeting materials can be used alone, or in combination, to create an even wider range of carpeting and characteristics. Acrylic, once dominant in the industry, is especially long-wearing. Nylon, which has overcome its static-electricity problem, is valued for its resistance to stains. Polyesters have a luxurious feel and resist

Timesaver
Have your carpenter only lightly tack your baseboards on so they can easily be removed for laying not only tile but all the floor coverings. If your scheme calls for quarter-round molding (or "base shoe") at the bottom of your baseboard, this might suffice for your floor-covering installers. Make it easy to remove.

abrasion, but they are not easy to keep clean. Polypropylene resists fading and is not absorbent. It can be used for both indoor and indoor-outdoor carpeting.

Carpeting falls into two general categories: cushion-backed and conventional. *Cushion-backed* is made with the padding as part of the carpet. It is usually cheaper and easier to install. It does not last as long as other types, however, and if it is laid down with adhesive, you will destroy it when you try to take it up. *Conventional* carpeting is made without a rubber backing. It usually is installed wall-to-wall and is stretched permanently over a separate underlayment of padding.

Carpeting types also differ in the way the fibers are stitched onto the backing:

- **Continuous pile** (or **level loop**) carpeting is stitched in one continuous thread. It is very durable and easy to maintain.

- **Cut-pile** carpeting is created when the loops of the continuous pile are cut off. If it is woven very tightly, it is known as **plush carpeting.** It has a very smooth look, and your vacuum will leave tracks.

- **Shag** carpeting is less dense and often has fibers of varying lengths. It is a less formal carpet and might not last as long as the more expensive types.

- **Sculptured** carpet is created by shaving a pattern into a cut-pile carpet.

One of the best measures of carpet quality is the *face weight.* This is the measurement of how high the pile is and how many tufts of yarn there are per square inch. The face weight might not be marked

on the carpet, but your salesperson should be able
to tell you. The more dense, the better. It will wear
better because the fibers are closer together and,
thus, support each other better. You will stand on
the fiber's ends rather than their sides. The most
luxurious carpets have a face weight of 30 to 40
ounces or more.

You shouldn't buy new carpeting without investing in good padding. It sometimes is included in the
price of your carpet, but it might be better to pay a
little extra or to negotiate for a better pad. Thicker
and softer padding is not necessarily better for your
carpet because it offers little support for its backing,
which might break down. Felted hair-and-jute
padding is the strongest; 40-ounce padding is usually enough for home use, even in the high-traffic
areas.

If your carpeting is going into potentially damp
areas (such as the kitchen or a bathroom), you
might want to go with foam-rubber or urethane
padding.

It probably comes as no surprise that the best
way to maintain your carpet is to vacuum it regularly. The bad news is that you should do it twice a week
or more in heavy-traffic areas. Small area rugs can
be taken outside and beaten to remove the deep
dirt particles that cause most of the wear on carpets.
Wall-to-wall carpet, however, should receive heavy
cleaning at least once a year to restore its freshness
and colors. This annual cleaning can be done in
three ways:

- **Shampooing** is the easiest way. You can rent a
  rotary brush that works the detergent into the
  pile, loosening dirt and holding it in the foam.
  Don't get carried away and over-brush any area;

it can harm the fibers. Let the foam do the work. When the solution dries, you simply vacuum it up.

- The **hot-water-extraction system** (often called **steam cleaning**) provides better cleaning. It should replace your annual shampooing perhaps every third year. You can either hire a professional or rent a machine and do the work yourself. The machine dispenses a nonfoaming detergent into the carpet under pressure and immediately sucks it back up with the loosened dirt. Don't overdo this method either; too much water will harm your carpet.

- **Dry cleaning** can be done between your annual deep cleanings. You can sprinkle a powdered compound on the carpet and then brush it down into the pile. This loosens the dirt, which you simply vacuum up. One advantage of this method is you can do it right before company comes. With the two water systems, you should allow at least two or three hours for the carpet to dry before walking on it. Unfortunately, dry cleaning does not clean as effectively as the other two methods.

Laying it all down

Just when you decide to have hardwood floors in your new den, vinyl on the kitchen floor, carpet in the living room, and tile in the shower, someone complicates your decision by telling you that each of these floor coverings can be used virtually anywhere. Not only that, you still have literally hundreds (maybe thousands) of choices in color, texture, weight, finish, pattern, design, and price still ahead of you.

The intention of this chapter on floor coverings is not to confuse you but to alert you to some of the dramatic and creative options available. The reason floors present a unique problem is that you not only look at them as you do your walls and windows, you also walk on them. You want something that looks good and wears well.

For more information on flooring options, read or contact some of the following:

Floors, Walls & Ceilings, by Graham Blackburn. Consumer Reports Books, 1989.

The Simon and Schuster Complete Guide to Home Repair and Maintenance, Bernard Gladstone. Simon and Schuster, 1984.

The National Wood Flooring Association Web page, www.woodfloors.org.

Also on the Web, look for the trade associations representing the various floor products and some of the manufacturers. Some Web surfing is required, but you may also find some local distributors and contractors listed on the net.

Just the facts

- Make sure you have clean, level, smooth, strong subflooring.

- You need at least three coats of quality urethane on your wood floors for them to last.

- Remember that your rugs and carpets need to be cleaned on the surface weekly and deep-cleaned at least annually.

- Don't skimp when it comes to flooring—the long-term benefits of quality products far outweigh any immediate savings in price.

Protecting Yourself and Your Home

GET THE SCOOP ON...
Silent killers: carbon monoxide and radon ▪
Unclogging your heat ducts ▪
Your chimney sweep ▪ The value and treatment
of smoke detectors

PART VII

Fire, Fumes, Radon, and Dust Mites

Sometimes what you don't know *can* hurt you. Most serious accidents occur in the home. Many of the dangers around a home are obvious. You know you shouldn't run your car in the garage with the doors closed or let your fingers get too close to the sharp edge of a carving knife. Even most kids know not to use a hair dryer in the bathtub.

You probably already recognize the potential danger from accidents, fire, and break-ins, but some hazards are more subtle. This chapter covers some of the often invisible dangers you might encounter: carbon monoxide, radon, smoke, fire, and dirty air. You'll learn about the devices and services available to lessen your exposure to these dangers. I'll also tell you how to find reliable installers or services, what you can expect them to do for you, and about how much it'll cost.

Chapter 15

Bright Idea
If you're purchas-
ing carpet in a
roll, ask the
dealer if he'd be
willing to unroll
it for a couple
weeks before it
is installed in
your home. This
will allow many
of the fumes to
dissipate.

Fumes: from unpleasant to potentially lethal

Remodeling, which often involves tearing out old, dirty, dusty, and mouse-dropping–filled walls, creates a temporary but potentially hazardous pollution problem. Many products used during remodeling give off odors that run from unpleasant to harmful; the odors can linger from the time the products are applied until some time after.

Dealing with unpleasant or unhealthy fumes is pretty much a matter of common sense, as anyone who has regained consciousness in the emergency room can attest. If you're already half-gassed and find thinking difficult, here's what you need to know:

▪ When using paints, solvents, varnishes, and adhesives, closely follow the directions on the containers. When they call for "adequate venti-lation," have your contractor open all the windows and use an industrial-strength ventilating window fan to pull the polluted air out of the room. Just opening one window is not enough.

▪ The odor you smell after the application of a product is called *outgas*. How long outgas lasts after the initial application depends on the product. If you are still getting odors a month after it is applied, however, something is wrong. Contact your contractor. I suggest using water-based paints and adhesives and nontoxic strippers. Always make sure the containers are tightly sealed after use.

▪ Carpeting is a source of fumes that can last up to several weeks after installation. If you buy 100-percent wool or cotton carpeting with glueless backing, you can avoid most odors. Otherwise, try to purchase a carpet with a stitched backing, with very little glue, and without any surface treatments such as stain guards.

If you can't justify the cost of wool or cotton carpeting or if you want stain guard, you will end up with some fumes. Your best bet is to open the windows of the room where the carpeting is installed and to get some serious cross-ventilation going. Fans can speed the process, but only time will cure it.

Carbon monoxide: the silent killer

Carbon monoxide has been getting more attention lately as a danger in the home. Oprah Winfrey has featured it on her show, and the medical profession has begun to alert its members to the common symptoms. As a homeowner, you should be aware of how carbon monoxide gets into your house. You need to recognize the early warning symptoms and know how to avoid carbon monoxide poisoning through preventive maintenance and alarms.

What is carbon monoxide?

Carbon monoxide (chemical symbol CO) is a flammable, colorless, odorless, tasteless gas produced by the incomplete burning of any fuel such as natural gas, oil, coal, wood, or kerosene. "Carbon monoxide poisoning from the use of fuel-burning appliances kills at least 200 people each year and sends more that 5,000 to hospital emergency rooms for treatment," says Chairperson Ann Brown of the Consumer Product Safety Commission (CPSC). *The Journal of the American Medical Association* (JAMA) estimates somewhat higher numbers—1,500 deaths annually and 10,000 who seek medical attention.

Watch Out!
One reason for the discrepancy in the carbon monoxide figures is that, according to medical experts, the symptoms of carbon monoxide poisoning resemble many other common ailments.

What are the effects of carbon monoxide on humans?

Carbon monoxide inhibits the blood's capacity to carry oxygen. In your lungs, carbon monoxide quickly passes into your bloodstream and attaches itself to hemoglobin (the oxygen-carrying substance in red blood cells). Hemoglobin readily accepts carbon monoxide over the life-giving oxygen atom and forms the toxic compound carboxyhemoglobin. By replacing oxygen with carbon monoxide in your blood, your body poisons itself by cutting off oxygen to your organs and cells. This can cause varying amounts of damage, depending on the length of exposure.

Low levels of carbon monoxide poisoning (carboxyhemoglobin levels of 10 percent) result in symptoms commonly mistaken for the common cold or flu: shortness of breath upon mild exertion, mild headaches, and nausea. At higher levels of carbon monoxide poisoning (carboxyhemoglobin levels of 30 percent), the symptoms become more severe: dizziness, mental confusion, severe headaches, nausea, and fainting upon mild exertion. If the level of carboxyhemoglobin climbs to 50 percent, unconsciousness and death can result. Carbon monoxide poisoning is insidious because it can happen gradually over a long period of time. The poison can accumulate in your body like a speeded-up aging process.

How does carbon monoxide get into your home?

Improperly adjusted furnaces, hot-water heaters, boilers, stoves, space heaters, and even fireplaces can produce carbon monoxide. Warming up your car in an attached garage, even with the garage door open, can build up dangerous levels of carbon monoxide in your home because it can enter through the kitchen door or through nearby windows. Ann Brown from the CPSC suggests, "Modern heating equipment is sophisticated and requires special training and tools for proper maintenance. The CPSC recommends that consumers should not service their own appliances. Instead, have a qualified professional perform an inspection."

Other sources of carbon monoxide are chimneys, flues, and vents. Blockages caused by creosote buildup, soot, or debris from bird or squirrel nests can back up your system's exhaust and can cause leakage of carbon monoxide into your living spaces. Even without blockages, improperly sized flues connected to high-efficiency furnaces and water heaters can contribute to carbon monoxide spillage.

Part of the problem, particularly in new homes, comes from efforts at heavy insulation and airtight construction. These are wonderful techniques for saving on the heating bill, but with little in-flow of fresh air, we breathe our own exhaust and the effect of fumes and carbon monoxide is heightened. Replacement windows and additional insulation can create the same problem in older homes. In either case, a furnace, which has the same need for oxygen to function as you do, can starve for lack of air or oxygen.

Preventing carbon monoxide poisoning

Have your chimneys, flues, and vents inspected annually by a professional, preferably before each heating season.

One of the better buys a homeowner can take advantage of is the service contract offered by an oil or fuel dealer. These contracts usually call for an annual inspection and include servicing, parts, and

Watch Out!
Black stains on the outside of your chimney or flue could indicate a creosote buildup or a blockage, and potential carbon monoxide problems.

cleaning. Yes, they cost you some money, but this is also a good deal for you. These contracts mean someone else is keeping track of your needs and will remind you when an inspection is due.

Detecting carbon monoxide

Although carbon monoxide is a serious problem, it is not difficult to deal with. Carbon monoxide detectors can be purchased from any hardware store and can be installed with a couple screws at the top of your basement stairs or in the rafters above your furnace. Some models simply plug into an electrical outlet. A carbon monoxide detector can save you and your family from serious harm.

Consumer Reports magazine tested carbon monoxide detectors and reported the results in the July 1995 issue. The magazine recommends the plug-in variety over the battery-operated types. A plug-in detector gives an audible warning whenever the carbon monoxide level reaches a level prescribed by a UL standard. A reset button quiets the alarm as you try to correct the problem by airing out your house. The unit continues to monitor your air, however, and will sound again in 10 minutes if the problem persists. When the problem is corrected, the detector shuts itself off.

A good detector should include the following features:

- An alarm that stops automatically when fresh air is supplied
- A manual hush or reset button
- A digital display or warning light
- A power-on indicator light
- A power horn of 85 decibels
- A test button to verify that the detector's electrons are working

Moneysaver
Carbon monoxide detectors cost between $30 and $90. Several in the $40 range were rated "best buys" by *Consumer Reports*.

Consumer Reports recommends that you have at least one detector if you have a fireplace or a appliance. (Make sure to have such appliances inspected about once a year.) It is recommended that you install it in a hallway or sleeping area.

Radon

When I first heard about radon gas a few years ago, I considered it part of the health-scare-of-the-month media blitz. I know better now: Radon is a legitimate concern for homeowners.

As a percentage of the population, the number of people affected by radon is small. Radon, however, does cause lung cancer and can be deadly.

Fortunately, the devices for detecting radon are simple and inexpensive. Corrective measures, if necessary, are effective and cost about as much as a small remodeling project.

The following sections provide more information about radon gas and how to detect and prevent it in your home.

What is radon?

Radon is not a man-made risk like asbestos or nuclear waste; thus, there's no one to blame when radon is detected. This might account for the lack of publicity it gets. Radon is part of our natural environment. It's an invisible, odorless gas that seeps up through rock and soil from subterranean uranium deposits. According to an article in the June 1995 issue of *Consumer Reports*, radon quickly decays into minuscule radioactive particles that, when inhaled, can become deeply embedded in the lungs, where they give off carcinogenic alpha particles.

Scientists learned most of what they know about the effects of radon from studying thousands of uranium miners who were exposed to radon on

Unofficially... According to a 1990 National Safety Council report, annual radon deaths equal half the number of deaths caused by drunk driving and three times the number of deaths from drowning or fires.

the job. According to the Environmental Protection Agency (EPA), radon is second only to smoking as a cause of lung cancer; it causes 14,000 to 30,000 deaths per year. High radon levels have been found in every state and in every type of house.

How does radon get into your house?

Radon enters your house through cracks in the foundation or through openings around water and sewer pipes; it can also be present in well water. Radon levels are almost always highest in the basement or the lower levels of a house and decrease rapidly in the upper floors. If you frequently use a finished basement with a playroom or a den, you should be more concerned than if your basement is used only for laundry and storage.

Radon levels can vary widely from month to month and even from day to day. They can be influenced by your use of bathroom and kitchen exhaust fans or by the amount of precipitation and barometric pressure. Don't relax just because your neighbors tested their homes and found no radon. Levels can vary from house to house on the same block.

If you don't try to detect radon, you won't know whether you're being exposed to radon for years. Even then, you'll only find out if you develop cancer. Luckily, there are better detection systems.

Radon detectors

You can't guess whether your house has radon; you have to test. Testing is easy, yet most people only do it when buying or selling a house. Detectors cost between $10 and $30, including the lab analysis and a written report. The detectors are available at your local hardware store or building-supply house, and you can install them yourself.

Put the detector in the lowest part of your house. Although the concentration of radon in a home can vary with temperature, weather, and even barometric pressure, the only question a homeowner should be concerned with is, "Do I have *any* radon?" A radon tester can answer that question. If your test proves negative, you can move on to other concerns in your life. If the presence of radon is detected, you have more work to do.

Two kinds of detectors are available: short-term and long-term. *Consumer Reports* recommends using the long-term kits unless you're closing on the sale of your house in the near future. Common short-term detectors include a charcoal-containing canister, an envelope, or a tray. These track radon levels for up to seven days. Long-term detectors provide an average concentration for up to 90 days. The alpha particles emitted when radon decays leave imprints on a small piece of specially formulated plastic.

Radon testing services

If your detectors record a high level of radon (4pCi/l or higher), you might want to confirm this finding by calling a professional testing firm. These companies are highly regulated and can be found by contacting your state radon office, which also can supply you with the booklet "Radon Reduction Techniques for Detached Houses."

Fixing a radon problem

If you have a radon problem, you need to call in a radon remediation firm. These firms, like the radon testing companies, are highly regulated. Their first step is to seal large cracks. This step probably won't entirely solve your problem, however, because the

Unofficially... Because radon levels vary widely over time, the EPA does not demand that they be extremely precise and repeatable. In fact, readings are allowed to vary by as much as 25 percent. All you're looking for is evidence of a serious problem.

gas can sneak through fissures too small to be seen. More work is necessary.

The most common method of venting the gas is installing a pipe through the foundation slab to suck radon gas away before it ever gets into the house. Typically, a small fan pulls the gas up to the roof, where the radon dissipates harmlessly. According to the EPA, remedial efforts cost between $1,000 and $1,500. On a more positive note, the remedial action is permanent and is not overly disruptive to your home.

Contrary to my perception before I investigated the radon problem, there are enough people who die of radon-caused cancer every year to make it worthwhile to spend the $10 to $30 to get a radon detector for your home. I recommend that you go along with *Consumer Reports* and choose the 90-day tester. If you get a low or zero reading, radon is one less problem to worry about.

Heating ducts

It is only a coincidence that I have actually employed some of the services and purchased several of the big-ticket items that I describe in this book. It has been 10 years since my wife and I remodeled our 50-year-old ranch house, and time eventually requires work on appliances and other maintenance tasks. We now have a new furnace, a new water heater, new gutters, a rewired workshop, a repainted interior and outside trim, and more recently, newly cleaned ductwork. Combine these items with the complete revamping of my mother's condominium with new carpet, paint, and appliances, and I'm starting to feel like a one-man testing laboratory.

I first became aware of the potential problems presented by dirty heating ducts through a newsletter sent out with the fuel bill from my heating oil company. The newsletter warned of flu-like symptoms: runny noses, watering eyes, and lingering colds. It mentioned higher fuel bills, long-running furnaces, and an abundance of dust. We had enough of these warning signs present that I ordered the company's duct-cleaning service.

Why should you clean your ducts?

Ducts should be cleaned every five years. The two main reasons for cleaning your ducts are better health and more efficient heating. Your heat ducts can harbor allergens such as dirt, dust, and pet hair and can continuously recirculate them as well as cold and flu germs.

Apparently, I added to an already excellent breeding ground by installing an in-line humidifier. One look at the unit's encrusted, perforated water wheel at the end of the heating season should have alerted us to the folly of this particular experiment. Even the addition of bleach to the water tank did little to clean it up. Following the strong advice of our installer, when we got our new furnace, we did not reinstall the humidifier.

Even those of you who feel fine might choose duct cleaning to improve the circulation of the expensive hot or cold air you are producing. In some older homes, ducts have so much accumulated crud that duct cleaners can barely get their cleaning tools inside. Just like the buildup in your galvanized water pipes, this cuts down on the amount of air that can be forced through your system. Clean ducts can improve both air flow and efficiency.

Watch Out!
When you think about it, what better environment could you create for the growth and propagation of mold, mildew, and any number of nasty, fuzzy things than your heating ducts? Be sure to clean the ducts at least every five years.

What causes dirty ducts?

In addition to dust and material accumulated over time (the major culprit), another potential cause of duct problems is remodeling activity in your house. If you've been tearing out walls, sawing wood, or sanding floors, your system has undoubtedly ingested considerable plaster and sawdust particles. The fan in your furnace is not powerful enough to pull these particles all the way to the filters, so it settles and builds up over the years. One sign that you need a clean-out is a dusty smell when the heat comes on.

In an article in *Home* magazine, Linda Mason Hunter describes a do-it-yourselfer who carefully sealed off a room where he planned to remove lead-based paint along with his walls. When the heating system cranked up in the fall, bushels of lead-laden dust were blown into every corner of his house. He had neglected to seal the vents.

Children and pets add another dimension to the foreign particles that end up in your ducts. Children spill, drip, dump, and even hide everything from their least favorite foods to toys in heat ducts. Pets add enough hair to your home's atmosphere to stuff pillows; much of it, along with its dander, enters your heating system. It's not wise to count on your furnace's air filters to catch these invaders because many items deposited in the heating ducts don't pass through the filters. They simply collect and then are blown out into the room when the fans come on.

Duct-cleaning service

Duct cleaning is one of the more impressive services you can employ. The cleaner's truck, which is a giant vacuum cleaner on wheels, parks in your driveway. The driver hauls a 6-inch-diameter hose into your basement and, after he removes your air filters, hooks it up to the return area of your furnace.

When he turns on the vacuum, six 2-foot-wide black bags rise out of the roof of his truck. Our dogs just sat in the yard and watched in amazement. You'll be tempted to run inside to see whether there is any furniture left in your house.

The cleaner puts newspaper over all the hot-air registers and cold-air returns, blocking the air flow. He then removes the paper from one outlet at a time, forcing all the vacuum power into that one duct. He sprays a powerful disinfectant into each duct as he uncovers it.

The next step involves tapping into each duct either by taking it apart at the joints or by drilling 2-inch holes and inserting a compressed-air hose. This hose has a 10-inch rubber wand or whip on the end that flails around inside the duct as he pushes the hose into it. This breaks up and loosens any encrusted matter, which then is sucked out. He also has tools similar to those for chimney cleaning, which are used for long straight sections. He finishes this operation by screwing galvanized patches over the holes he has made. The entire job takes three to four hours to complete.

How do you locate a reputable duct-cleaning firm? The answer once more is the Yellow Pages. The company that cleaned my ducts was independent, but it worked on a contract basis with my heating oil supplier. I have confidence in my oil company, so I accepted their selection of duct cleaners.

There are, however, some questions you can ask before hiring a duct-cleaning service. Less effective companies clean ducts using portable vacuums. My cleaner suggested that this is not the most effective way to clean ducts. He also suggested that a home-owner should check to see whether a cleaner plans to use compressed-air cleaning tools and hole cutters. He has been in the business long enough to have gone from the wire brush stage to pneumatic power, and he knows the difference air power can make.

You can count the number of inlets and outlets you have to come up with a ball-park figure of what duct cleaning will cost. Our cleaner's basic cost was $350 for up to 10 registers and $15 for each additional register.

I had our ducts cleaned because we met several of the "duct cleaning time" criteria: We remodeled 10 years ago, it had been anywhere between 10 and 50 years since the last cleaning (depending on which ducts were selected), and we were feeling flu-like symptoms in the fall and winter. If any of this sounds familiar, you might want to have your duct-work cleaned.

The ancient art of chimney sweeping

There seems to be a strict division of labor in the business of cleaning the various pipes, ducts, chimneys, and flues in your home. The duct cleaners take care of your heating and cooling system's transport system. Your annual furnace service's cleaning and adjusting cleans the furnace and its flue from the furnace to the chimney, clearing accumulated soot. Cleaning the chimney seems to be reserved solely for chimney sweeps.

All chimneys get dirty, some faster than others. If your oil- or gas-burning furnace has slipped out of adjustment, unburned fuel in the form of soot gets deposited on the walls of your chimney as the gases cool on their way upward. If you have a fireplace, its smoke and soot go up a separate flue, probably in the same chimney as your furnace.

If you can't remember when you last had your chimney cleaned, it's probably time you had it checked. Most likely, your fuel delivery company suggests a once-a-year cleaning in the fall before the onset of the heating season. That might be overly cautious, but a couple of annual checks will let you know what your cleaning schedule should be.

What you can expect from a chimney sweep

Chimney sweeping is not a high-tech business. First the chimney sweep looks up your chimney (if you have a fireplace) to see what is needed. The idea is to dislodge all the soot, creosote, bird's nests, and squirrel remains from your chimney's flues and to let it all fall to the bottom. (This can be done from the top of your roof or from inside your house.) Everything that falls is cleaned out of your fireplace (which is usually covered with a tarpaulin) and from the clean-out door in your basement. The chimney sweep vacuums and sweeps up around each area, and that's it.

Because the chimney sweep has seen more of your chimney, both inside and outside, than anyone else, he or she (yes, I have met a female chimney sweep) might notice cracks, separations, and leaks you didn't know about. This can be tricky because a less-than-honorable sweep might attempt to instill in you a sense of imminent danger that only he can correct while at your house.

There are, however, some valid reasons for immediate repairs. If your chimney needs relining, it can often be done on the spot with materials in the truck. A sweep also can recement the hinges of the cast-iron clean-out door in your basement. (This

Unofficially...
Chimney sweeps are a traditional lot. Many will actually show up with a long-tailed tuxedo coat and a top hat (but probably won't sing and dance like Dick Van Dyke in *Mary Poppins*). Many of the tools they use are the same as those used for generations, such as long-handled wire brushes and ladders. Other items, such as nylon brushes and vacuum cleaners, have been added in recent years.

Moneysaver
If a chimney sweep (or any repairman, for that matter) finds additional problems that will cost you more than a few dollars to take care of "while he's there," pass on the offer. Get additional opinions and bids unless you already have checked the person's reputation.

is not an expensive operation.) Your chimney might need a new cap, repointing (recementing between the bricks), repairing of the flashing (the copper or aluminum sheets at the bottom of the chimney that run under the shingles), or waterproofing.

I asked Linda Johnson of the Chimney Doctor in Prospect, Connecticut, how homeowners can protect themselves from unscrupulous chimney sweeps. She recommended the following:

- Deal with an established firm (at least five years in business).

- Check for membership in the National Chimney Sweeps Guild.

- Get references and check them out.

- Believe the firm you call. Have doubts about a sweep firm that solicits your business over the phone.

What will a chimney sweep cost?

This is by no means the most expensive work you can have done on your home. In the Connecticut area, for example, cleaning a chimney with one flue costs about $90. A second flue can be done at the same time for an additional $50 to $75. If you've ever seen a chimney fire in which the built-up creosote catches fire, and if you've witnessed the blast furnace effect, you will not hesitate to get your chimney checked.

Smoke detectors

Statistics and the nightly news offer a grim reminder of the loss of life and property caused by fire. There is, however, an inexpensive and dependable way to protect your family and your home—smoke detectors. They can provide you with an early-warning system that can alert you to a fire in your home.

Types of detectors

Two types of smoke detectors are currently on the market: photoelectric and ionization-chamber. The photoelectric type uses a photoelectric bulb that emits a beam of light. When smoke enters the unit, light from the beam is reflected from particles in the smoke into a photo cell and the alarm sounds. The ionization-chamber smoke detector contains a small radiation source that produces electrically charged air particles called *ions*. The presence of these ions allows a small electric current to flow in the chamber. When smoke particles enter the chamber, they reduce the flow of the electric current. The change in the current sets off the alarm.

Installation

Smoke rises, so the best place to install a smoke detector is high on a wall or on the ceiling. If you have a multilayer, air-conditioned home, a detector should be installed on each level. In sleeping areas, a detector should be close enough to your bedroom that you can hear the alarm, but it should be at least 3 feet away from any warm or cool air registers that might blow smoke away from the detector.

If you install multiple detectors, you might consider interconnecting them so that, if one detector is triggered, they all will sound. There are two ways to interconnect detectors. One way is by wires run through the walls, which will probably require the services of an electrician; the other way is a wireless system that works like an intercom.

There are two ways to power your devices. The first is by house current, using either a cord plugged into an outlet or by wiring it into your household electrical circuits. An electrician should be called in to hook up these units. You might consider including provisional detectors while you are remodeling.

Unofficially...
Ionization detectors respond more quickly to open flame; photoelectric detectors respond faster to smoldering fires. The differences are not critical, however. Just make sure any detector you buy has been approved by Underwriters Laboratories (UL).

Watch Out!
Remember, a smoke and fire detector alerts you to a fire but doesn't put the fire out. Your family should have pre-arranged escape plans to help you exit your home with fires in various locations. Having fire extinguishers handy to put out a fire in its early stages could save your home. Your first consideration, however, should be getting your family out of the house safely.

The second way is by battery. Battery-powered detectors are certainly the easiest to install because they require no outlets or connections to your wiring. They do, however, require periodic checking—about once a month—to make sure they are functioning and are clean.

Batteries last about a year, and most detectors have an early, low-battery warning system that periodically emits small chirps. These chirps will continue for about seven days. (This should give you plenty of time to figure out where the annoying noise is coming from.) If you've been away on an extended vacation, you should test all your detectors when you get back.

The most common cause of fire- and smoke-detector failure is dead or removed batteries. The most common reason people remove batteries is to prevent annoying false alarms caused by simple cooking excesses such as boiling water or burning toast. If you are getting too many alarms from innocent occurrences, consider relocating your detectors to adjacent rooms or lower down on the wall.

Just the facts

- Detecting carbon monoxide and radon can save your health and your life.

- Cleaning your heating ducts can cut down on allergies and communicable illnesses, and it can improve your furnace's efficiency.

- Get a chimney inspection every two years; a chimney sweep visit is an inexpensive, effective safety measure.

- Buy and install smoke detectors if you haven't already; they're an easy, affordable way to be warned of a fire. Remember to test them monthly and equip them with fresh batteries as needed.

GET THE SCOOP ON...
Security systems—fad or necessity? ▪ Bringing
in pest control professionals ▪
Getting your home inspected

Security, Pests, and Inspections: Getting Professional Help

Y ou might be able to fix a leaky faucet or replace a window pane, but when it comes to protecting your home from vermin, insects, and burglars, you're probably out of your league. This chapter explores how to make your home more secure. It looks at the hoopla surrounding home security systems and helps you differentiate between hope and hype.

After dealing with the big varmints, we'll give you some tips on how to protect your home from smaller six- and eight-legged critters. In the process, we'll discuss both the pests and the pest controllers, commenting on how difficult it sometimes is to tell them apart.

Finally, this chapter provides some guidelines for having your home professionally inspected. These inspections often are necessary in preparation for repairs or remodeling, in anticipation of selling your home, or in pledging it as collateral.

Security systems

A burglar-alarm system can give you a sense of security, not only when you are away but while you are in the house, awake or sleeping. Some even incorporate a heat and smoke detector for added protection.

Security systems come in the following levels of complexity and protection:

- Motion detectors simply turn on spotlights outside your home. They serve both to deter thieves and to alert homeowners.

- The next level is a security system hooked up to a couple doors and some windows that sounds an alarm or siren outside your house. The siren is designed to frighten away a burglar and to alert your neighbors. This type of system can also be connected to smoke and fire detectors.

- The final practical level of sophistication involves the automatic dialing of an outside service: the fire department, the police, or a system monitor. This service is discussed later in greater detail because it involves a greater outlay of money both to install and to maintain.

A burglar-alarm system usually consists of the following:

- A main control (usually located in your basement)

- A remote keypad that allows you to shut off the system as you enter and to reset it when you leave

- Detectors or sensors on each door and window easily accessible from the outside

- A motion detector

- A siren

- Speakers, microphones, and video cameras

How security systems work

What happens when an alarm is tripped? Let's say a door has been opened in the back room, setting off the alarm. The system dials your central control monitor. A notice appears on their computer screen, stating that customer 341 (you) at your address has a Code 4 alarm. (Code 4 is your backroom motion detector.)

The control monitor first calls you to see whether you know what is happening. If you answer with, "I just came in and forgot to turn off the damn detector," they say, "Fine. What is your password?" You have to give the correct password to stop the alarm.

Some security systems have you respond to a verbal challenge by punching in your code number on the keypad of your telephone. What happens if you are being held hostage in your own home or if a burglar is in your house and is threatening you? You can simply give the wrong password or punch in the wrong number. "Okay, thank you very much," will be the response from the control monitor, who will then call the police for you.

Some new systems can be activated and deactivated by remote control. You just punch a button on a remote as you enter your driveway. The garage door opens, the outside lights turn on, and your alarm system is deactivated. On some new two-way remotes, a signal or message on a screen will alert you if your detection system has recently been triggered. That way, you don't walk in on a robbery in progress.

Bright Idea
The installer I talked to recommends that you pick the name of a present or past pet as your password—it's one word you'll always remember.

This same system can flash messages to your beeper (if you have one) if your system is activated. This is a nice feature for latchkey kids. When your child comes home from school, he just punches in the deactivation code. You then get the message that he has gotten home safely and on time.

"Remember the book *1984* [by George Orwell]? It's getting mighty close," my security system installer warned me. "I have a customer who owns a Dunkin' Donuts with video surveillance cameras. He wants to be able to dial up the store from his home computer and tap into the video images of the store." Security systems are getting more and more technologically advanced.

How do you find a reputable security company?

The average homeowner should contact three or four alarm companies and should invite their salesmen in for a presentation. The Yellow Pages once again are a prime source, but the most reliable source is a recommendation from a friend or neighbor who has had a system long enough to learn its advantages and disadvantages. The independent alarm-firm owner I talked to told me he gets 99 percent of his business from word of mouth.

Sit down with the various representatives and figure out the best way to protect your home. Count the outside doors and the number of accessible windows. Add an indoor siren, an outdoor siren, and a smoke detector. Decide which package you want and then get comparable bids from each firm.

Look out for "freebie" deals. A "free alarm system" and "free installation" can sound quite attractive, particularly if you haven't done your homework. Before deregulation, Ma Bell got very wealthy by leasing telephones and collecting usage

Unofficially...
How do you know you need an alarm system? Not surprisingly, the primary trigger for installing an alarm system is if your house or a neighbor's house has just been broken into and robbed.

fees. Some large alarm firms are doing nearly as well using this same approach.

American District Telegraph (ADT), one of the largest alarm companies, recently was sold for $6.6 billion. ADT installs about 500 systems a week and has its own monitoring service as well. (The independent alarm firm I talked to has 600 customers after 12 years and is doing well enough.)

ADT leases its equipment and signs you up for a minimum of a 36-month lease ($24.95 per month) and monitoring service. At the end of the lease, you will discover you can't switch to another monitoring service because the ADT equipment is incompatible with any other monitoring system. You can either buy and install a new system, a new control panel, or stay with ADT.

When properly designed, installed, and monitored, most alarm systems will provide the security promised. My advice is to carefully read and understand the contract and compare service.

One approach used by scam artists is to collect payment for your system in advance. They then slap in a junk system and are gone. Others lead you to believe you are buying the equipment, but the agreement you sign is a lease agreement.

You should check each alarm firm's state license to install alarm systems. Ask for and check the references of previous and current clients, and make sure they have workman's compensation insurance and liability insurance. Remember they are working in your home. If a worker for an uninsured firm gets injured on your job, you could be liable.

The offer of free equipment and installation has limits. It typically includes:

Watch Out!
Security systems are full of hidden expenditures. When you add the cost of additional sensors and keypads and a sometimes inflated telephone-hookup charge, don't be surprised if your "free" installation costs around $150. An ADT monthly central monitoring service of $24.95 per month for 60 months will add up to $1,497 over the life of your contract, or $300 each year.

- A central control box
- One keypad
- Two door sensors and one window sensor
- A motion detector
- One indoor siren

Careful analysis of your situation probably will indicate the need for additional keypads, window sensors, and perhaps an outdoor siren. It also makes little sense to have an alarm system without heat and smoke detectors tied into the monitoring service. Check to make sure they are included.

You might find that any additional devices beyond the basic offer are charged at double what they should cost. Service and installation labor might be very high—$65 an hour or more. Your job during initial interviews with the alarm-firm salespeople is to get straight answers to your questions about these extras. And read everything you sign very carefully.

Compare "free" offers to the many local independent alarm firms that typically include purchase and installation of the following:

- The control panels
- Two door sensors
- Six window censors
- An indoor and outdoor siren
- Smoke and heat alarms
- Telephone hookup to the control center

The cost for equipment and installation in the average home should run between $800 and $1,200. The annual fee for the monitoring service runs about $180.

Moneysaver
You don't have to go with a huge alarm company to have a well-monitored service. There are many highly qualified and competitive firms in the monitoring business. Local alarm firms tend to keep tabs on two or three competitors to stay on their toes for service and better pricing.

Do alarm systems work?

In a survey of police chiefs sponsored by the Security Equipment Industry Association, 90 percent of the responding chiefs said they believe homes and businesses with alarm systems are less likely to be burglarized than comparable establishments without alarm systems. The same percentage believes an alarm system increases the probability of a burglar being apprehended.

The alarm industry was created by ADT around 1840 as a safeguard for night watchmen. It has since developed into a multibillion-dollar business. Anything with a big cash flow tends to attract some less-than-honorable characters and some less-than-fair sales techniques. Determine exactly what your home needs and then get bids from three or four alarm firms. The bids should include the equipment and installation plus the central monitoring service.

Hiring a pest control professional

This section covers what a pest control professional does before entering your house with all his equipment, what he does as he goes through your house, and what you can expect as a final result. You'll learn where to find and how to check on reputable pest control firms and what to look out for from the less-than-reputable pretenders. I'll also give you an idea of how much various treatments can cost and how long they will take.

A termite inspection is the closest most people come to hiring a pest control firm. They're not called termite inspections anymore, however; they're now *wood-destroying insect inspections.*

Knowing that the house you are about to buy (or sell) is wood-eating-insect-free offers peace of mind.

Unofficially...
Ninety percent of all alarms sounded from homes and businesses are false alarms. For this reason, most police and fire chiefs in larger cities prefer alarms that alert a 24-hour monitoring company to those that report directly to police or fire departments. The central monitor contacts you before the police are notified. This helps prevent the police from wasting limited resources.

It also can be a real money saver because you can either avoid buying a home with real problems or renegotiate a price that will allow funds to fix the problem.

How do you know you need a pest control expert?

If you are selling your house, you don't need a pest inspection because your buyer will probably retain a wood-destroying insect inspector to go over your house in the 10-day window between the sales contract agreement and the final signing. This is often the only inspection required by lending institutions.

If you are living in the house and are not planning to sell your house, the first indication of a pest problem might be a long trail of little red or big black ants or a swarm of winged bugs that look like ants. It could also be piles of what looks like sawdust around your foundation. (This is not a good sign.)

What you can expect from a pest control service

When you call to request a visit from a representative, you will be asked to describe the creatures causing you concern. The pest control specialist comes prepared to solve your problem, but he will probably want to confirm the extent of the infestation and the exact type of insect you are harboring.

- **Termites.** The more famous of the wood-destroying insects accomplish their destruction by actually eating the wood. They cannot be eliminated with a single treatment; they require treatment once a month for 12 consecutive months.

- **Carpenter ants.** These insects come in various subtypes, but they all are in the wood-destroying insect category because they dig their way into your beams to create their nests. You are most

Timesaver
Try to capture one or two of the invading insects to show the serviceman when he comes. This will help him determine more quickly the exact nature of your problem.

likely to see them in the spring when they are swarming and mating. You should save a specimen because they disappear after an initial flurry. Carpenter ants go through four cycles from eggs to adult, lasting 10 months. Your pest controller will want to come back every month for a year to catch each generation as it matures.

■ **Little red ants.** You might be fascinated by the long line of ants leading to and from your sugar bowl, but they really aren't very good guests. They can usually be eliminated with one or two treatments.

■ **Meal moths.** These insects resemble moths. When you flatten one, it leaves a dark dusty smudge on the wall or ceiling. They seem to come into your home through various grains: bird seed, cereals, and so on. They are hard to get rid of because they crawl into the cracks and crevices of the cupboards to breed and lay eggs. Getting rid of any open grain packages and washing down the cupboards can help, but it won't get them all. You must spray to get into their nests.

■ **Rats, mice, and other larger visitors.** Elimination of rodents seems to be a service often thrown in with a termite, carpenter ant, or other insect-treatment program. My wife and I set traps and reluctantly check them when we find corners of cereal boxes chewed open, droppings, or other evidence of mice. Professionals have more efficient baits and eliminators.

How do you locate a reputable exterminator?

The size and number of ads in the Yellow Pages is startling. Extermination is both a highly popular vocation and a highly controlled industry. (It has both state and national standards.) Each firm must be licensed, and each service person must be trained and licensed. I suggest calling a couple firms and then checking their credentials by calling your state's licensing board, your local Better Business Bureau, the National Pest Control Association, and your state chapter of this association.

This is an industry that, in the past, has had some shady operators—usually not the licensed firms, just individuals pretending to be qualified and licensed.

Possible scams to look out for

If someone comes in and says he can eliminate your termite or carpenter ant problem with one treatment, you are dealing with a scam artist. You probably won't know it for a year, however. After the ants' initial spring fling, they virtually disappear for another year as they go outside for their preferred food. A year later, they will make their presence known again.

The one-shot claim is impossible because EPA regulation stipulates that all pest control agents must be biodegradable within 24 days. Unless he is using illegal sprays, the 10-month incubation period will outlast the spray.

What warranties are offered?

Warranties vary according to what is being treated and how it is treated. Your red ant problem will be solved for 60 days. The much more extensive and difficult termite treatment might be guaranteed for five years.

How long does a treatment take?

You can expect the exterminator to be in your home no longer than an hour or two for the first termite

Bright Idea
Accompany your pest control service person on his tour of the house. In addition to the verbal explanations you pick up, you will learn what problems to look for and where to look for them.

treatment and 20 to 30 minutes for each of the 11
monthly visits that should follow. Other bugs can be
handled in shorter times.

Approximate costs

A half-hour treatment for red ants for two consecutive months might cost you $180. A full termite
riddance process could run from $1,200 to over
$2,000. Variables include your type of foundation,
ground cover (ivy, bushes, and so forth), accessibili-
ty of the affected area, and so on.

Benefits to the homeowner

Aside from the warm feeling of knowing that termites and carpenter ants are no longer eating away
at your foundation, you will be rid of creatures that
are more annoyance than hazards. The pest control
companies I contacted said that, as an additional
service, they invariably leave other traps and pesti-
cides around to hit the mice, beetles, ticks, fleas,
silverfish, and spiders that are our uninvited coha-
bitants.

In summary, most people really do not like to
see any bugs taking up residence in their cupboards.
Most pest control visits do not take a long time and
are not overly expensive. The fears of antipesticide
groups are sometimes over-blown. The EPA has a
strong say in what chemicals can be used in
your home and the length of time they can pose a
hazard.

Most wood-destroying insect inspections are
purchased by home buyers during the 10 days (stipulated in most agreements) between the time of a
purchase agreement and the final signing. If you
have any outward signs of termites or carpenter ants
in your home, don't wait to sell to get it inspected.
These problems can be easily corrected.

Bringing in a nitpicker: getting your home inspected

For a profession that is only about 20 years old, home inspection has become very important in the real estate market and, to a lesser degree, in construction. A trained and licensed home inspector has replaced novice evaluations by your drinking buddy's uncle of the property you are about to buy.

This section discusses what an inspector does as he goes through your house and what you can expect in his final report. You also will learn where to find reputable inspectors, what to look out for from less-than-reputable pretenders, and how much an inspection might cost.

For most buyers, an inspection offers peace of mind. For some, however, it can also be a real money saver. From a neutral, third-party perspective, an inspector can offer reasons to renegotiate a price, by locating faults and problems even the owner might not know about.

When do you need an inspector?

If you are selling your home, you probably don't need an inspection because the buyer must retain an inspector to examine your house during the 10-day period between the sales contract agreement and the final signing.

Most inspections are purchased by home buyers. The buyer's lawyer can use the inspection report to add a list of items to be repaired or replaced by the seller; these items become contingencies to the purchase agreement. The seller can choose to fix the items in time for the closing, negotiate further, or call the deal off. No matter which direction the negotiations eventually go, the buyer is now at least aware of potential problems before they become his sole responsibility.

More about the inspection process

A home inspection is a walk-through, visual process. It is not a take-it-apart-and-test-it procedure. Glaring problems are usually found, however, and financial surprises are held to a minimum. Inspections are about reducing risk. Inspectors don't have x-ray vision, but they can:

- Make observations
- Consider implications
- Evaluate interactions
- Weigh risks and probabilities
- Draw reasonable conclusions
- Make recommendations

The following classes of findings get the inspector's highest priority of attention:

1. Things (items or situations) that are dangerous
2. Things that cause rapid, costly damage
3. Essential things that don't work

An inspector's job is to distinguish between what is potentially important (costly, dangerous, doesn't work) and what is unimportant (on a cost and risk scale).

Home inspectors perform a complete visual inspection of your house—inside and out. This includes:

- Foundation
- Heating and air-conditioning systems
- Plumbing
- Electrical setup
- Shingles
- Rain gutters
- Siding

Unofficially...
Oddly enough, *the purpose of an inspection is not to find defects.* Your inspector might point out minor defects as a courtesy or even as an added service, but the purpose of the inspection is to reduce the chances of a costly or very dangerous surprise.

- Attic
- Garage

What home inspectors do not inspect

A home inspector does not inspect or report on systems or components that aren't readily accessible, such as a chimney flue or insulation hidden inside a wall cavity. You can request, for an additional fee, some specialty inspections that are not usually included:

- Water wells
- Septic systems
- Swimming pools
- Water-quality testing
- Radon testing
- Termite inspection

A home inspector does not confirm property lines or acreage. If you require these services, an inspection firm can probably arrange a qualified professional to handle these items for you.

The written report you receive pinpoints any household systems or components in need of immediate repair and indicates problems to come. This report also outlines any health- or safety-related concerns the inspector might have about your home. One home inspector I interviewed makes a copy of his 16-page checklist along with his notes and presents it to his client at the end of his inspection—no waiting for a written report.

As he takes his tour, the home inspector might have the following problem-classification system in mind:

1. **Lowest priority.** Consider but do not report . . . premature.

Watch Out!
Home inspectors do not give you an opinion on whether a particular property is a good deal or fairly priced. These judgments are outside their area of expertise and in fact are prohibited by their code of ethics.

2. **Medium priority.** Report potential defects to client with advice to watch and investigate.

3. **High priority.** Report likely defects to client and advise as to further action.

4. **Extreme priority.** Report and identify virtually certain costly or dangerous conditions.

Even if they are not a high or extreme priority, subtle defects, modifications, historical data, and site conditions might suggest the presence of a costly or dangerous problem in the future. The probability is high enough to justify a warning to the client.

An inspector should always be asking these questions: What's different here? What surprise is waiting? What's holding that up? How do air, moisture, and people move in the building? How does that work? What has changed here? Why? Did it work? What is this little anomaly? Could it point to something important?

How to locate a reputable home inspector

As with most home-building specialists, if your neighbors or a friend know of a reputable home inspector, that is your best lead. The Yellow Pages (look under "Building & Land Inspection Services") can offer more help than usual for this category because the listings often include the inspector's affiliations with national professional associations:

- American Society of Home Inspectors (ASHI)

- National Association of Home Inspectors (NAHI)

- American Inspectors Association (AIA)

Members of these associations are bound by their codes of ethics and are barred from doing follow-up repair work or renovation for their clients.

They are also prohibited from dealing with realtors, which would be a conflict of interest. These associations also require members to meet certain professional standards and to keep their skills current through continuing education.

Moneysaver
Before you hire a home inspector, make sure you understand what exactly is included in the basic inspection. Decide whether you need any "special" inspections and determine their cost. Have a contract.

Look for inspectors with at least two (and preferably five) years of experience and some 200 inspections under their belts. Interview two or three inspection firms. Check their references. Make sure they are appropriately insured and look over some of their inspection reports. (Inspectors need insurance for their own protection. If they fail to report a fault, they can be and have been sued by new homeowners. Moreover, they are covered for any injuries sustained during the home inspection. After all, they are poking around in potentially dangerous areas.)

What you can expect from an inspection

In a presentation given in Toronto at the national seminar of the Ontario Association of Home Inspectors in October 1997, Dan Freidman of Poughkeepsie, NY, outlined some home inspection philosophies. "Inspections are not about eliminating risk . . . We cannot reduce risk to zero. To attempt to do so would be to tear everything apart, replace everything, and in the course of putting back together, probably make new errors which would lead to still more problems.

"Inspections are about reducing risk . . . We identify visually detectable problems—visually detectable risks for which there is sufficient data to suggest attention—and select levels of response appropriate for economic and safety reasons.

"For example, a bad burner on a range, while annoying, is (1) excluded from ASHI scope and (2)

very unlikely to be connected to a significant
expense at the property. Focus on this clue builds an
inappropriate expectation in the mind of your
client that the purpose of the inspection is to assure
that trivial items are in order: stove burners, oven
temperature accuracy, dishwasher cycling, gate
latches. These are absolutely not the purpose of
your inspection, and not only does attention to
them miscommunicate to your client, it also dilutes
your total attention and risks an increased probability that you fail to attend to something costly or
dangerous."

According to a member survey conducted by
ASHI, water-related problems were the most common problem reported. Water problems involve
improper surface grading which, in turn, causes wet
basements and crawl spaces. Water also plays a role
in roof damage, faulty plumbing, and flaws in the
home's exterior walls. Improper electrical wiring,
particularly in older homes, and malfunctioning
heating systems were also frequently mentioned by
the ASHI members.

Inspections are not a high-cost item, and they
can be done within a couple hours—time is not a
big factor. The time required for a survey varies.
The size of the house and its general state obviously
affect the time, but most inspections run between
two and four hours. Home inspection fees usually
start at about $175 and increase with the location
and complexity of the house. Specialty inspections,
if necessary, also increase the cost.

Possible scams in home inspection

A fair number of scam artists and incompetent
inspectors are scattered throughout the trade. They
use the homeowner's invitation to inspect the home

and the credibility of a professional to go on a repair-job shopping tour of the house. They are apt to find foundation leaks, chimney problems, and furnace problems that do not exist, all of which his firm or a friend's firm would be willing to come in and fix.

Home inspection is a growing profession in this country. Inspectors can be retained by homeowners for their own peace of mind or by people planning to do extensive remodeling or new construction, but primarily they are employed during the sale of homes, so that the buyer has confidence about the soundness of their investment.

Just the facts

- Security systems offer many ways to feel safer in your home, but look out for "free" deals.

- Bring in pest control professionals when you notice uninvited company.

- A home inspection can help you find items that need repairing. If you are looking to purchase a particular house, a home inspector can alert you to obvious problems that could be hazardous and/or costly to repair.

Taking Care of the Outside of Your Home

PART VIII

GET THE SCOOP ON...
When it's time for a new roof ▪ Re-siding pros
and cons ▪ Repainting the outside of your home
▪ Replacement windows

Putting on a Good Front: Exterior Maintenance and Repairs

U p to this point, we have discussed many options for improving the living conditions inside your home. Now we come to the outside, where an improved appearance often benefits your neighbors more than you. Driving up to your newly painted or re-sided home can give you a warm feeling of pride and maybe some additional warmth when you get inside, thanks to better insulation and higher R-valued windows.

You should remind yourself that paint and re-siding preserve your house's wood, and the roof is your first line of defense against the wind and rain that nature hurls at you.

When to put a (new) lid on it

The most common indication that you need a new roof is water leaking through a ceiling. This can start

349

Chapter 17

with the simple staining of the walls or ceiling after a particularly heavy rain combined with high winds. Another indication is when the shingles begin to curl, cup, lift at the edges, and dry out.

You can also learn a lot by checking your calendar. If it has been more than 20 years since you last resurfaced your roof, maybe it's time to do this again. On the other hand, maybe you've decided just to give your home a lift, and a new roof would enhance the look. Whatever the reason, you certainly don't want to make any costly mistakes.

Not surprisingly, homeowners fall victim to a number of pitfalls, including evaluating and hiring a contractor without a personal interview, judging estimates on price only, selecting products without comparison shopping, and failing to understand reroofing basics. Being prepared and knowing what to expect when reroofing work begins will help ensure your ultimate satisfaction with your new roof.

How to find a reputable roofing contractor

Referrals are the best place to start. If your neighbor recently had his roof replaced, ask about the contractor and whether he was happy with the work done. Short of personal references, check the roofer listings on the Contractor Network Web site (www.contractornet.com).

The next best place to seek out a reputable contractor is to go to your local building distributor or lumberyard and ask for recommendations. I'm not referring to large home centers or retail store chains, but professional roofing material distributors who work with reputable contractors on a regular basis. The Yellow Pages is usually the third place you can look. Be prepared, however, to make a substantial number of follow-up calls before you get a contractor to actually come out and look at your job.

You should interview two to three different contractors whether they are referrals or names from the Yellow Pages.

You might use the following points to evaluate the contractors:

Watch Out!
Do not consider any bids from contractors you have not met, interviewed, and checked out.

- Repeat business in the nearby area

- Length of time in business (preferably at least five years)

- Willingness and ability to handle complaints quickly and fairly

- Completeness and professionalism of estimate offered and presentation given (roofers often have pictures of the jobs they have done)

- Proof of proper workman's compensation and liability insurance, a state contractor's license, and 8 to 10 references (job-site locations or names of homeowners)

- Membership in professional associations

- Knowledge and thoroughness of roofing procedures

What is the best way to judge an estimate?

Although you might receive a reliable, fair estimate from the first contractor you interview, you should usually obtain two additional estimates to help you determine which one is best. In judging the cost of a job, you should consider the following issues:

- Your evaluation of each contractor's reputation for standing behind his warranty and providing the service promised.

- The quality and completeness of the roof system recommended. Make sure the job includes

Bright Idea
Judge the value of proposals using the criteria I discuss throughout this book: don't rely only on the lowest bid. A low price can signal discrepancies and shortcomings in the reliability of the contractor.

ventilation and waterproofing underlayment (if appropriate to your region and home structure).

- The quality of the product choices offered. Expect to pay a higher price for designer or architectural shingles.

- The completeness of the contractor's insurance package. Make sure you are protected from involvement in worker injuries, third-person liabilities, and damages consequential to the work being performed.

What to expect from a roofing contractor

After a contract or agreement has been signed, the usual time delay before the job starts is two to six weeks, weather permitting. This period can vary a great deal depending on the season and the contractor's backlog. Job-start delays and postponements are a fact of life in a trade so highly dependent on the weather. The contractor also has a responsibility to you, however, to be honest and straightforward about his availability right from the start. He should also advise you on a timely basis about any changes in the original schedule.

What reroofing involves

I recommend hiring a professional contractor to reroof your home, but you still should familiarize yourself with certain aspects of the reroofing process. Various conditions about your roof might limit your product choices or affect the cost of your job, so you need to be familiar with your options.

Here's a list of questions relevant to the reroofing process:

- Do I need to obtain a permit to install a new roof on my home?

- What is my roof slope? Does the slope of the roof limit the choice of shingle that can be used? The slope of the roof is measured by the rise (vertical distance) versus the run (horizontal distance). Some roof slopes can limit your choice of shingles. For example, a roof slope below 2/12 (2 inches per foot) cannot use shingles.

- Will it be necessary to tear off existing shingles before reroofing? If they are torn off, who is responsible for cleaning up the yard and disposing of old shingles? Most areas have codes regarding the allowed number of roofing layers. The weight is sometimes too much for wooden rafters, especially in areas where snowfall can add more to the load.

- Is the roof properly ventilated? Research has shown that proper ventilation is required if shingles are to last their warranted life. This requires small vents in the *soffit*, under the eaves, that allow air to flow under the shingled roof. Other kinds of vents include roof vents (metal vents inserted into the roof surface, usually on the back of the house) and ridge vents (shingle-topped venting systems installed along the roof peak).

How long should a roofing job take?

The time it takes to finish a roofing job varies widely depending on the size and complexity of the roof. A small, uncomplicated roof job can usually be finished in a day or two. A large, complex project can last a week or more, particularly if several layers of old roofing must be removed. Once started, however, a job should not be interrupted for any reason other than weather.

The effect of weather is considerable. It is a common practice among contractors to discontinue roofing work in wet or windy weather for both the workers' and your home's safety. Depending on the roofing being applied, cold weather might also halt work. Organic shingles (as opposed to fiberglass shingles) available in colder climates are typically more robust for handling in cold weather and can be applied later into the winter season. Hot weather can also present application problems such as marring of the granule surface from foot traffic on the hot shingles. Each contractor's expertise will determine his approach to these problems.

How to protect yourself

You can expect to pay a percentage of the job up-front upon signing the contract. Contractors have to protect themselves from homeowners also.

Deposit requirements vary from contractor to contractor. It is not considered unreasonable to pay a deposit, but you should never pay up-front for the total job. The deposit and progressive payments should not equal more than 75 percent of the total price of the job. (Some state laws regulate this amount.)

It's recommended that you not give any deposit to a contractor whose track record you have not verified by references from recent work.

Roofing material options

Selecting roofing shingles is no easier than purchasing a major home appliance. There are a lot of choices. You should investigate your options carefully, do some comparison shopping, and weigh the costs against the features and benefits you desire.

Just like choosing a car, the overriding factor in selecting a roofing shingle is knowing whether your

Moneysaver
Before signing the contract or agreement, make sure the price covers all materials, ventilation, cleanup, dumping fees (if applicable), and labor for specific repairs (such as replacing rotted wood, flashing around a chimney, and so on).

primary goal is function only or function plus aesthetics. With a car, you should know whether you want a sporty, knock-'em-dead model or a practical sedan with room for several passengers. It's the same with roofing shingles. Your choices of material include asphalt/fiberglass, wood, metal, clay, concrete, and slate.

Asphalt/fiberglass

When contractors talk about asphalt shingles, they are actually referring to organic, felt-based shingles. Organic shingles are saturated and coated with asphalt. They offer excellent resistance to blow-off (they won't get blown off the roof in a strong wind) as well as outstanding tear and nail-pull resistance.

Fiberglass shingles are also asphalt shingles; the difference is that they're made on a fiberglass base. Properly sealed and correctly applied, many fiberglass shingles offer the same standard of tear and nail-pull resistance as their organic felt counterparts, in addition to excellent wind resistance.

Both organic and fiberglass shingles can be good choices for your home. About 80 percent of all homes are roofed with this type of shingle. The main advantages are versatility, performance, and comparatively low prices. Most also have Underwriters Laboratories (UL) Class A fire resistance ratings (the highest).

The three-tab shingle, also known as a strip shingle, is most common and has been applied to homes since the early 1900s. Since the invention of the Hallmark Shingle by CertainTeed Corporation in 1965, however, shingles have taken on a much more sophisticated, dimensional appearance with a variety of color blends to choose from.

As a result, manufacturers today provide a range of product choices, from strip shingles carrying

Unofficially...
When discussing roofing, contractors and roofing suppliers always talk in terms of "squares." One square will cover 100 square feet of your roof.

20-year warranties to more durable and appealing products carrying warranties of 25 years and longer. Major differences among these products that are discernible by the homeowner are usually reflected in the construction of the shingle, which determines its appearance.

Fiberglass shingles are made by a variety of manufacturers and are constructed to duplicate the appearance of wood shakes. One of the most dramatic looks is found in GAF's Timberline Ultra shingle. The shadow lines are so deep that the shingles are often mistaken for real wood. They also have a series that resembles slate. This product comes with a whopping 40-year warranty.

The cost for these shingles ranges from a low of $28 per square up to $80 per square for a designer series. The lowest installed price is about $90 per square. This depends on the type of roof, the accessibility, and the amount of work involved, such as ripping off all the old shingles and underlayment.

Wood shingles

Cedar shingles or shakes are often considered a luxury item. (Shakes are split from blocks of wood; shingles are smoothly sawed.) They run about $75 per square and have a lower fire rating. If properly maintained, however, they are extraordinarily durable.

Maintenance consists of keeping them clear of moisture-retaining debris and treating them with a preservative spray every five years to prevent moss and fungus growth. They can also be treated with an effective fire retardant.

Cedar is not the only wood available for shingles. Pressure-treated southern pine shingles from the Southern Forest Products Association (SFPA) are

Bright Idea
Ask your contractor to show you the good, better, and best choices in the line of products he offers. This range of choices allows you to see all the options available and helps you make the best choice by comparison shopping.

gaining more acceptance. They last 30 years, and the only downside reported by contractors is that they weigh more than cedar.

There is also a man-made, composition-wood shingle from Masonite. It is a wood fiber, self-spacing, side-lap shingle that looks like natural wood. It is easy to maintain and even weathers to a natural gray.

Metal

Shingles can also be made of steel, copper, or aluminum. They are designed to go over a solid deck and are fire safe, durable (lasting 30 years or more), and energy efficient.

The metal roofs I'm most familiar with are on farmhouses and barns in Vermont and are made of 30-foot-long strips of galvanized steel. They seem to work just fine and shed snow well, perhaps thanks to steeply pitched roofs. Precoated colors, such as barn red and dark green, have recently been added.

Metal roof manufacturers are also showing some creativity these days. Mel-Tile, Inc., for example, has combined the strength of steel with the look of Spanish tiles. Lightweight copper shingles are also available. They combine copper's beauty and durability with asphalt-shingle technology, and they come with a 30-year warranty.

Clay and concrete tiles

Clay and concrete tiles are traditionally associated with the southwestern U.S., but they are beginning to move outward as they take on new shapes, such as cedar shake and the traditional "S" or half-round configuration. Other selling points are that clay tiles can withstand wide temperature ranges, are virtually immune to decay and erosion, are fireproof, and have a 50-year to lifetime warranty. They

Unofficially...
Because snow, condensation, and rust buildups can be harmful, manufacturers recommend that metal shingles be used only on homes in warmer climates.

are also expensive—costing as much as $10 per square foot—and are very heavy.

Slate

Slate is generally regarded as the ultimate roofing material, with good reason. It still survives on centuries-old mansions and castles in Europe. It also weighs in at 800 pounds per square, so it should only be used on steeply pitched roofs.

With this much weight, it is best if you live near a slate quarry, because the price tag, including shipping, comes in at between $240 to $1,100 per square. Even used slate salvaged from old buildings can cost between $195 and $900 per square, depending on its color.

Now you know. There are no simple aspects to getting things replaced or remodeled around your home—reroofing is no exception. Selecting the right grade and material to meet your functional or aesthetic roofing needs takes some study and decision-making skills. (One advantage to getting a new roof is that it usually does not affect the inside of your house. You can go on with your daily life.)

I've covered how to locate a contractor, but you should probably decide ahead of time what general type of roofing material you want. That way, you can ask whether your contractor is skilled in applying it. Ask questions and get answers before you hire the contractor. Make sure the contract covers all aspects of the task at hand before you sign it.

New siding on the outside of your home

I'll admit it up front—I'm not a big fan of aluminum or vinyl siding. Although design and application techniques in recent years have made improvements

Bright Idea
For more information on roofing products, contact the CertainTeed Home Institute, Roofing Products Group, P.O. Box 860, Valley Forge, PA 19482 (610-341-7000). You can request *The Homeowner's Guide to Reroofing.* You might also read "Home Report" by James Lomuscio in *Home* magazine, June 1993.

in appearance, I still don't think they have solved the problems of fitting existing windows and doors to the thicker walls created by the siding.

There are, however, some compelling reasons to put siding on your home, and in this section I'll review some of them. If you already have siding, this section offers some hints for maintaining it. I'll also try to give you enough information to be able to judge the differences between companies and products, and I'll give you some idea of the relative costs. To many people, the words "aluminum siding" have become synonymous with "rip-off." I'll also give you some advice on how to avoid becoming a victim of con artists.

How do you know you need it?

The best reasons for choosing re-siding are if you have an older home with very poor or no insulation in the walls, if your clapboards are in very poor shape, or if you have peeling paint and you've discovered just how much paint and labor that nice old Victorian cottage requires. If you add these considerations to the shortened time between paint jobs that the new, environmentally friendly paint formulas bring us, siding begins to look better.

The virtually maintenance-free characteristics of vinyl siding mean less exterior upkeep for your home because painting is never necessary. Over time you save the costs of repainting, making vinyl siding a cost-efficient alternative to more traditional wood and composite lap sidings.

How do you locate good siding contractors?

Re-siding contractors are easy to spot as you drive around your local area. Any reputable firm will welcome an inquiry from a prospective client and should be willing to show you a little of how they

Moneysaver
You'll still have to wash vinyl siding, but a light soap-and-water cleanup is all that is ever required for vinyl siding, soffits, fascia, installation components, and accessories.

work and what the job entails. Go to your neighbors, friends, and your local lumber dealer. If you need more names to complete your list for estimates (get at least four), you might try the Yellow Pages. I could not find a listing under siding contractors, aluminum siding, or vinyl siding. Some GCs listed siding as one of the services they perform.

Now you really need solid references from your bidders, and you should check them out thoroughly. Check the firms with the Better Business Bureau and go with companies that have been in business at least five years.

How to spot the con artists

The first clue that you might be dealing with a shady operator in any number of fields is if he comes to you either at your front door or by phone and offers you a deal that sounds too good to be true. If the salesperson then pressures you to make a decision immediately ("or else you'll lose this wonderful price"), say good-bye. That is a dishonest tactic.

The best protection against fraud is to keep your money in your wallet or bank account until you are completely happy with the completed job. A percentage for a down payment might be necessary to protect the installer's interests, but make sure enough money is left unpaid so the contractor has incentive to finish the job.

What you should expect when the contractor comes

Any mess created by new siding should remain nicely outside your living area. The amount of mess or dumpsters required depends on what you decide to do with the old siding. You can cover it up with a layer of insulation board and a insulating wrap of some kind and just add the new siding, or you can tear it off.

Before starting work, your contractor should clean and repair the underlying surface. Any new siding, shingles, or clapboards should be installed on a level, nailable surface. All vinyl panels interlock. This hides the nails, and the lapping offers weather-tightness. For horizontal or vertical siding, nails should be centered in the nailing slots just loose enough to allow for thermal movement of the siding. Siding should never be applied directly to studs; sheathing boards should be installed.

Upon completion, your contractor should clean the siding and soffit work to remove fingerprints and soiled areas. (When you stand under your roof's overhang and look up, you're looking at the soffit.) He also should remove all scrap materials.

Siding options

We tend to think of siding as man-made metal or vinyl, but there are a variety of ways to add traditional siding to an existing building. One way is to sheath the house in a insulating wrap, add a layer of 4 × 8–foot sheathing panels, and cover this with a vertical board-and-batten siding. Board-and-batten is made up of 8- or 10-inch boards nailed vertically to the building with 3-inch boards nailed over the cracks between them.

If the only reason you're getting the house re-sided is to avoid most of your painting chores, you might consider re-siding with cedar shingles and simply staining them or leaving them to weather.

I think you should rule out aluminum or other metal siding. The metal variety is subject to dings and dents, and it has a coating that can wear or be scraped off. Vinyl siding has color all the way through the material, is resistant to fading, is virtually chip-proof, and seems to last forever. It is also a

Bright Idea
Before you tear off old asphalt shingles or dented, torn aluminum, take a look at what's underneath. It's not uncommon for people to have covered up beautiful original clapboards with something that doesn't require extra work. You might find a gem worth salvaging.

better insulator than aluminum, which is a conductor.

A variety of vinyl sidings are currently available, as shown, for example, on the Georgia-Pacific Web site (www.gp.com). This site offers a wide variety of durable, attractive vinyl-siding products including siding, soffit, fascia, a line of accessories, and vinyl-siding installation components for any architectural style. All are available in today's popular designer colors.

Paneled or louvered shutters are available in a wide variety of colors with a baked-on acrylic finish and authentic wood-grain design. Should it become desirable to change the color over time, vinyl shutters can be painted with a quality exterior latex paint.

Unofficially...
You and your siding contractor should treat siding as if you are getting ready to paint. Do all the careful prep-work such as caulking around windows and doors, setting popped nails, smoothing, and sanding where necessary.

A great advantage enjoyed by vinyl siding over painting is the opportunity to apply a layer of insulation (or at least a wind-proofing wrap) to an old, leaky house. One example of insulating board is Owens Corning Fanfold, available in both ¼-inch and ⅜-inch thicknesses. It is an extruded polystyrene insulation that provides a smooth, even surface over the old siding for easy installation of the new siding. The product's fan-fold design virtually eliminates gaps to reduce air infiltration and helps create a total insulating envelope around your building.

PinkWrap house wrap is an energy-saving house wrap from Owens Corning, engineered as an air infiltration and moisture-protection barrier for use in residential sidewall construction. In addition to minimizing air leakage, which maximizes a home's overall energy performance, PinkWrap house wrap doesn't trap problem-causing moisture in your walls. Its design allows water vapor to pass through.

How long should it take to side a house?

In a race with painters, the crew putting on siding
would probably win if they were each working on a
large barn. The prep work should take about the
same amount of time, but the siding contractor has
to install insulating board or wrap and then has to
measure, cut, and fit vinyl covering around all the
windows, doors, dormers, porches, and so forth.

What is it going to cost?

The final cost is going to depend on the size and
complexity of your house, the amount of prep work
and insulating material you need, the quality of the
siding you select, and of course, your ability to drive
a hard bargain in the bidding wars. Remember to
weigh the cost against the money you save from not
having to repaint your house. In fact, unless you wait
until just after you paint your house to put on the
new siding, you should be able to mentally credit
your bank account a few hundred dollars each time
you see a neighbor out repainting his house. In a
few years, you should be feeling pretty good about
your decision. (I hope you picked a color you and
your spouse can live with.)

With the ever-shortening life span of exterior
paints, vinyl siding is beginning to get new consideration from homeowners. Take particular precautions when selecting a siding contractor. I suspect
they have worked hard to help clean up the negative
industry image (as depicted, for example, in the
movie *Tin Men*). You don't want to be the last suck-
er taken, however. If you get competitive bids, check
references, and pay most of the money after the job
is done, you should do all right.

Bright Idea
By ordering new,
vinyl-clad
replacement win-
dows when you
order vinyl sid-
ing, you can add
additional depth
to replacement
windows to
match the added
thickness of the
siding plus insu-
lation.

Repainting outside: a face-lift for your home

Much of the basic information discussed in the section about painting inside your house (see Chapter 13) also applies to the outside, with some notable exceptions. The biggest difference is that everyone can see whatever you do to the outside. There are few improvements you can make to the outside of your house that will add more value than a new coat of paint.

In this section I will go over some of the clues that tell you your house needs attention and some of the things that can save you a paint job for a couple of years. I'll try to help you find a painter who is an artist rather than a con artist, and I'll alert you to a few of the shortcuts some take. I'll take you through the job a painter does so you'll know what to expect. You'll also get a feel for your options, such as color, type of paint, and even how much to paint.

How do you know you need to repaint?

If your house has cracking, blistering, or peeling paint, you're probably due for a paint job—particularly if you are trying to sell your home and get a good price for it. If the paint is in good shape but your house looks grimy and dirty, a good washing (rather than a full repainting) can bring back the color and luster of the original paint job.

There are several products and devices on the market for washing your house, from the basic scrub brush and a pail of soapy water to a whirling brush attached to your garden hose by a long pipe.

My painter suggested I take a shot at cleaning the trim and shingles (both asphalt roofing and cedar siding) using a rented power washer. Now here is a powerful tool that even Tim "the Tool

Man" Taylor could appreciate. First, it took the dirt off the trim and siding and cleaned the fungus off the garage roof shingles. Second, I tried it on my very weathered deck. It took the gray out, right down to the fresh wood.

If you choose to paint, you might not have to do all the painting at one time. Take a walk around your house and look at the paint on all four walls. In northern states, north- and west-facing walls seem to bear the brunt of the weather, and the paint often shows it. In southern states, the sun is the enemy and the south-facing wall gets it the worst.

You can save yourself some money by painting only the worst side(s) of your house and by hosing down the rest. You'll probably have to paint the whole house eventually, but if you can spread the cost out over two or three years, it won't hurt as much. Another partial approach to the painting problem is to do only the side that faces the street, the one the world sees.

You can paint just the trim around the windows and doors and at the eaves and corners. This isn't just a cheap trick: The trim paint on our house seems to fall off every two years. If the trim looks bad, the whole house looks bad. We did the trim last summer; the rest of the walls, which are painted shingles, looked fine.

How to locate good painters

Again, go to your neighbors and friends for their recommendations. This time you also can add your local paint-specialty stores to the list. A paint-store manager knows most of the painters in your area and would probably give you the names of four or five. You still have to check their references by talking to past clients. Look for someone who has been in business for at least five years.

Watch Out!
If you hold the nozzle of a power washer 12 to 16 inches away from a surface, it is a cleaning tool. If you hold the nozzle 4 inches away from the surface and don't move it quick enough, it becomes a powerful cutting tool and can take wood off weathered features.

The lead time needed to start a painting job is much less than that required by most contractors in construction. Work can usually start whenever you want, depending on your painter's availability. In the middle of summer, this could prove to be a problem. The better he is, the longer you might have to wait. You still need a proposal or contract in which your painter outlines the job tasks, an estimated schedule, and an estimate of the cost of labor and paint.

How to spot con artists

Outside painters often are the same people who paint inside. They can be professional and well-meaning, and can be incompetent, simply inexperienced, or outright dishonest. The techniques for taking advantage of homeowners on the inside of the house can also be used on the outside. The most common technique is to charge the client for the best paint and then buy the least expensive.

What you should expect when the painter comes

When getting your house painted on the outside, the inside of your house is yours to live in as usual. There is no mess, no dust, no furniture to move, and no vital appliances to live without. There might be some dirt tracked, however, in because you have to give your painter access to the various facilities.

Here is a list, more or less in order, of the steps in painting your house:

1. The painter, possibly with a partner, first covers the shrubbery under the area where he plans to start prepping the surface and painting.

2. He next starts his prep work. Prep work on the outside is just as important as on the inside, but it need not be quite so meticulous. The first

Timesaver
Make sure you give your painter permission to enter your home to use the bathroom. You could also include the refrigerator, sink, and microwave on your list of available services. A pot of coffee might go a long way toward getting the work day started earlier.

effort should be with the hose to remove loose dirt and dust. Next come scrapers, electric sanders, wire brushes, and even torches in the effort to get loose paint off and to create a relatively smooth surface.

3. Your painter next starts to sandpaper all the rough surfaces created and any hardened drips and runs left by previous painting. He countersinks any nails that have worked out from the siding and putties the dent. He cleans the accumulated grease, grime, cobwebs, and dust off the surface once more. The last step in the prep process is to caulk around every door and window frame and along the eaves. This keeps out water and continues your war on heat loss and cold-air infiltration.

This is a good time to check your gutters for any leaks or low spots that fill up and spill water down the side of your house. (You will be able to see where this is happening.) My personal recommendation, if you have gutters that have been riveted together, is to replace them with seamless gutters. Take off the old gutters that undoubtedly leaked. Paint the wood behind them and then install the new seamless gutters.

I had the gutters on my second story removed when I installed seamless gutters on the first floor. I couldn't reach those top gutters, but the surrounding maple trees could. The gutters were continuously clogged, and they rotted the soffits behind them. The water from the top roof now drops freely onto the overhang on the first floor and away in my new seamless gutters. I'm singing in the rain.

Watch Out!
Never attempt to cut corners by painting on a surface that hasn't been prepared. If you paint over blistered, peeling, and flaking old paint, it eventually will fall off and will take the new paint with it.

Moneysaver
Never paint over
mildew. The
paint job won't
last and you'll
have to do it all
over again. If
you seem to
have a particu-
larly stubborn
case of mildew,
ask your paint
dealer for
mildew-resistant
paint or for addi-
tives for your
new paint. He
might also have
more-powerful
mildew removers.

4. Check for mildew. As a professional, your painting contractor should know whether the stuff
   that looks like dirt is actually mildew. Mildew is
   a living fungus and can't just be washed off. It
   must be killed and scrubbed off with a mixture
   of one part bleach and three parts water. Add
   some powdered detergent to the mix and,
   after scrubbing, let it dry before hosing it off
   thoroughly.

5. Only now is your painter ready to open a can of
   paint. First he will apply a primer coat of paint
   to the walls. If you are moving from a darker
   color to a lighter color on the outside walls, he
   will probably recommend a "heavy primer" (a
   special formula of primer paint with better "hiding" qualities).

6. Finally, your painter will get to the part you
   thought you hired him for—painting your outside walls. Invariably, two coats of paint will be
   necessary.

What are your paint options?

Picking the color is only the first of many decisions
you get to make, but it can get you into the most
trouble with your neighbors. Just as you try to have
each room blend or harmonize with the rooms or
spaces around it inside your home, your house
should blend in with the general color tone of your
neighborhood.

If the homes around yours are painted in earth
tones (browns, yellows, tans, reds), don't paint yours
blue. If the neighbors' homes are in cool colors
(grays and blues), yours will stick out if it's not
done similarly. You might not want to go along
with this philosophy of togetherness, but you should

be aware of how the color of your home relates to others.

There are simply too many variables in effect to pick a color with complete accuracy. Be sure to be around when the first coat of your color goes on and after it dries. There's a chance you will be happy with the actual color and will be able to adjust. If you aren't and you can't, talk with your painter. The paint dealer can make subtle adjustments to lighten or darken the shade of the unused paint.

Some exterior paints are good for a wide range of surfaces and conditions, but no paint is perfect for all surfaces. Check the label on the can before you put it on your house. Like interior paints, exterior paints come with either a latex base or an oil or alkyd base. Here are some of your options:

■ **Water-based latex or acrylic paints.** This is the formula of choice for most do-it-yourselfers because it goes on fairly easily, it dries quickly, and the cleanup of brushes and equipment can be done in the kitchen sink. You can start painting with them while the surfaces are still damp after a rain or are covered with early morning dew. Latex exterior paints have another advantage over oil or alkyd paints—they are semipermeable. This means that water, or more likely moisture, can escape through it without causing bubbles or peeling. Oil paints are not permeable, so any moisture that gets into the wood behind the paint literally pushes the paint off in its effort to escape.

■ **Oil-based paint.** You might want to use oil-based paint outside in much the same way you use it inside and for the same reasons (see Chapter

Timesaver
With the fast drying time of acrylic paints, two coats can be applied in the same day. Oil-based paint must be applied to dry wood surfaces (a minimum temperature of 50 degrees Fahrenheit for both the air and the surface is recommended) and should dry overnight before applying the second coat.

13). It flows more evenly and works well on the door and window trim. It also has a slightly higher gloss and thus is easier to clean. Because your trim color is often lighter than the house paint, it shows the dirt sooner.

- **High-end paint versus low-cost paint.** You will get better coverage with good paint, and it will stand up to repeated washings better. Its price, however, can be as much as double the price of cheaper paints. Talk this point over with your painter and factor in the length of time you plan to remain in your home.

- **Spray painting.** Both water-based and oil-based paints can be applied with a spray gun and compressor. Spray painting the outside of a house is easier than spraying inside as long as it isn't windy. This is something best left to professionals. The advantage is that the painting goes much faster. The disadvantage is that the coats are thinner. Rolling or brushing results in a somewhat smoother application, but the difference is not exceptional.

How long should it take?

This depends on the size of your house, the condition of the outside walls, how many painters show up, the type of paint used, and the speed of the painters. Your painter, who will know most of these variables, can give you the best time estimate.

What is it going to cost?

There are several different approaches your painting contractor can take for establishing a price.

- **A flat-rate or firm bid.** Based on your contractor's estimate of the paint quality you want, the time needed, and the going local rate.

- **Time and materials.** Probably the fairest approach, with time charged at an hourly rate plus the cost of the paint.

- **Different approaches to the same method.** Some painters, according to my paint dealer, buy the paint and pass on their contractor's discount to the client. Others take their discount and charge the customer the retail price, thus giving themselves a little extra profit.

- **Combination of professional and do-it-yourself.** By doing some of the less demanding work yourself, you can save money. By using a professional, you get help with the work and can achieve professional results.

Getting someone to paint the outside of your house is a fairly straightforward project. With recommendations from friends, neighbors, and the local paint-store proprietor, you should be able to get three or four painters to look at your project and make bids. Check the references each painter gives you by at least calling the people. Preferably, you should go see what the contractor's work looks like. You might also get more straightforward answers to your questions in person.

Hiring an honest, quick, and experienced painting contractor should assure you of getting the level of preparation that a good result requires, a tighter house with all the necessary caulking, and a fair price for the materials and labor involved.

Replacing your windows

The need for new windows will be obvious if you're remodeling and cutting holes where no windows were before. The need for replacement windows is equally obvious if your home is drafty or if your old

Timesaver
Here are three labor-saving devices for painting. *Paint pads* can replace rollers for walls and trim. *Paint sticks* suck paint directly from the bucket into the handle. Paint is then fed into a roller by pushing down the plunger in the handle. This saves countless trips to the roller pan. *Foam paint brushes* are cheap, hold more paint, and make neater straight lines than other brushes.

windows are rotted, warped, and difficult to open (if you can't raise them in the summer or close them tightly in the winter).

One question to ask yourself is why you are considering a window job. If you are planning to sell your house within a year and you want to get a better selling price, you should consider some other alternatives. A study by *Remodeling* magazine shows you will only recover 69 percent of the installed cost of new windows when you sell. Replacement windows rank twelfth on the list of remodeling projects in terms of cost recovery. Working on your kitchen or bath will benefit you more.

If you are planning to stay where you are for at least five years, however, other factors come into the picture. Given time, your energy savings will begin to offset the cost of new windows. Once you have stopped cold air and water from flowing into your living spaces through your old windows, you have gained most of the energy savings you will realize with your new windows. There are also the less tangible reasons: a better-looking house, more light in your rooms, enhanced views, less upkeep, and ease of seasonal changes from screens to storms.

How to find a reputable replacement-window contractor

Windows are almost always a part of any construction project, whether new or remodeling. This means that almost any moderately experienced carpenter can take out your old windows and can install new ones. To find a contractor, referrals are again the best place to start. If you know a neighbor who recently had his windows replaced, ask about the contractor, the make of the windows, and whether he was happy with the work and the product.

Watch Out!
If you choose to replace your windows, beware of false economies to which homeowners can fall victim—judging window replacement estimates on price only, selecting products without comparison shopping, and not understanding window basics. Be prepared and know what is involved. It will help ensure your satisfaction with your new windows.

The next best place to seek out a reputable contractor is your local building-supply house or lumberyard. Most lumberyards have a model-window display area in which you can tour the vast number of choices in window materials, styles, manufacturers, and even glass type. The Yellow Pages is usually the third place you should look. You should interview two or three different contractors, whether they are referrals or from the Yellow Pages.

Investigate on your own to find out what a good window looks like and costs. A few replacement-window firms might call or come to you with specials. You should be wary of these firms because they might be offering thinly clad aluminum or vinyl windows at a premium price.

The cost of replacing windows primarily is determined by the quality of the product and the manufacturer you choose. Replacing a window is not a lengthy process, so installation fees should not raise your costs considerably.

When you question contractors during your initial search, you should find out the following:

- Length of time in business (preferably at least five years)

- Willingness and ability to handle complaints quickly and fairly

- Whether they offer a warranty for their work

- Proof of proper insurance, a state contractor's license, and two to four references

- Knowledge and thoroughness of replacement-window procedures

What is the best way to judge an estimate?

Although you might receive a reliable, fair estimate from the first contractor interviewed, you should

Moneysaver
Do not consider any windows with a warranty of less than five years on the glass seal. A warranty of 10 to 20 years is even better.

usually obtain two additional estimates to help you determine which one is best. In judging the cost of a job, you should evaluate the following:

- The reputation of each contractor for standing behind both his work and the manufacturer's warranty and for being there to provide the service he promises.

- The quality and completeness of the window system recommended. Make sure the job includes replacement trim both inside and outside and complete insulation around the windows.

- The quality of the product choices offered. There are hundreds of standard windows sizes and configurations. Custom orders are not unusual, but you can expect to pay a higher price for designer or architectural windows. You also can expect to wait two to three weeks for delivery (longer at the height of your local construction season).

- The completeness of the contractor's insurance package. This is designed to protect you from involvement in worker injuries, third-person liabilities, and damages consequential to the work performed.

What you can expect from a replacement-window contractor

After a contract or agreement has been signed, a good contractor leads you through a virtual maze of options. Our contractor went with us to the lumberyard and took us through the displays. He, along with the salesperson, explained the various features available and the costs.

If he has any eye for aesthetics, your contractor can help you select a window style that complements

Bright Idea
The most critical aspect of window replacement is getting the correct measurements for the window openings. Get an experienced window firm or contractor to measure and order your windows, even if you plan to install them yourself. If you order the wrong size and the windows are delivered . . . you're stuck with them.

your home. With an older home, it is probably best to duplicate the original windows. You certainly don't want to mix and match window styles. It can adversely affect your sales value.

How long should a replacement-window job take?

One new window of the same size as the old one can probably be replaced in a couple hours or less. You don't, however, have to multiply the number of windows by two hours to get the total time. After your contractor is set up, the second, third, and fourth windows will go in faster.

For more complicated replacements, such as larger windows or new windows in former walls, you have to listen to your contractor, but it will probably take less time than you imagine.

What replacing windows involves

If you are adding windows that were not there before, you probably need a local building permit and a visit from the building inspector.

After the windows have been ordered and delivered, your contractor will come in and remove your old windows. This involves removing the wood trim from both the inside and the outside of the window. He will then *cut* all the nails holding your old window. (Most do-it-yourselfers do not own the correct tools to remove the nails—a very difficult job.)

The simplest replacement job is if your new windows are the same size as your existing windows. The new ones can be popped in immediately. There isn't even much of a mess created, and you only have to clear enough space to move the new windows into the room. The next-easiest adjustment (if your home is not brick or stone) is if you kept the same width window but want them a foot or so longer (closer to the floor). It is fairly easy to cut

Watch Out!
Don't let your contractor start removing your old windows until their replacements are leaning against the wall beside them. Deliveries can be delayed or wrong, and windows leave a large hole in your house.

studs and put in a new footer. (A footer is at the bottom of a window; a header is the overhead beam.)

Complications arise when you replace your old window(s) with wider windows or a picture window. This calls for removing the old header, cutting studs, and replacing the header, footer, and sides. Now you're creating sawdust, and your workers need more room to operate—but you still don't have to move out.

The installers should be sure to:

- Nail the window into solid framing lumber and install a new header if necessary.

- Install a proper vapor barrier (plastic sheet or building paper).

- Pack the voids around the window with insulation or use a foam filler.

- Install good head flashing over the top of the outside of the window. Flashing is aluminum or copper sheeting pushed up under the siding and then brought out over the top of the window to keep water out of cracks and crevices. (It is also used around chimneys and where roof lines meet.)

- Carefully caulk all the seams around the window.

- Replace the inside and outside trim and paint if necessary.

I recommend hiring a professional contractor to install new or replacement windows in your home. You still should familiarize yourself, however, with certain aspects of the process. Here's a list of relevant questions:

- Do you need to obtain a permit to install new windows in your home? If so, who will apply for it?

- Do your new windows blend harmoniously with other windows and the style of your home?

- Have you increased the glass area so much that it will affect your heating bill?

- Will the additional sunlight fade your furniture and carpeting? If so, should you order ultraviolet light-shielding glass?

- How many years' warranty does the manufacturer offer on the seal in your new windows?

How to protect yourself from a replacement-window scam

It is considered reasonable to pay a percentage of the cost up-front upon signing the contract, but you never should pay for the whole job in advance. The deposit and progressive payments should not equal more that 75 percent of the total price of the job. (Again, some state laws regulate this amount.) Never give a deposit to a contractor whose track record you have not verified by references from recent work.

An additional precaution you might take if you live in a historic district or a town that holds architectural approval rights is to check on the town's policy regarding aluminum-clad or vinyl-clad windows. Some towns do not allow them at all.

Your replacement window options

Selecting windows is probably the most complicated process in remodeling. You should investigate your many options carefully, do some comparison shopping, and weigh costs against the features and benefits you desire.

Windows aren't like appliances or wall coverings, which can be replaced fairly easily if you change your mind or get tired of their features or

Bright Idea
When selecting window styles, be sure to consider the basic architecture and the effect of the windows on the overall appearance of your house, inside and out.

looks. New windows will be a part of your house for many years, affecting your home's looks, comfort, maintenance, and economy.

Keeping that in mind, you should avoid no-name window companies that arrive at your doorstep or on the other end of an unsolicited phone call. Stay with the companies (and there are many) that have worked years developing their names and reputations. They also offer a strong warranty on their windows—at least 10 years on the glass seal and all parts.

With today's high energy costs, only if you live in a temperate area does it make economic sense to go with anything but double-paned glass rated A by the Sealed Insulated Glass Manufacturers Association (SIGMA). The A rating means the seal that bonds the two panes of glass into a unit has met SIGMA's standards. You might save a few bucks with B or C windows, but the problems down the road when water or dirt gets in between the panes will outweigh short-term savings.

The style

Literally hundreds of style options are available in replacement windows. Here are just some of the options:

- **True divided lights.** These are traditional windows made up of individual panes of glass separated by wood called *muntin bars* (often pronounced *muttin bars* or just *muttins*). The style is called *mullioned windows* (very few people can keep all these terms straight).

- **True divided lights with wide or narrow muntin bars.** You now can buy windows with individual dual-pane glass, but they are expensive.

Unofficially...
Consumer Reports magazine, evaluating double-hung replacement windows, referred to single-pane windows as "dumb windows." "Smart windows" are double-glazed (insulated glass) with a vinyl frame, or are wood-clad with aluminum or vinyl; the extra pane of glass cuts heat loss. "Smarter still" are double panes coated to make the most of your home's heat in winter; these can also have an inert gas between the panes.

■ **Snap-in grilles.** These consist of a single sheet of dual-pane glass with snap-in wooden muntins. Purists hate this compromise, but most of the objections arose when the grilles were first made and were molded plastic that looked fake and cheap. Now these grilles are made from wood and are attached both inside and outside the window.

■ **Button-on storm windows, outside.** For people whose partners insist on true divided lights but can't swing the large cost difference of individual dual-pane glass, the industry offers a single sheet of glass with metal edging that fits over the outside of the window and is held in place by small metal or plastic turn buttons. Ours have never fit properly, and I was startled to find that the small panes still get dirty inside these storm windows, thus creating four surfaces of glass to be cleaned.

Faced with this problem when we replaced two big picture windows in the front of our house with true divided lights, I had a local glass company measure and install a single sheet over the entire outside of each window. They were sealed well enough to keep dirt out of the interior space, and they seem to work well.

■ **Button-on storm windows, inside.** If you are faced with trying to preserve a historic outside appearance, you can have your local glass company measure and cut storm windows to fit inside your old windows. You will be faced with the annual spring chore of taking down and storing these sheets of glass, but at least you will be inside your home instead of hanging on a ladder outside.

Timesaver
Objections you have to snap-in grilles might fade when you calculate the cost savings or when you think of the ease of snapping out the grille work and washing a single sheet of glass.

- **All the rest.** At this point, I have to leave you on your own. Literally thousands of special designs and shapes are available, and specialty shops are willing to make precisely what you want if it isn't standard. You can have round, fan-shaped, oval, stained glass, bow . . . anything is possible for a fee.

The glass

The insulation value of your walls should be between R-17 and R-19. (The higher the number, the better; for more information, see the section about insulation in Chapter 11.) A single sheet of window glass has a rating of R-1. If you go to double-glazing, it jumps up to R-1.7.

Here are some general glass rules to guide your choices:

- **Single-pane.** Best reserved for the garage.

- **Double-pane.** Consists of two sealed sheets of glass separated by an aluminum spacer that includes a desiccant to keep moisture from condensing between the panes. (Once moisture gets in, the only solution is to replace the glass.) The wider the air space between the sheets of glass, the better the insulation.

- **Argon-filled.** The air space between the panes is replaced by an inert gas. Krypton is also used sometimes. This steps up the R rating a little and the price a lot. It works best with an air space of a half-inch to an inch wide.

- **Low-emissivity glass.** Low emissivity glass (or *low e*) refers to a coating that alters the way the glass transmits visible and invisible light. Light is energy or heat. In northern states, low e glass is formulated to let heat in and to keep it in. In southern states, the formula is turned around to keep heat out and cool in.

▪ **Triple-pane.** Triple panes provide a little better insulation, but almost no one can lift them. Not only are they heavy, they're expensive. The Pella Corporation offers a window with triple glazing and shades that fit inside the windows between two panes of glass. Using them can reduce heat loss by as much as 52 percent and can reduce summer heat gain by as much as 42 percent.

▪ **Plastic sheeting.** For the first two years, I covered our picture windows with clear-plastic sheets from a storm-window kit I picked up at the hardware store. Double-sided tape is provided in the kit for around the window. The sheeting is applied right to the outside frame (or to the inside, for that matter). Wrinkles can be removed with a hair dryer. The sheets create a trapped air space and might even do some good. Just don't try to put them up in a high wind and be sure to have an extra pair of hands.

The frames

The frame has a significant effect on a window's thermal performance, price, and upkeep. There are many kinds, of course, including the following:

▪ **Wood frames** are still the staple of the industry. They often come preprimed with one coat of paint. If you plan to stain the inside of your windows, be sure you order them without the priming on the inside. Wood windows are the least expensive, but they require maintenance and repainting in a few years.

▪ **Wood frames clad in vinyl or aluminum**, usually only on the outside surfaces, tend to be more

Unofficially...
In October 1993, *Consumer Reports* reported the results of an exhaustive study comparing conventional double-glazed windows and low-e/argon-filled windows. They found that in a typical 12-room house it would take nine years to recover the additional cost of the low-e/argon-filled windows with energy savings.

expensive than all-vinyl or all-wood windows. They require only minimum maintenance, however—usually washing instead of painting. Be sure you pick a color you want to stay with such as white.

Unofficially...
You might have to limit your selection of vinyl windows to one of many standard sizes, because vinyl windows are formed in molds and can't be custom-made for every opening.

- **Aluminum** is too good a conductor of heat or cold to be a good choice in colder areas. In the right region, however, it is a lower-cost window with minimum maintenance needed.

- The **better-quality vinyl** windows have welded corners rather than screws. Stick to the welded variety. Vinyl might offend the sensibilities of your town fathers and architectural purists, but they probably won't notice the vinyl-clad variety. Other than not needing painting, not wearing out, ease of cleaning, better insulation, and better appearance, vinyl windows are coming closer and closer to pure wood.

- Other features to look for include **solid, smoothly working locks and hardware**, ease of opening and closing, self-storing screens and storm windows, and pull-out and swing-down windows that allow you to clean outside surfaces from inside.

In summary, unless your present windows are a complete disgrace—rotting, peeling, loose, or inoperable—the monetary rewards of a higher sale price for your home or vast energy savings are not available in replacement windows. Good reasons for replacing your windows fall into the less-tangible categories of enhanced beauty, lighter rooms, increased comfort, and if you go for the aluminum- or vinyl-clad variety, the satisfaction of not having to paint your windows ever again.

Find a reliable contractor or window-replacement specialty firm and then pick a window manufactured

by a nationally known firm. Select a style that blends
with the rest of your windows and your home. If
money is tight and you are buying one of the thousands of standard windows, you can do one room or
side of your house at a time. As your financial well
refills, you can take on another room or side without any noticeable changes.

Here is a partial listing of some major window
manufacturers and where to write for more information:

Anderson Windows, Inc.
P.O. Box 3900
Peoria, IL 61614
800-426-4261

Marvin Windows & Doors
P.O. Box 100
Warroad, MN 56763
800-346-5128

Peachtree
P.O. Box 700
Norcross, GA 30091
800-477-6544

Pella Corporation
102 Main Street
Pella, IA 50219
800-847-3552

Pozzi
P.O. Box 5249
Bend, OR 97708
800-547-6880

Weather Shield Manufacturing, Inc.
531 N. 8th Street
Medford, WI 54451
715-748-2100

You can also read more information in the following articles:

Don Best, "Window Sense," in *Home*, June 1993.

Mervyn Kaufman, "Home Report," in *Home*, November 1994.

"Replacement Windows," in *Consumer Reports*, October 1993.

Just the facts

- An incredible number of roofing choices are available. Know which type you want and how much it costs before you start collecting bids.

- Go the extra distance and buy the extensions that make your windows and doors look right when you put vinyl siding on your house.

- Prep work for repainting the outside of your house is not a simple task, but it is essential for lasting paint.

- Replacement windows might not increase the value of your home or save much energy, but they can add a degree of comfort and beauty to your home.

GET THE SCOOP ON...
Creating a deck design ▪ The ABCs of deck
building ▪ Construction material options ▪
Maintaining your old or new deck ▪ Adding a
swimming pool or hot tub ▪ The price of
swimming pool fun . . . maintenance

Maintenance and Protection of Swimming Pools and Decks

Chapter 18

N ow that the inside of your home is remodeled, refurbished, and insulated and the outside is cleaned up, repainted, or resided, you might want to consider creating some recreational and entertainment spaces on the outside.

It started as the front porch and then became the utilitarian back porch. Now this outside space is called the back deck, and it has become an integral part of a home's design. Decks can furnish the extra room you thought you needed and save you from expending on expanding your house.

In the southern United States, the Florida room fills the same role as a deck and has the advantage of being available for use year-round. With the obligatory screens and, in many cases, glass walls and

French doors leading into the house, it is really a full-use, dramatic, extra room and a greenhouse for exotic greenery.

A swimming pool, to many people, is the ultimate luxury. A Florida room often contains a swimming pool, which is considered a necessity by many residents of the hotter southern states. Elsewhere, a swimming pool can be surrounded by a portion of a deck or can sit by itself in the backyard surrounded by a fence.

In this chapter I will discuss various design possibilities for both decks and pools, different construction methods and materials, and tips for maintaining these structures.

Creating a creative deck

A creative deck furnishes you with an outdoor living area that serves as an extension of your home. It can match your family's lifestyle and give you the flexibility for socializing, recreation, gardening, or just relaxing. A creative deck can turn an ordinary yard into a beautiful showplace.

What kind of deck do you want?

The following considerations can help determine the size and shape of your deck:

- **The slope of your land.** If your land drops steeply away from your home, you can create useable deck space by erecting a platform and holding it up with wooden pillars as tall as you need them from the ground to the deck. It is common in San Francisco to see entire homes with decks that appear to be anchored to only a few feet of solid land; the rest is supported by steel pillars rising out of the hillside.

Bright Idea
If your land drops away from your home in the back or the front, it might be difficult to maintain a lawn. It could, however, be perfect for a creative deck.

Your lot is probably not as steep as those surrounding San Francisco (and you might not have to contend with heavy rains and mud slides). With only a few feet of supports, you can have a level, useful backyard that you won't have to mow.

A level deck, however, might not be the most creative use of your property. Multilevel decks are definitely popular now, with one level serving as your outdoor dining area. You then can go up a few steps to a hot tub area, down a few steps to the barbecue and entertaining area, and finally, a few more steps to ground level.

- **The activities you want to accommodate.** What exactly do you want to do on your deck? These activities can help determine its design. If you want to work on your tan, for example, you'll want your deck to be open and out of the shadows. Conversely, if you want to enjoy meals on your deck, you'll probably want a roof or at least some shade. You might even want insect screening. Although not all activities are mutually exclusive, you do need to think about how much and what kind of space each activity requires.

- **Taking your neighbors into account.** If you have several young ladies sunbathing and lolling around the hot tub, your neighbors might not object to a view of your deck. Most people, however, prefer privacy for such moments. Even if you aren't blessed with acres of woods, you can still have a deck that allows for fairly unfettered activities. You have the option to include fencing, trellises, screening, latticework, railings, and even planters with heavy foliage in your deck plans.

Moneysaver
It isn't necessary to build a wall all the way around your deck to achieve seclusion. Just check out the sight lines from the street and from neighbors' houses and erect attractive visual barriers on those lines.

You can also achieve a good degree of privacy by keeping hot tubs low or even set into the deck by building a solid railing. Even better, build your railing with slanted slats in a louvered effect that allows a breeze to cool your deck and still keeps your activities out of view.

The basics of deck building and design

At its most basic level, a deck is a square or rectangular wooden platform held up by 4 × 4–inch, cement-imbedded posts every 6 feet or so and attached to your home at or near a door. At the other extreme, it can be a highly engineered, architecturally designed work of art with clever angles. It even can be built around trees, which then extend up through it.

The range of possible materials includes:

Unofficially...
The protective qualities of pressure-treated wood tend to be over-sold as the final solution to deck weathering. All decks turn gray, however, and still need periodic (usually annual) maintenance with a coating of sealer.

- **Pressure-treated wood.** This wood usually is a form of pine or fir. This treatment, applied at the lumber source, is designed to prolong the life of the wood. It tends to give the wood a slight greenish color that fades with time. It also makes a load of lumber very heavy and tends to dull saw blades very quickly.

- **Untreated pine or fir.** Less expensive and easier to work with than pressure-treated wood, these woods need the most protection and maintenance. They could be your choice, however, if you plan to paint and repaint your deck.

- **Natural water- and sun-resistant woods such as redwood and cedar.** These woods are more costly initially and provide a more pleasing color, but they too need to have sealers applied to prolong their beauty and life.

- **Metal or plastic decking on a wood frame.** Most expensive material initially, this option comes closer to living up to the claim of maintenance-free use.

Initial sealing of wood decks

An unpainted wooden barn seems to last forever as the wood weathers to a pleasant gray. When wood is laid flat on a deck, however, it takes the full brunt of the sun, standing water, and snow. If left untreated, your deck will deteriorate within a couple years.

I asked Peter Fox of Sun Frog Products, Inc., for answers to the most frequently asked questions concerning coatings and sealants. These are his answers:

1. **When should I seal?** Only seal when the wood is thoroughly dry. New wood should be allowed to season for 30 days before sealing. Older woods should be allowed to dry for 48 hours after cleaning and color-reviving but prior to sealing. When dry, the wood will be "thirsty" for an oil seal, thereby achieving maximum penetration. Do not seal during hot, direct sun conditions, however, because the sealer will dry before full penetration is achieved.

2. **Is resealing all I need to do?** No! If you want your project to look as good and perform as well as possible, the wood should be clean and free of mildew before a sealer is applied. On previously sealed and weathered woods, we recommend cleaning with Deck Cleaner and color-reviving with Born Again prior to sealing.

3. **How should I apply a sealer?** We recommend a stain pad for optimum application. It works the sealer well into the wood, avoids surface excess, and provides easy application.

4. **Can I apply more than one coat?** No! First-coat, wet-on-wet application while the wood is absorbing is great. After the first coat is dry, however, a second coat will not penetrate and should not be applied.

5. **What is the dry time?** Typically it takes 12 to 24 hours. Avoid getting water on the surface during dry time or the surface will water spot.

6. **What color should I use?** We recommend using the color that corresponds to the type of wood being sealed (cedar on cedar, redwood on redwood, and so on). Color versions provide more UV protection than clear versions. Although graying is slowed with clear sealer, it is slowed more appreciably with the color versions.

7. **Does deck sealer bead water?** No! It sheds water. Beading is usually a function of wax, which wears off quickly at the surface and can prevent recoating. Deck sealer does not contain wax. Deck sealer sheds water because of the penetrating drying and nondrying oils. These oils give the wood a deep, rich look.

8. **How long will it last?** Speaking for Sun Frog, his company's own product, Peter Fox predicts the following: On decks, expect one year of excellent performance. Depending on sunlight exposure, standing-water frequency, and foot traffic, however, two years is possible. On vertical surfaces, three to five years is expected. Performance depends greatly on wood quality, preparation, and application techniques. Follow label directions.

9. **When do I reseal?** When the sealed area lightens, looks dull, or loses its ability to hold out

Unofficially...
A sealer covers approximately 250 square feet per gallon on new woods, 200 square feet on older woods. Hardwoods such as mahogany get more coverage. Weathered, rough-sawn woods (fences, siding, and so on) can take as much as 1 gallon per 100 square feet.

water, clean it with a deck cleaner and reapply
deck sealer.

10. **Can a sealer be reapplied when necessary?**
Some products, such as Sun Frog Sealer, reapply well; others do not. Be sure to read the manufacturer's instructions.

What happens to wood out on that deck?

External woods are exposed to incessant attack
from sunlight, water, microorganisms, pollution,
and physical wear from wind, dirt, and foot traffic.
Inside the tree, wood is protected from these elements by bark, a stable moisture content year-
round, natural oils, and decay-resistant constituents.
Stripped of its bark and laid bare in the outdoor
environment, however, its new fresh color and condition do not last long. To slow the process of
weathering and to prolong its natural beauty, wood
needs protection.

A wood deck has many enemies. Check the seal's
label to see whether its ingredients fight the
following:

- **Sunlight (UV radiation).** Transparent oxide pig-
ments in some sealers absorb significant ultraviolet light to stabilize and prolong the life of seal
solids.

- **Mildew and wood rot.** Fungus-fighting, broad-
spectrum mildew inhibitors resist wood rot by
the water repellency of the seal.

- **Cracking and checking.** This is caused by
wet/dry (swell/shrink) cycles and can be
controlled by water-repellent oils. A high proportion of drying-oil solids "get there first"
when applied to dry wood. Water invasion/
evasion is significantly reduced, promoting
prolonged shrinkage control.

- **Physical wear from foot traffic.** Drying oils in the sealer polymerize to fortify the dirt- and wind-damaged wood fibers and to reduce abrasion.

Getting your deck ready to seal or reseal

If you have never put a sealer on your deck and you still have a deck in fairly good condition—meaning you can still see all the wood without obvious rotting areas—you can save what's left by applying a deck sealer now. Most decks that are left untreated and many that are sealed become covered with green fungus, mold, and moss.

Cleaning a deck in preparation for sealing is an adventure in itself. I speak with some authority on this subject because I have a deck made from pressure-treated yellow pine that I have been maintaining for 10 years. I waited the prescribed 30 days before applying a sealer (a TV-advertised brand that I can't remember). Two years later, thanks to overflowing nonseamless gutters, I had problems with moss, fungus, and gray-to-black weathering, all of which I had expected to avoid.

I bought a deck-cleaning product and went at it with a long-handled scrub brush. It seemed to remove the majority of the bad stuff, but with a lot of effort. I then applied another TV-advertised sealer that lasted a year. Because I purchased a 5-gallon can, I also reapplied it the next year. Last summer, my deck was back to looking like the floor of a rain forest—lots of moss, blackening boards, and fungus. When I rented a pressure washer to clear up some mildew problems on the outside paint and roof of my house, I also tried it on the deck.

I now know more about pressure-washing a deck. Because it is important to remove all dirt, mold,

mildew, and moss from a wooden deck before sealing it, follow these steps for every pressure-washing
job:

1. Wet the deck completely.

2. Apply a solution of trisodium phosphate along
   with the water. Allow this mixture to sit for two
   to three minutes. This loosens the mold, dirt,
   and mildew and prepares the surface to be
   pressure-washed.

3. Pressure-wash each board. You'll get the feeling
   you are spray-painting your deck as the muck
   and gray color disappear under the pressure
   nozzle of the washer. Don't get carried away and
   get too close to the surface, however. As I've
   mentioned before, a pressure washer can actually cut the wood away.

4. Carefully rinse any remaining soap from the
   entire area with your garden hose.

The deck-sealing quandary

As I talked to paint-store owners, looked over manufacturers' literature, checked the Web, and tried to
recall my own experiences, I kept getting conflicting
information. Some say to put the sealer on pressure-
treated wood immediately; others say to wait a
month until the wood treatment has dried.
Different sources recommend different methods:
brush it on, scrub it on, roll it on, put it on with a
pad, spray it on, cover all six sides of the boards. (I
imagine this would be much easier before you build
the deck.) I frankly could not decide what to recommend to you.

I then got hold of the June 1998 issue of
Consumer Reports magazine. It started a five-year
study of deck coatings in 1996 with a 55×21–foot

platform of 1 × 6–inch yellow pine deck planks in Yonkers, NY, and a second identical test platform in the Miami, FL, area. The study started with 36 products, and after less than a year, some fared so badly they were replaced. Now, after 20 months, some are doing quite well. (You'll find an interim report in the magazine's May 1997 issue.)

Here is part of what the study has shown so far:

Watch Out!
The ability to make water bead is not an indication of a good water repellent. The real test is how well the product keeps the wood from cracking.

- Semitransparent products and "toned" finishes (those with a hint of color) have performed best overall.

- The clear finishes performed the worst by far. (Only 5 of the original 19 are still in the test.) Expect to renew a clear treatment every year.

- Solvent-based products started better but have now lost their advantage over water-based finishes.

Expect to clean your deck every year

Part of the test conducted by *Consumer Reports* involved cleaning the entire patchwork surfaces each year. This is something the homeowner must also do. Some products cleaned easily; some still held onto their dirt and grime after 10 strokes of a stiff brush and Red Devil TSP Phosphate-Free cleaner. The cleaning was followed by a thorough hosing with water. Some of the tinted finishes gave up a portion of their color when cleaned; others held up better.

To clean an old deck, you might follow *Consumer Reports*' advice and use a mixture of 1 quart bleach, 3 quarts water, and 3 ounces Red Devil TSP Phosphate-Free cleaner. (For your own deck, however, you need not limit yourself to 10 strokes per brush load.)

What you can expect to pay for a deck sealer

The prices of the 36 tested products ranged from under $10 to over $50 a gallon. The cost of a product did not necessarily indicate product performance, although the highest-cost finish had the best overall rating and the worst-rated was the lowest priced.

If you are interested in the product ratings from the test, you can check out the June 1998 issue of *Consumer Reports* from your local library. Although the magazine gave me permission to discuss their tests and general findings, they do not want the product ratings reproduced, and for good reason. Manufacturers constantly change formulas and improve their products. *Consumer Reports* is a monthly magazine and can update a report as a product improves and testing continues.

Other methods to create a better deck

Choosing the best deck sealer is one way you can have a better-looking, longer-lasting deck, but there are other considerations. A sealer that permits the wood to "weather" might allow you to have the warm gray color you are trying to achieve. Decide what you are after when making a sealer selection. Other steps you can take for a better deck before you seal the deal include:

- For a longer-lasting and stronger deck, use 2 × 4s on edge for your decking. They are less likely to cup (curl along their length) than wider, thinner boards.

- Although the contractor probably does this as a general practice, be sure to fasten your decking with galvanized screws rather than nails. Screws hold more securely, and you won't get any nail pops as the wood moves with the seasons.

Bright Idea
Don't just order lumber for your deck. Go there, pick the wood out yourself, and reject boards that are cracked, warped, or have too many knots—especially if you plan to let the grain show through your sealer.

You might consider showing your metal

Wood is not the only product available for decks. I came across the following descriptions of steel decking in a brochure from the manufacturer of E-Z Deck. In addition to the usual benefits you might expect from metal decks—strength and extended life—they also offer the following benefits:

- The closed or nonporous surface reduces dirt and stain entrapment. Most of the time, the only cleaning necessary is an occasional hosing down with water. Grease from the barbecue is not a problem because it does not penetrate the surface.

- If you're working with angles, E-Z Deck miters easily. (You have to switch to a carbide blade on your skill-saw.) Because steel decking comes in traditional lumber lengths of up to 40 feet, there is usually no need for joints.

- One considerable advantage is that you won't be saddled with the chore of painting your decking. With E-Z Deck, there is no need to paint. Color pigment is evenly distributed through the profile and is designed to be fully functional for 40 years.

- According to the manufacturer, steel decking is easy to install. It can also replace your current worn-out wooden boards right on the existing frame, provided that it's still in good condition, level, and square.

Locating a reputable deck building and maintenance contractor

The design and construction of decks has become sufficiently popular that some contractors specialize in these projects just as others specialize in kitchens and baths. Visits to deck specialists' showrooms offer you the opportunity to see hundreds of possible designs. The designs are often on a computerized program that lets you see various possibilities for your site.

Should you even consider building your own deck?

After all this discussion, you might well be intimidated by the thought of building a deck yourself, with some justification. However, The Home Depot offers complete materials packages for decks that include materials for the supporting structure, the deck, railings, and three steps. They seem to think do-it-yourselfers can handle the job. The wood is pressure-treated yellow pine, but selection and application of the sealer is still up to you and costs extra.

Many books and woodworking magazines contain detailed, step-by-step drawings, pictures, and instructions about the design and construction of decks. If you have the basic skills in hole digging, cement pouring, post-setting, and carpentry and if you have the tools to handle the job, go for it. It is, after all, a fairly simple structure.

Do you need a contractor?

Be aware of your own skill level before starting a deck project. When it comes to maintenance, some products are available only to professionals. If you plan to do your own maintenance, try for a sealer that gives you long life and good cleaning properties. If you hesitate to take on the task, people who specialize in decks already have the specialized equipment you might have to rent. Additionally, some products lose their manufacturer's warranty if not applied professionally. There are not many of these, but you still should check it out.

Moneysaver
You might consider buying a precut kit of the wood deck materials and railings from a lumber-supply store. These are available for a variety of deck sizes. If you possess the basic skills and have access to a truck, you could build your own deck.

Locating a deck building contractor

Unlike remodeled kitchens and bathrooms, decks tend to be visible from the road. You can tell just by looking around who you might approach for recommendations and advice. Deck contractors are also listed in the Yellow Pages and show up in seasonal newspaper building supplements and at home shows. Ask for and check references and look at their picture galleries of decks they have built. This can give you ideas for your project and can help you gauge their skills. Look for a minimum of five years in business.

Don't overlook the carpenters in your town. I'm sure most of them could handle even a complicated deck design. It probably wouldn't be their first choice for a project, but you might catch them between house jobs or in need of some sunshine after spending six weeks cooped up working in someone's attic.

Protecting your pocketbook

As for deck-building contractors, the most common scam is to collect in advance either the entire cost of materials or a sizable advance and then disappear. Don't pay for building materials or sealers until they are in your yard. If your contractor doesn't have enough credit to purchase your materials from a building supply store or a lumberyard, you don't want him on your job.

Swimming pools and hot tubs

If you already have a pool but have been waiting for a book like this to come out before you start maintaining it, you're in serious trouble. This section is for people who are contemplating installing a pool or hot tub (possibly in conjunction with a new deck)

Watch Out!
Some sharp operators will bill you for a high-priced spread and then apply colored water. Check the containers of sealer and insist on seeing unopened cans of the product you selected.

and need to know what their construction options are and what is involved in pool maintenance.

Above-ground pools

These pools are made of plastic or sheet metal with a plastic liner. In some towns, an above-ground pool is considered a temporary structure; therefore, it will be included in your property taxes. An above-ground pool requires all the maintenance and chemical treatments that an in-ground pool requires.

I have owned two above-ground pools, one in Pennsylvania and one in Vermont. We thoroughly enjoyed them for the most part. Our children were young and all could swim. Both pools were out of the sight lines of neighbors, thus opening them up for night usage. Great fun.

I learned the following vital facts about above-ground pools, however:

- The ground under a pool must be perfectly level and flat. We were instructed to dig the sod out of a shallow pit (4 inches deep) and fill it with sand. Stretch a string between stakes, hang a level on it, and then move the sand around to get a level pool base. Take the time to do it right.

- A pool that's 3½ feet deep lets you do everything you can do in a deep pool—except dive. You only use the top 3 feet to swim, and you use even less to float with a cool beer in hand. Also, the kids can stand up in it, which lessens the worry factor.

- Never drain an above-ground pool by unhooking the plastic siding and folding it over the water. One memorable Labor Day, I decided to

Bright Idea
To drain an above-ground pool slowly and safely, fill a hose with water, crimp it at both ends, and lower one end into the pool. Place the other end in the area you want the water to drain (somewhere below the level of the pool). Release the crimps. You have created a siphon—slow and undramatic but safe.

drain our pool this way. (The water would not drain through the plug, which was pressed tightly against the bricks of our patio). Forty thousand gallons of water came cascading out all at once . . . down over a steep embankment and onto the road 30 feet below. It looked like a tidal wave as it hit the roadside ditch, surging up and flooding 200 yards of the road with water, woodsy debris, rocks, and mud just in front of a passing bus. I turned to my wife and asked, "Do you think Homeowner's B covers idiocy?" She got on the phone and called 10 friends to "come quick and bring a snow shovel." They came, no questions asked. It was an adventure but, as they say on the video shows, "nobody got hurt."

- Above-ground pools come in all shapes and sizes, from kiddy wading pools to large 4- or 5-foot-deep oval and circular pools. Larger sizes have more geometric and elaborate structures around them. The structures must also be stronger to handle the increased weight of the water. Costs can run from a couple hundred dollars at Kmart for a 3-foot deep by 12-foot diameter pool with all the pumps, filters, and hoses to several thousand dollars for a dealer-supplied pool.

- Hot tubs and spas don't come in kiddy sizes or prices, but they give you somewhere to relax with friends. They usually come with heating units that can heat the water to over 100 degrees F. This can mean possible—but not probable—all-year use, even in northern states. They still have to be chemically balanced because microbes love warm water, but cleaning is less of a chore because such units are smaller than pools.

In-ground pools

In-ground pools are a permanent part of your property and are generally taxed as such. They can be anywhere on your property, including inside your house or, as is common in southern states, in a screened-in area that is an extension of your living space. (I am told that the screen functions as much to keep tree droppings out of the pool as to keep bugs out.) They can be built in virtually any shape, size, or depth, depending on the size and depth of your wallet.

Should you buy a pool?

The answers to this question vary for different parts of the country. Developers of high-end housing in southern states regard pools as a necessity. Real estate agents in northern states report that up to 80 percent of people looking at homes for resale do not want a pool on the property. The reality of having an "attractive nuisance" and the liability and fencing that accompany it deter many potential pool owners. A pool is probably regarded as an asset by home buyers who have never had a pool.

You should ask yourself the following questions:

- **Will the kids use it?** If you have young kids of swimming age, you will get a lot of use from your pool, at least until they grow tired of it.

- **Will you use it to exercise?** Swimming is the best all-around exercise. If you have family members who are conscientious exercisers and will stay with their program, a pool can save you the cost of a health club membership. As one pool-builder observed, however, "After a season of the cost and time of maintaining a pool, the beach or a health club looks like a good deal."

- **Do you entertain business associates and friends?** A pool builder who puts in two or three 25 × 50–foot, $100,000 pools each year in Greenwich, CT (complete with fiber-optic lighting, heaters, and elaborate tile work) reports that these pools are used mostly to impress others and to provide a congenial backdrop to the cocktail party.

- **Can you afford it?** This same builder said, "I can build a pool for $30,000 but, when you add fencing, heating, lighting, and a patio or deck around it, the cost will be closer to $50,000."

Unofficially...
One of the axioms of luxury buying is "If you have to ask, you can't afford it." The same might be said of a fancy pool.

- **Are you willing to devote the required time and attention to maintaining the pool?** You should test the water two to three times a day in the height of summer usage, adding chemicals as necessary. Cleaning and vacuuming are required weekly, even with a skimmer and filters. There are also winter shut-down procedures and spring reopening chores. There are some who thrive on the pool maintenance procedures. (I've noticed that the best pool keepers can avoid actually having to go swimming.)

- **Are you adding a pool to increase the value of your property for resale?** Don't. The cost of a pool is seldom realized when a home is sold. Do it only for your own long-term enjoyment.

Building and maintaining your pool

About the only good thing about the building of a pool is that the construction takes place outside, so your life is only marginally disrupted. Ditto for maintaining a pool. It's hard to ignore algae growing in your tub, but if the pool gets a little yucky, there's always next weekend.

Finding pool building and maintenance contractors

Like deck owners, pool owners are easy to spot. Ask pool, spa, or hot tub owners for their recommendations. Check out potential contractors' references and look at their photo albums of past jobs.

To find a good pool-maintenance contractor, check with pool owners in your neighborhood. You might be able to get a good rate for multiple jobs close together. Another good source for cleaner leads is your pool builder. It's to his benefit for his pool to be well taken care of.

Pool and hot tub construction options

If you want a pool or a hot tub, have passed the preceding basic questionnaire, and are willing use it, here is further basic information for your consideration and education. There are three main types of pool construction:

- **Gunnite.** Gunnite is a cement mixture pneumatically applied over an excavation dug to any size and shape you desire. The process has recently been improved with a system called Shotcrete, which employs the same delivery system but is less labor intensive. The procedure involves a steel mesh or steeltex outside liner, a maze of re-bar supports inside the cement, and a crushed-stone base, all of which are installed before the cement is applied. Properly done, this method produces a pool that should last 30 to 40 years. The gunnite method can also be used for hot tubs.

- **A steel (or other metal) box with a vinyl liner.** A competitive gunnite pool builder pointed out that the vinyl liner can be cut with a sharp toenail and can cause a catastrophic leak. He also admitted there is only a tiny chance of this

Timesaver
It won't be long before you tire of the cleaning job. Hiring a pool-cleaning contractor is a valid and popular option . . . and it's well worth the reasonable cost.

happening. (You might, however, take the precaution of clipping your toenails.) This method
is about half the cost of a gunnite pool. The useful life of this pool type depends on the liner.

- **Fiberglass (often called plastic).** This pool type
comes in prefabricated portions that are low-
ered into your excavation. Fiberglass is the
material of choice for hot tubs, which usually
come in one piece. It affords a smooth, plastic-
like surface that is easier to keep clean and
holds up to rough usage.

Recommended maintenance program for pools

Note: The following material was derived from literature supplied by Aqua Clear Industries, Inc., the
makers of SUN Pool and Spa products. It has been
excerpted with permission.

You'll discover early on that pools do not maintain themselves. After you resign yourself to this, it's
only a tiny jump to setting up a regular pool-
maintenance schedule. The following tips can help
you organize your effort:

- **Cycle time.** In general, the longer the pool
water is filtered, the cleaner the water. As a minimum, run the circulation pump continuously
when bathers are in the pool and for 4 hours
out of 12 at all other times.

- **Filter.** The purpose of the filter is to trap suspended particles and to stop them from getting
back into the pool. It is essential that the efficiency of the filter is not impaired. Follow the
manufacturer's instructions and backwash it
(reverse the flow and drain any dirt that has
accumulated). This should be done at least
twice a month, but watch the pressure gauge

and do it more often if necessary. Sand needs renewal every 7 to 10 years. Make sure that flow through the pump strainer is not impeded by rubbish as part of the backwash routine.

■ **Skimmers.** Clean the skimmers once a week, taking out leaves and anything else that could obstruct the water flow.

■ **Vacuuming.** If you are not operating an automatic pool sweep, vacuum the pool once a week to remove solids not floating in suspension. Some (aluminum-based) water clarifiers drop accumulated solids to the bottom of the pool. Vacuuming might be required shortly after treatment—see the instructions on the pack. Fill the vacuum hose with water before connecting it to the attachment in the skimmer.

■ **Brushing.** Brush the sides and bottom of the pool frequently; make sure any algae discoloring the tiles, grouting, or liner is removed (look for this around the steps, any underwater lights, and "dead spots" where water movement is minimal). Brush towards the drain so that debris and dirt are drawn into the hopper and onto the filter.

And now for a chemistry class . . .

All chemical calculations depend on the size of your pool or, to be more accurate, the number of gallons of water you use. The following list shows you how to properly size your pool; this is a critical step in determining a chemical program for you to follow. If you use the proper amounts of chemicals, the result is crystal clear water.

■ **Circular.** Diameter × Diameter × Average Depth × 5.9 = Total Gallons

Bright Idea
Clean dirt from the water line of your pool with a chlorine-compatible tile and liner cleaner. Greasy deposits can act as breeding sites for algae.

- **Oval.** Long Diameter × Short Diameter × Average Depth × 5.9 = Total Gallons
- **Rectangular.** Length × Width × Average Depth × 7.5 = Total Gallons

To determine the amounts and types of chemical required, your pool should be tested daily for pH and free chlorine. It also should be tested periodically for alkalinity, stabilizer, and hardness. Your dealer has chemicals to treat and cure any problem that might arise.

Sanitation

Proper filtration removes most suspended debris from your pool; however, filtration alone is not enough. Chlorination is required to disinfect pool water. The proper combination of filtration and chlorination is necessary to keep pool water sparkling clear.

Chlorine

Chlorine must be added to kill bacteria and algae present in the water. It also supplies a residual or active supply of chlorine to kill new bacteria and to prevent the growth of algae. A chlorine residual of 1.0 to 3.0 parts per million (PPM) must be in the water at all times.

Algae

If the chlorine level drops below 1.0 PPM, unsightly algae might appear. Algae can discolor water and can give off unpleasant odors. This condition might also an indication of improper sanitation. Should this problem occur, consult your professional pool dealer.

Shock treatments

As foreign matter enters your pool, your chlorine demand increases, resulting in decreased chlorine residual. Foreign matter can enter your pool as the result of swimmers, wind, and rain. This matter can consist of organic wastes such as perspiration, urine, saliva, suntan lotions, and pollutants. Periodic shock treatments are required to maintain the proper level of chlorine residual. This can be accomplished by using a heavy dose of chlorine (three to five times your normal daily dosage). Shock treatments should be done once a week during peak season when temperatures and bather-loads are heavy. Cloudiness or strong chlorine odors are indications that a shock treatment is necessary.

pH

The measure pH is the degree of acidity or alkalinity in pool water. It is measured on a numerical scale from 1 to 14.7; the middle of the scale is considered neutral. Readings below 7 are increasingly acidic, and readings above 7 are increasingly basic or alkaline. Under normal conditions, the proper pH for pool water is approximately 7.5, although pH 7.2 to 7.8 is an acceptable range.

Water balance

Balanced water is a term used to describe the ideal condition of pool water. Water is "balanced" if it contains just the right amount of pH, total alkalinity, calcium hardness, and dissolved solids. Unbalanced water can have scale-forming or corrosive tendencies.

Stabilizer

To achieve maximum chlorine efficiency, your pool should be properly stabilized. Stabilizer (cyanuric acid) "holds" chlorine in pool water, screening it from loss caused by ultraviolet rays from the sun. Stabilizer helps maintain an active chlorine residual in your pool at all times.

Unofficially...
As you struggled with the lab assignments in your high school chemistry class, you might have wondered what you would ever do with the information. Now that you have a pool and have to monitor chemical levels, you know.

Without a properly stabilized pool, chlorine is broken down by the sun's ultraviolet rays. Consequently, you will need to use more than your normal daily requirement of chlorine to maintain the proper level of chlorine residual. Chlorine stabilizer is generally added once at the beginning of each season.

Total alkalinity

Alkalinity represents the amount of alkaline minerals in water. It is the measure of water's buffering capacity or resistance to a change in pH. It minimizes changes in pH, making pH easier to control.

People often confuse alkalinity and pH. pH is a measure of degree of acidity or basicity of water. Alkalinity is a quantitative measure, telling you the total amount or quality of alkaline minerals present. The proper alkalinity range is 80 to 120 ppm. If alkalinity is allowed to drift, corrosion or scaling can result. Have your pool water tested periodically for alkalinity by a qualified dealer.

Calcium hardness

Total hardness refers to the total amount of dissolved calcium and magnesium bicarbonates—as well as smaller quantities of other minerals—in water. Unbalanced water, if high in hardness, can cause water to become cloudy. Scale can form inside pipes, restricting water flow. It can cause calcification of sand in filters, reducing their efficiency. Scale can also discolor a pool's interior.

On the other hand, low hardness and unbalanced water can contribute to corrosive water conditions. Therefore, a certain amount of hardness is desirable. The desired range is between 100 and 400 ppm. Again, your water should be tested periodically for hardness.

Total dissolved solids

Total dissolved solids refers to metals that have dissolved in your water. They can interact with chlorine, resulting in a color change of your pool water. Total dissolved solids should not exceed 2,000 ppm. Should this or any other problem occur, consult your authorized professional pool dealer. They're ready to help!

Helpful hints for pool or hot tub owners

Though pools and hot tubs are for the good life, your good life can look like a mill pond if you don't keep an eye on things. The following sections contain suggestions for keeping the workload manageable and the pool or hot tub inviting.

Opening your pool

- **Check filtration system.** The heart of any pool is its filtration system. Before adding any pool chemicals, make sure all components are in working order and that the filter is running.

- **Shock your pool.** At the beginning of each swimming season, it is necessary to superchlorinate the pool to establish a chlorine residual. Shock your pool with a chlorine shock product or simply add three to five times your normal daily chlorine dosage.

- **Stabilize.** Chlorine stabilizer (cyanuric acid) should be added to pool water to protect the chlorine from UV breakdown by the sun. Have the pool water tested to determine how much stabilizer should be added to maximize chlorine efficiency.

- **Balance.** Pool water "balance" is determined by pH, total alkalinity, and calcium hardness. Your pool professional has the equipment and the expertise to analyze your pool water. He can recommend exactly what you need to balance your pool water.

During the swim season

The swim season is the time to be especially attentive. Pool-water chemical levels and requirements are constantly changing due to weather, pool location, and the types of chemicals used. Periodic water tests, either at home or at your pool center, are essential to avoid water problems before they occur or to correct them.

After a heavy rain, prolonged periods of hot weather, or a heavy bather load, it is recommended that you shock your pool. Shocking the pool helps destroy visible algae, restore low chlorine levels, and burn off accumulated organic wastes (chloramines).

Putting your pool to bed

The method you should use to winterize your pool depends on where you live. In a climate where the pool water does not freeze, it might not be necessary to shut down and cover your pool. In colder regions, you can protect your pool from damage caused by freezing water by using large rubber floats or logs floated along the sides. Covering your pool is critical if you choose not to drain it. Check with your pool dealer for winterizing instructions for your area and your yard.

If you live in a region where it is necessary to cover your pool for the winter, the addition of a winter algaecide and a soluble granular or liquid chlorine can help ensure that your pool will be sparkling clear when it is opened the following spring.

Unofficially...
If you live in Florida or anywhere with a high groundwater level, do not drain your pool in the winter. When empty, your pool can become a cement or fiberglass boat and can float right out of the ground.

Note: Information about deck-protection products and deck maintenance has been supplied by Sun Frog Products, Inc., and is cited with their permission. For more information about Sun Frog Products, Inc., contact sunfrog1@ix.netcom.com or write to Pete Fox, Sun Frog Products, Inc., 17865 SE 82nd Drive, Gladstone, OR 97027. You also can call 800-488-3764.

Much of the chemical information and pool-care advice was obtained from Aqua Clear Industries, Inc., makers of SUN Pool and Spa Products, 2550 9th Avenue, P.O. Box 387, Watervliet, NY 12189-0387. You also can call 800-346-CHEM. Excerpts are used with permission.

Just the facts

- A deck can greatly increase the living and entertainment area available to your home; with a creative design, it can also be a decorative plus.

- Sealing, cleaning, and resealing your deck might seem like a difficult annual chore, but it covers up grass you would otherwise be mowing every week.

- Before you dive into the world of pool or hot tub owners, check with friends to see how much they enjoy and use their pools.

- To relieve yourself of the weekly duties of chemically balancing the water and cleaning the pool, hire a maintenance contractor who already works on pools in your neighborhood.

Resource Guide

For more information and help you can write, call, fax, or e-mail some of organizations listed.

For general information on remodeling, and to locate NARI (National Association of the Remodeling Industry) in order to find the names of member remodeling contractors in your area, contact NARI on the Web at nariinfo@nari.org

To locate your nearest design/remodeling firm, call your local or state Home Builders Association and ask for a list of those closest to you. You can also call the National Association of Home Builders at 800-368-5242.

The World Wide Web has become an easy way to find contractors in various specialties. National associations will list the names and numbers of members in your area right on the screen. Tap into the Web or ask a friend to do it for you. NAHB (www.nahb.com) and NARI (nari.org) are good places to start your search; also check out Contractornet (www.contractornet.com).

For information on plumbing and plumbing fixtures, try the Internet sites created by the Ball Plumbing Supply Company:

www.a-ball.com

www.plumbnet.com

www.oldhouse.com

Much of the information in our chapter on heating and air-conditioning systems was based on fact sheets prepared by the NAHB Research Center (400 Prince George's Boulevard, Upper Marlboro, MD 20774), with support from the U.S. Department of Energy and the National Renewable Energy Laboratory. You can obtain more information on this and many more remodeling subjects at www.nahbrc.org.

For an excellent source of information on products and appliances and how they stand up to rigorous testing, check out back issues of *Consumer Reports* magazine at your local library or use their Web address: www.consumerreports.com.

I am indebted to The Consumers Union Edition of *The Complete Guide to Home Repair and Maintenance*, by Bernard Gladstone, for some of the information on preparing walls for and removing wallcoverings. If you do decide to do your own hanging of wallcoverings, the book offers detailed, step-by-step instructions and many illustrations showing this fine and demanding art.

For more information on flooring, read or contact some of the following:

Floors, Walls & Ceilings, by Graham Blackburn.
Consumer Reports Books, 1989.

The Simon and Schuster Complete Guide to Home Repair and Maintenance, by Bernard Gladstone.
Simon and Schuster, 1984.

The National Wood Flooring Association Web
page, http://woodfloors.org

Also on the Web, look for the trade associations
representing the various floor products and some of
the manufacturers. Some Web surfing is required,
but you may also find some local distributors and
contractors listed on the net.

For information on ductwork and many other
aspects of home building and remodeling, contact
the NAHB Research Center, 400 Prince George's
Boulevard, Upper Marlboro, MD 20774; 800-638-
8556.

The Home How-To Institute book, *A Portfolio of
Decks,* published by Cowles Creative Publishing, Inc.,
of Minnetonka, MN, contains over 50 color pictures
of decks, from the simple platform to many-layered
masterpieces. It should give all the inspiration you
will need.

Information on deck protecting products and
deck maintenance for this chapter has been supplied by Sun Frog Products, Inc., and is cited with
permission. For more information from Sun Frog,
contact sunfrog1@ix.netcom.com or write: c/o Pete
Fox, Sun Frog Products, Inc., 17865 SE 82nd Drive,
Gladstone, OR 97027; 800-488-3764.

Much of the chemical information and pool
care advice was obtained from Aqua Clear
Industries, Inc. makers of SUN Pool and Spa
Products—cited with permission. For information
on the chemistry and water purification products
for swimming pools and spas, contact Aqua Clear
Industries, Inc., 2550 9th Avenue, P.O. Box 387,
Watervliet, NY 12189-0387; 800-346-CHEM or 518-
274-9777; fax 518-274-9782; e-mail istig@albany.net.

Remodeling Expenditure Charts

With nearly 30 percent of current housing stock built before 1940, the remodeling industry will remain strong and stable as homeowners continue to add space and amenities to their homes. However, the rate of growth in remodeling has slowed. The remodeling market is expected to grow 4 to 5 percent per year during the course of the 1990s.

TABLE B.1: RESIDENTIAL REMODELING EXPENDITURES, 1978–1995 (IN BILLIONS OF DOLLARS)

Year	Total	Maintenance/Repairs	Improvements
1978	$37.5	$12.9	$24.6
1979	42.2	14.9	27.3
1980	46.3	15.2	31.2
1981	46.4	16.0	30.3
1982	45.3	16.8	28.5
1983	49.3	18.1	31.2
1984	69.8	28.9	40.9
1985	80.3	35.4	44.9

Year	Total	Maintenance/Repairs	Improvements
1986	91.3	36.0	55.3
1987	94.1	38.2	55.9
1988	101.1	40.9	60.2
1989	100.9	42.7	58.2
1990	106.8	51.3	55.5
1991	97.5	49.8	47.7
1992	103.7	45.2	58.6
1993	108.3	41.7	66.6
1994	115.0	42.9	72.1
1995	112.6	42.3	70.3

Due to rounding, numbers in the last two columns will not always equal the numbers in the "total" column.

Source: U.S. Census Bureau

TABLE B.2: REMODELING EXPENDITURE FORECAST, 1996–2000 (IN BILLIONS OF DOLLARS)

Year	Total	Maintenance/Repairs	Improvements
1996	$118.5	$43.5	$75.1
1997	125.3	45.3	80.0
1998	130.6	47.3	83.3
1999	136.6	50.0	86.7
2000	143.0	53.4	89.7

Source: NAHB

Getting Your Closets Organized

In this section I will tell you about the range of services offered by closet organizer manufacturers and installers in the U.S. Home design for closets has come a long way from the simple hanger rod across the back of the closet. Walk-in closets now use the side walls for hanging clothes, and the single rod has become two rods, with shorter areas for shirts and coats and a smaller but higher hanging area for longer clothing.

Having caught our attention with the original closet organizers, manufacturers and designers have turned their attention to other rooms and areas in the house.

How do you know you need an organizer?

Remember when you were planning your remodeling project and you had to choose between a larger closet for the master bedroom and a little more room in the bathroom? If you chose a smaller closet, closet organizer firms might be able to help you utilize the space more efficiently.

My wife and I had to choose between closets and a larger guest bedroom. We chose the option that we thought would give us two huge walk-in closets. We learned two things. First, never have a closet door that opens into the closet; it really doesn't work. You either cut off ready access to half the closet by leaving the door open, or you go in, close the door and shut yourself up inside the closet. Second, we had more stuff than would fit in the space built for us by the contractor. I had seen pictures of closet organizers and visited a few home show displays and thought I might be able to build something suitable for our needs. I did, and it has worked.

I'm convinced everyone could use a better system for their storage areas. Fortunately, there are several approaches you can take:

Build it yourself

This is perhaps the one area where I will suggest you can achieve respectable results on your own. The first thing you should do is put in another layer of clothes rod. Don't just measure the length of your shirts—also allow for the hanger size when you reposition the rods. The secret of these systems is that they create a lot of smaller cubbyholes. You can create these mini-storage areas by stacking plastic crates available at stores such as Kmart. For instance, crates will help you divide a big pile of sweaters into smaller, more accessible piles of sweaters.

It isn't asking too much of the handyman of the house to step into the closet and draw up some plans. In our case, I started by keeping intact the shelves the contractor put in—these were high above the clothes racks and on the three walls of the closet. I added a second clothes-hanging bar below the first one. (Take note of how the first one is installed and do the second one the same way.)

I then cut half-inch plywood into 10-inch × 8-foot boards. These can serve as the sides of whatever shelving arrangement you devise. On the left as one enters the closet, using the front wall as one side of the shelf unit and a vertical board as the other, I created a stack of shelves for my shoes; each shelf is a shoe height above the other.

The next stack contains a clever laundry bag holder with a swing-down door that leaves a 6-inch slot for laundry entrance. I built five bins above the laundry chute using some of half-inch plywood as shelving. I then created three slanted shelf bins above the laundry for my socks. I keep my socks in the bins, where I never have to sort them into pairs. To the right of the door I built a 16-inch-wide cabinet with a clothes bar about forty inches up to hang pants on hangers. There are two shelves above the pants for shirts and folded pants.

I'm by no means a neat freak. This closet organizer is an example of one of my best projects: several weeks of planning, drawing, and measuring, and only about two hours of actual work. Incidentally, most lumberyards will cut up your plywood or lumber to length for you if you have the dimensions. You don't have to wait until your workshop is finished before taking on your closet organizer.

Put it together yourself

Closet organizers and general organizers are available in kit form at your local building supply store or hardware store. Look at the pictures and pick out the arrangement you think will work for you. The kits will ask you what size you need. So, before you buy, go into your closet and measure the walls. Do the same for the spaces you want to fill in the garage and between the washer and dryer in the basement.

Shelving and drawers by the foot

In the stores, probably on display near the storage kits, you will see wire shelving, up to 16 feet long, along with brackets to put it up. Using these products, you could shelve the entire back wall of your garage. You will also find some metal drawer systems. These consist of a metal rack with slides to hold wire baskets of various sizes.

Hanging closet organizers

These resemble garment bags, can be hung from the bar or placed on the shelf, and offer an easy way to organize closet space. Check out catalogs from companies that specialize in items to make your life easier room by room. I have seen rod-hanging bags in the form of shelves for shoes or sweaters and over-the-door bags for shoes, belts, ties, and much more.

Personalized organizer design service

You can also invite to your home one of the many organizer companies or franchise operators. They will both design and build you a system in any location where you need help.

How to locate a reputable company

You will find several companies listed in your Yellow Pages under "Closet Equipment & Accessories." By inviting two or three companies to talk to you, make suggestions, and offer estimates, you should be able to weed out any con artists that might show up, particularly if you pay nothing down or in advance of the finished work.

What you can expect from an organizer firm

There is more available under the general heading of "Organizers" than you ever thought possible. They are usually willing to visit your home and bring samples and pictures of the available units. The salesperson will also take the necessary measurements and possibly act as the designer for your system.

Suppress your basic instinct to clean your closet, garage, attic, basement, pantry, or office in anticipation of the visit of the organizer salesperson. She will be able to do a much better job of designing your space if what actually goes in it is still there when she sees the room.

Of course, closets are not the only space you can organize. Some other rooms that may need organizing include:

The laundry room

Washing, drying, and ironing with various soaps, softeners, and starches make a laundry room cluttered. An easy-to-use, swing-down ironing board can be conveniently installed inside a cabinet. You can also add a sink to wash the really hard stains. If your washer and dryer are in the basement, you often can gain shelf or cabinet space by hanging a shelf from the rafters. Make sure you screw the sides in well, because there is a limit to what a couple of small nails can hold, and shelves can fall down. Many container-oriented stores and catalogs sell storage options to fit all the little nooks and crannies (such as the space between your washer and drier) with some clever pull-up or slide-out arrangements.

Pantry

Pantries can be located anywhere near the kitchen for additional food storage, and don't have to take up more kitchen space. Many variations of pantries exist, including ones with a china hutch.

Garage

If you are pressed for space from the amount of "stuff" stored in your garage, having a row of closet organizers might be your answer. In fact, you might even be able to park your car in the garage for the first time! You can also free up your house closets by filling your garage closets with off-season clothing and equipment.

The garage is so obvious a place to store stuff that I almost overlooked it. When you look at your garage, think of it as having three walls available for storage. You could have one or several clothes closets for your off-season stuff, but there are more seasonal items to store than just clothes. The shape of the shovels change from snow to dirt diggers as spring comes, and the bags of sand, ashes, and rock salt give way to fertilizer, grass seed, and mulch. Golf clubs and tennis racquets take over the space from skis, sleds, and ice skates.

I don't think there's a garage big enough to hold all the stuff we all seem to need, but if you devise a sensible schedule twice a year to move half of your things from some deep storage area to ready access, your garage should be able to accommodate it. There have been many clever inventions to replace the old nails-in-the-wall method of hanging tools. Peg board systems have become very advanced, and there are numerous clips and holders available for shovels, rakes, and hoes. There are also systems for hanging things from your garage ceiling; these will take care of everything from bicycles to canoes.

With its large, open floor surface, the garage can mislead you into thinking that everything will fit, so you just keep moving things in. That philosophy will give you only one layer of stuff. The trick is to build shelving, from floor to ceiling if necessary, and put up clips and holders for your garden tools, golf clubs, lumber, and so on. If you still can't get the car (or even the lawn mower) in the garage, it may be time to go shopping for a tool shed building for your backyard.

Bedroom

We spend up to a third of our life in our bedrooms. Why not start and end the day in an organized room? Options include space-saving beds and organizer dressers. Much of the furniture designed for bedrooms is actually part of an organizer system. There are armoires with filing systems of small drawers, plus some extra hanging space. The various dressers, whether tall, long, or side by side, are other examples of the organizer philosophy. Some new gadgets slide or roll under the bed, designed to hold off-season stuff. You can also order wheeled boxes from organizer catalogs, but if you're only going to pull them out twice a year, you might consider the large, flat, plastic storage boxes available for under $10 at stores such as Home Depot and Kmart.

What warranties are offered

Much of the literature from organizer firms guarantees customer satisfaction, but doesn't say much about what the firms would do to make it happen. They warranty their organizers against defects of workmanship and missing parts, but collecting on these promises is probably best done at the place you bought the units. These are pretty straightforward installations, so you'll probably know immediately whether they are right or not.

How long does an installation take?

Installation is not a lengthy process with the right tools and knowledge. If you are doing your own installation of a kit or pre-cut system, I can't predict how long it might take you. A lot depends on the driving time between your closet and the hardware store. If you use professional design and installation, the actual installation will probably take no more than two or three hours after the initial sales and measurement call.

Approximate costs

Organizer systems are not cheap. For example, I just spent over $100 for 6-inch pine boards for a nearly floor-to-ceiling bookcase. Shelving, drawers, and bins eat up a lot of material, so these costs are probably not exaggerated. Organizers will run between $45 and $90 per linear foot installed. So an organizer for one end of a 5-foot-wide closet will run between $225 and $450, depending on the sophistication of the units you select. If you then take advantage of the space at the sides of your closet, the costs will increase, but so will your storage space.

In California, those tip-up-and-away bed units with a twin, full, or queen-size mattress run from $1300 to $1900 installed.

Benefits to the homeowner

You have a chance to make good on that old promise, "Next week we've got to get organized." Hire someone to come in and create space for your stuff. If you are in the market to sell your house, closet organizers will give your house an up-to-date look and recoup at least part of your investment.

Organizing closet space can be like adding additional floor space to your home or office—the more that fits into the closet, the less there is in the room.

In summary, the basic purpose of organizers, whether in your garage, basement, home office, bedroom, or closet, is to utilize more of the wall space for storage. Most of us live with storage facilities with the capacity of a bench. A storage system is like stacking 10 benches on top of one another. You wouldn't be able to store many glasses and plates if your kitchen cabinets had only a bottom shelf. Storage systems bring this kitchen cabinet philosophy to the other places in your home.

You can spend a much as you want for a storage system, but with a little imagination you can certainly improve on what you have now. Creating a space where there's a place for everything may not get your teenagers to pick up or do their laundry, but it will increase the odds (at least for a while!).

Energy Terms and Concepts

ACH (air changes per hour)   The air-leakage rate of a building. Specifically, the number of times each hour that the air in the building leaks out and is replaced by outdoor air.

AFUE (annual fuel-utilization efficiency)   The percent of purchased fuel that ends up as useful heat in a home. The higher the number, the more efficient the heating system.

backdrafting   Potentially hazardous condition in which the exhaust from combustion appliances does not properly exit the building. This can be caused by a number of factors including blocked flues or pressure differences.

CDD or CDH (cooling degree days or hours)   A measure of the severity of the summer climate. See also *HHD*.

CFM (cubic feet per minute)   A measure of air-flow rate usually used in heating and cooling systems or for exhaust fans.

COP (coefficient of performance)   A measure of the efficiency of electrically operated systems such as heat pumps. It is the ratio of useful-energy output to purchased-energy input. Electric resistance heating has a COP of 1.0; heat pumps have COPs ranging from about 2.0 to 3.5.

EER (energy efficiency ratio)   A measure of the efficiency of air conditioners, not including cycling factors. It is the amount of cooling provided per unit of electricity purchased. The higher the number, the more efficient the unit.

EF (energy factor)   A measure of the efficiency of a water heater. It is the amount of hot water produced per unit of gas or electricity purchased. The higher the number, the more efficient the unit.

HDD (heating degree days)   A measure of the severity of the winter climate. Degree days equals 65 degrees Fahrenheit minus the average daily temperature, added up for a year. See also *CDD*.

heat gain   Solar energy acquired. It can help offset heating needs in winter and must be removed in summer if excessive.

heat loss   Heating energy lost to the outside.

HSPF (heating seasonal performance factor)   A measure of the efficiency of a heat pump in heating mode. It is the amount of heating provided per unit of electricity purchased. The higher the number, the more efficient the unit.

HVAC   Heating, ventilating, and air-conditioning.

Pascal   The unit used to measure pressure equal to one Newton per square meter.

R value   The resistance of a material to heat flow. The higher the number, the greater the resistance to heat flow. For components such as walls and roofs that are made up of several layers, the total R value is related to the R value of each layer.

SEER (seasonal energy efficiency ratio) The over-all seasonal efficiency of a central air conditioner. It is the amount of cooling provided per unit of electricity purchased. The higher the number, the more efficient the unit.

shading coefficient The relative transmission of solar energy through glass. Single window glass has a shading coefficient of 1.0. The lower the shading coefficient, the less solar energy comes through.

SHGC (solar heat gain coefficient) Another relative measure of the solar energy transmission of glass or windows. An opening with no glass and no frame has a SHGC of 1.0.

thermal envelope The portions of a building (or *shell*) that contain the insulating and air-tightness elements. Properly constructed, these elements are located next to each other to eliminate thermal bypasses, in which air leaks past insulation.

U Value The conductance to heat flow or the inverse of the R value. The lower the U value, the greater resistance to heat flow.

Source: This fact sheet was prepared by NAHB Research Center, 400 Prince George's Boulevard, Upper Marlboro, MD 20774 (800-638-8556) with support from the U.S. Department of Energy and the National Renewable Energy Laboratory.

Detailed Information on Ductwork

Many remodeling projects involve some addition to, or modification of, the HVAC system, which in many cases includes ductwork. Leaky and poorly insulated ductwork located outside the sealed and insulated building envelope (i.e., in exterior walls, garages, crawl-spaces, and attics) is very common. As many as one home in twelve has major ductwork problems, such as disconnected ducts, pinched or crushed duct-work, missing or badly torn duct insulation, or poor duct layouts. Remodeling is an excellent time to consider ductwork improvements, when existing ductwork is accessible and new ductwork is being designed and installed.

Benefits of insulating ductwork include utility savings and better health. Reducing duct air leakage and improving duct insulation can reduce utility bills and prevent or eliminate associated comfort and health problems. Specifically, heating and cooling costs can be reduced by as much as 20 to 30 percent. Comfort can be improved by ensuring adequate delivery and return of conditioned air. Downsizing of heating and cooling equipment is possible. Finally, entry of mold, radon, dust, and moisture into the house can be reduced.

Factors to consider

There are several factors to keep in mind when considering changes to your ductwork.

Location

Ducts placed within conditioned spaces are more efficient than those placed in unconditioned spaces. If located within conditioned space, conductive and radiative losses, leakage losses, and equipment cabinet losses are reduced or regained into the building space. If possible, locate new ductwork and relocate old ductwork within the house envelope. This means avoiding exterior walls, garages, crawlspaces, and attics. In some cases, it may be easier to alter the location of the insulated and sealed (thermal) envelope so that the existing ductwork is then within the house where leakage is of less concern (i.e., crawlspaces). If it is not feasible to locate ductwork within conditioned space, the ducts should be properly sealed and insulated.

Sizing

With all ducts, take care that the ducts are large enough to deliver the necessary air volume. Smaller ducts tend to be noisier and more leaky than larger ducts because of higher air speeds and pressures. In order to deliver the same volume of air, flexduct and ductboard systems usually must be sized larger than metal ducts because their interior surface is much rougher, causing more restrictive air flow.

Any new ductwork should be sized according to recognized industry standards such as Manual-D, published by the Air Conditioning Contractors of America (ACCA).

Return air

Many homes have one or more supply registers in each room but often have a total of only one or two return registers, usually located in hallways. If interior doors are left open, this arrangement usually works well. When these doors are closed, however, as is often the case with bedroom doors, an adequate volume of air often cannot get back to these centrally located return registers. This causes higher pressures in the rooms with closed doors. This condition greatly increases the amount of heated or cooled air forced out of the house from these rooms. The higher pressures in these rooms may also make it difficult for the rooms to receive enough supply air.

The result can be an uncomfortable room and higher energy use. Meanwhile, the rest of the house is at a lower pressure, causing outside air to enter at a faster-than-normal rate. Backdrafting of exhaust gases from combustion appliances may then result, as unequal pressure causes air to be drawn down flues or chimneys. While undercutting doorways can improve air return, it simply may not be adequate in many cases. Alternatives include installing return ducts in each room, or installing transfer ducts or bypass grills which connect the affected bedroom(s) to the hallway, for example.

Installation issues

In order to achieve a good seal for a long time, ducts must be sealed with mastic and fiberglass mesh (where required). Flexduct should be adequately supported along its length and not pinched. Standard, 6-inch, round flexduct should not generally be used in lengths over 16 feet.

Tests of duct systems can identify leakage sites and confirm the effectiveness of sealing measures. To test, ducts are pressurized with a fan at a return register or the air handler cabinet. See the NAHB fact sheet "House Air Leakage" for more information.

Material and equipment options

Sealing leaks in ductwork involves the use of special duct "mastic" and mesh which is extremely durable and effective. This work may be done by insulation or general contractors or weatherization specialists. The cost of reducing leakage depends a great deal upon the number, type, and location of the leaks, as well as the particular contractor. A range of $200 to $400 would be typical for retrofit work.

Selection of duct material is based on its price, performance, and installation requirements.

The most common, **sheet metal**,

- is durable
- can be customized to fit odd sizes and locations
- has a smooth surface offering low resistance to air flow
- has many connections, joints, and seams, each having potential leakage
- must be insulated when located in unconditioned spaces

A second option, **flexduct**,

- is made with a plastic inner liner inside a tube of insulation, covered with a vinyl vapor barrier

- has few duct connections and joints, and low installation and material costs
- is easily torn, crushed, pinched, or damaged, with damage to inner lining not visible
- has higher resistance to air flow than metal ducts, and must be properly specified

Ductboard is made from stiff, high-density sheets of fiberglass with foil facing bonded to one side.

- Its insulation is integral to duct material
- Its material costs more than sheet metal
- Installed costs may be comparable when sheet metal must be insulated
- It is lightweight and particularly adaptable to attic systems
- Vapor barrier is part of the duct material
- It provides excellent sound attenuation
- Its durability is highly dependent on closure method (tapes and mastics)
- It may be damaged or crushed during construction
- It is relatively airtight when properly installed

Transfer ducts/bypass grills are

- used in lieu of individual returns for each room
- used to connect bedrooms, etc., to a hallway having a central air return
- typically made using short pieces of ductwork, or grills above a door or other location
- installed in attic or through walls

Ductwork sealants

There are also a wide variety of sealants on the market.

- **Mastic** is a paste applied to joints and connections in ductwork. It becomes hard and very durable when dry, and can be used on cracks up to a quarter-inch wide

- **Fiberglass mesh** is used to help seal holes larger than a quarter-inch wide.

- **Butyl-backed foil tape** can be used to seal holes or cracks but cannot be used to seal awkward connections, such as where a round duct meets a rectangular one. Its long-term durability not known.

- **Foil tape** has been shown to come loose after just a few years, especially in hot attics. Many joints cannot be properly sealed with tape at all, such as where a round duct connects to a rectangular duct.

- New options include duct sealing technology that seals the ducts from the inside with a **latex-based spray**. This will soon be available commercially.

Duct insulation

For metal ducts, insulation may be installed on the inside and/or outside of the duct. If on the outside, a vapor retarder, usually integral to the insulation itself, should cover the insulation. This is to prevent condensation on the duct, which could severely degrade the effectiveness of the insulation and can lead to damage of the house.

Remember that insulation does nothing to prevent air leakage—ducts must be properly sealed before insulating. For ducts of any kind located in an attic, insulation of the ducts can be improved by placing batt or blown insulation over the ducts. For flexduct and ductboard, insulation is part of the duct itself. R-4.2 insulation is most common on flexduct. R-6, R-8, and R-11 flexduct is also available. Ductboard is typically made from R-4.3 and also available in R-6.5.

Fiberglass duct liner (for metal ducts), used to line the inside of rectangular metal ductwork, is made of specially treated, rigid fiberglass insulation. Its typical R values are 3.6, 3.7, and 4.2 per inch; it is available in 1 and 2-inch thicknesses.

Fiberglass wrap insulation (for metal ducts), used to cover outside of ducts located in unconditioned spaces, has typical R values of R-3.6, 3.8, and 4.1 per inch. It is available in 1, 2, and 3-inch thick rolls, and with or without a vapor barrier (an outer covering of reinforced foil). It is insulated better than duct liner.

Remodeling scenarios

For existing ductwork, there are basically three options for improving any given portion of ductwork. Depending on where the ducts are currently located, their present condition, and the costs involved, you can:

- Relocate the thermal envelope
- Relocate the ducts
- Seal and better insulate the ducts

While it is generally preferable to locate the ducts within the thermal envelope, it may be physically impossible or very expensive to alter the location of the thermal envelope or the ducts themselves. If relocation is not possible, ducts should be sealed with mastic and possibly better insulated. This can be a highly worthwhile measure, even if it is necessary to remove and reinstall the existing insulation.

Finally, at the beginning of a project, be sure to consider: location of the ductwork, duct type and size, sealing method, insulation method, and R value.

Source: This fact sheet was prepared by NAHB Research Center, 400 Prince George's Boulevard, Upper Marlboro, MD 20774 (800-638-8556), with support from the U.S. Department of Energy and the National Renewable Energy Laboratory.

A

The *Unofficial Guide*™ Reader Questionnaire

If you would like to express your opinion about hiring contractors or this guide, please complete this questionnaire and mail it to:

The *Unofficial Guide*™ Reader Questionnaire
Macmillan Lifestyle Group
1633 Broadway, floor 7
New York, NY 10019-6785

Gender: ___ M   ___ F

Age: ___ Under 30   ___ 31–40   ___ 41–50
___ Over 50

Education: ___ High school   ___ College
___ Graduate/Professional

What is your occupation?
_____

How did you hear about this guide?
___ Friend or relative
___ Newspaper, magazine, or Internet
___ Radio or TV
___ Recommended at bookstore
___ Recommended by librarian
___ Picked it up on my own
___ Familiar with the *Unofficial Guide*™ travel series

Did you go to the bookstore specifically for a book on hiring contractors?   Yes ___   No ___

Have you used any other *Unofficial Guides*™?
Yes ___   No ___

If Yes, which ones?
_____
_____
_____

What other book(s) on hiring contractors have you purchased?

_____

_____

_____

Was this book:
___ more helpful than other(s)
___ less helpful than other(s)

Do you think this book was worth its price?
Yes ___   No ___

Did this book cover all topics related to hiring contractors adequately?   Yes ___   No ___

Please explain your answer:

_____

_____

_____

Were there any specific sections in this book that were of particular help to you?   Yes ___   No ___

Please explain your answer:

_____

_____

_____

On a scale of 1 to 10, with 10 being the best rating, how would you rate this guide? ___

What other titles would you like to see published in the *Unofficial Guide*™ **series?**

_____

_____

Are *Unofficial Guides*™ **readily available in your area?**   Yes ___   No ___

Other comments:

_____

_____

_____

_____

Get the inside scoop...with the
Unofficial Guides™!

The Unofficial Guide to Alternative Medicine
   ISBN: 0-02-862526-9 Price: $15.95
The Unofficial Guide to Buying or Leasing a Car
   ISBN: 0-02-862524-2 Price: $15.95
The Unofficial Guide to Buying a Home
   ISBN: 0-02-862461-0 Price: $15.95
The Unofficial Guide to Childcare
   ISBN: 0-02-862457-2 Price: $15.95
The Unofficial Guide to Cosmetic Surgery
   ISBN: 0-02-862522-6 Price: $15.95
The Unofficial Guide to Dieting Safely
   ISBN: 0-02-862521-8 Price: $15.95
The Unofficial Guide to Eldercare
   ISBN: 0-02-862456-4 Price: $15.95
The Unofficial Guide to Investing
   ISBN: 0-02-862458-0 Price: $15.95
The Unofficial Guide to Planning Your Wedding
   ISBN: 0-02-862459-9 Price: $15.95

All books in the *Unofficial Guide™* series are available at your local bookseller, or by calling 1-800-428-5331.

About the Author

Duncan C. Stephens can tell you everything you need to know about hiring contractors. He lives in Woodbury, Connecticut, where he and his wife Eileen remodeled her 750 square foot ranch style "weekend house" into the present 1600 square foot Cape Cod that is their home. It was that experience that triggered his first book, *Home Remodeling Pitfalls and How To Avoid Them*, published by the Globe Pequot Press in 1993.

During the course of his career, Mr. Stephens was placed in contact with the Home Builders Association of Northern Vermont, and later, the Waterbury Connecticut Home Builders Association. His work with the home builders gave him an appreciation of the complex home building and remodeling process.